A SIGN IS JUST A SIGN

Advances in Semiotics

Thomas A. Sebeok, General Editor

A SIGN IS JUST A SIGN

THOMAS A. SEBEOK

INDIANA UNIVERSITY PRESS
Bloomington and Indianapolis

The paper used in this publication meets the minimum requirements of American National Standard for Information Sciences—Permanence of Paper for Printed Library Materials, ANSI Z39.48-1984.

Manufactured in the United States of America

Library of Congress Cataloging-in-Publication Data

Sebeok, Thomas Albert date.
A sign is just a sign / Thomas A. Sebeok.
p. cm. — (Advances in semiotics)
Includes bibliographical references and index.
ISBN 0-253-35131-6 (cloth). — ISBN 0-253-20625-1 (paper)
1. Semiotics. 2. Linguistics. I. Title. II. Series.
P99.S344 1991
302.2—dc20 90-42289
CIP

1 2 3 4 5 95 94 93 92 91

For Jean

Rick (to Ilsa): But it's still a story without an ending.

—*Casablanca*

CONTENTS

A SIGN IS JUST A SIGN

Laszlo (to Rick): This time I know our side will win.

—*Casablanca*

Introduction

As time goes by, my *obiter dicta* about semiotic theory, inquiry, methodology, critique, *doxis* (exhortation) or *praxis* (consummation), and applications in diverse domains continue more or less factitiously to pile up. These include collateral remarks, some of which have remained stubbornly glottocentric, in a traditional, perhaps even fusty, mode, on a wide assortment of semiotic topics. Other, more recent observations conjure up Nature as an interpretive, hermeneutic problem: they contrive a world fancied as though encrypted on its surface yet bridled by a concealed deep structure, a decipherable code or a "language." Addressed to us all, it is palpably a hieroglyphic archive unsealed (cf. Blumenberg 1981; and Kergosien 1985). Galileo's pronouncement, unavoidably formulated in poetic imagery or metaphor, fires the imagination: "this grand book, the universe, . . . is written in the language of mathematics, and its characters are triangles, circles, and other geometric figures without which it is humanly impossible to understand a single word of it; without these, one wanders about in a dark labyrinth" (1957:328).

The cosmos is not, of course, unfailingly indited in deep mathematical idiom. As Jones recently called to mind, Cézanne, among others, had claimed that a painter, too, "is engaged . . . in the effort 'to read [the book] of Nature'" (1989:91). A few crumbs of cake dipped in tea, *la petite madeleine,* were all that Proust needed to actuate from his bed in the cork-lined room at 102 Boulevard Haussman his role as *tisseur,* weaving his wonderously complex tapestry so slowly, so painfully that he thought of it as textile for his shroud. Sherlock Holmes likewise asserted the primacy of metonymic movement in the detective story—from fragmentary clues to large-scale scenario—when he remarked apropos a fictive magazine article of his called "The Book of Life": "From a drop of water . . . a logician could infer the possibility of an Atlantic or a Niagara without having seen or heard of one or the other. So all life is a great chain, the nature of which is known whenever we are shown a single link of it" (Doyle 1967:1.159). And so also the begetter of a well-crafted song, a syncretic work of art fabricated out of a hierarchy of sign repertoires—verbal, including metrical, as well as musical—creates, I suggest, a controlled nonpareil world of its own.

In the recollections of many of my American contemporaries, and so also in mine, a handful of public happenings remain seared in memory.

You Must Remember This: Pearl Harbor Day, the commination of which caused intense trepidation as my father and I, listening together in Chicago in 1941 to a radio broadcast of a concert by the New York Philharmonic, heard an announcer interrupt with a flash to report the attack in Hawaii; the devastating news of FDR's death in Georgia, which reached me, on a fine April day in 1945, while I was teaching at the University of Pennsylvania, and which sent me into the streets of Philadelphia where thousands of citizens were milling about in our shared grief; or the moment in November 1963, when Margaret Mead, uncommonly flustered and still incredulous, told me in a San Francisco hotel elevator that she had just learned of JFK's assassination in Texas.

A reclusive scene from my past clings to the mind with surprising force, laden with symbolic presentiment. I vividly recollect the last evening of 1942, when, having taken the train from my campus town to Manhattan, I spent several pre-midnight hours celebrating New Year's Eve in the company of Princeton's Lillian, Madame Librarian—which rhymes with Marian, the Madame Librarian of *The Music Man*—at the Hollywood Theater (as I am pretty sure it was called). We enjoyed a first showing of the movie *Casablanca,* which, in the event, had less to do with exotic Casablanca than with my native Budapest. Hungary was also the birthplace not only of *Casablanca's* director, Mihály Kertész (aka Michael Curtiz) but also of several key members of his cast, including the talented comic Szőke Szakál. (Curtiz was reputed to have displayed a sign on his desk, "To Be Hungarian Is Not Enough.") Already humming "As Time Goes By," which would soon become *Casablanca*'s signature tune, we left the moviehouse for Times Square to embrace 1943.

Does Herman Hupfeld's name evanesce—a sign writ perhaps in water? Or is his epitaph an air? It was Hupfeld who composed the music for and set to words this banal pop song he called "As Time Goes By." Its three staves of six lines each were introduced by two performers, Oscar Shaw and Frances Williams, in a 1931 Broadway revue called *Everybody's Welcome.* Rudy Vallee then cut a recording, issued on the RCA Victor label (Ewen 1966:24), with little publicity and hardly any immediate effect. Murray Burnett, a Cornell undergraduate at the time, was among the few who chanced to buy a platter, and, although he never saw the show, "he fell madly in love with the song, whose poignant melody and lyrics seemed to him an appropriate and timeless philosophy on the mysteries of love" (Francisco 1980:41).

Nine years afterward, in the summer of 1940, Burnett, with another young playwright, Joan Alison, started to plot a play, to have been titled *Everybody Comes to Rick's.* Burnett still felt that, although "As Time Goes By" had failed to become a popular hit, it surely deserved another hearing. "It could be sung by the hero's black friend to set the mood for the bittersweet reunion of Rick and his former paramour" (ibid.). So he wove it into the first act of their play, which, however, was fated to remain forever unproduced on Broadway, or, so far as anyone knows, anywhere at all. But eventually the play was bought for $20,000 as potential movie material by Warner Brothers, where Hal Wallis retitled it *Casablanca*. This was released in 1942.

Wallis, moreover, also bought the rights to Burnett's favorite love song, "As Time Goes By." Max Steiner, an Austrian arranger and conductor of Broadway musicals, steeped in the works of the classic romantic composers of the nineteenth century, but then just fresh from his triumphant creation of the background music for *Gone With the Wind*, was assigned to score the motion picture (on Steiner, see Gorbman 1987, Ch. 4).

Nobody else objected to leaving "As Time Goes By" in *Casablanca*, this according to Francisco's lovingly detailed chronicle (ibid.:138). The main title of his book, *You Must Remember This . . .*, itself quotes the first six syllables from the song's seventh line, as its dedication (" . . . The fundamental things apply") consists of the second eight from the eighth—yet Steiner later, though luckily too late, became convinced that its selection as the picture's main theme song was a terrible mistake, since "the old tune was unnecessarily confining in its simplicity" (ibid.:185). The melody is indeed rather plain, although it does build up expectations in the listener and then plays with them in ways that do express the text.

Steiner, at any rate, wanted to substitute a stronger, more appropriate, more "significant" love song, one which he himself had composed. Accordingly, he demanded that the scenes in which "As Time Goes By" was played or sung be reshot with his new score. But he was overruled by Wallis, not just because the producer thought it a pleasant enough tune, but chiefly because Ingrid Bergman's hair had already been shorn for her next role as Maria, the earthy guerrilla in *For Whom the Bell Tolls*.

Ultimately, the success of *Casablanca*, critics generally agree, was in fact signally enhanced by Steiner's masterful overall scoring. This was clearly anticipated and recognized by the studio, which featured Steiner's name in the opening credits in letters as large as or larger than either Wallis's or those of Michael Curtiz, the director, or even those of the three stars (these credits are all reproduced in Anobile 1974:3).

Steiner succeeded in accommodating "As Time Goes By" in the film so that the song, both as sung by Dooley Wilson ("Sam") and as a recurrent musical theme mirroring and enhancing the narrative development, became its polysemous emblem. The music contributes to a sense of minatory suspense by Steiner's artful interlacing of Hupfeld's sentimental little tune with "La Marseillaise" on one side and "Deutschland über Alles" on the other. The rhythms seem to reconcile everyday speech with global political events. While, on the personal level, the tune itself modulates the shifting relationships of Ilsa and Rick, the rival anthems echo the overarching international conflict in the backdrop. Francisco rightly points out that it "requires a practiced ear to pick out some of Steiner's minute integration of music behind dialogue" (1980:187). For example, when Ilsa comes back to visit Rick, who is drunk and alone in the darkened cafe after their first, brief sight of each other earlier (depicted in Anobile 1974:135–139), their verbal dialogue is matched by an exchange of heavy, threatening music behind Rick and a bright, almost childlike ditty behind Ilsa, both derived from "As Time Goes By."

"As Time Goes By" became so popular after 1942 that RCA Victor revived its old recording, which then went on to become a best seller. Stores were swamped by customers asking for a Dooley Wilson recording, but no such track album was ever produced. The reason that a new disk version of the song could not be released was that James Petrillo, then the all-powerful boss of the American Federation of Musicians, had instituted a ban against all recordings. In December 1979, in a memorial broadcast originating from stage nine of the Warner Studios in Burbank, Frank Sinatra, standing in for Bogart, sang the song on network television while Ingrid Bergman sat at Dooley Wilson's battered piano.

Casablanca offers a rich terrain for semiotic analysis, or, as Eco remarked in "Casablanca: Cult Movies and Intertextual Collage" (the more interesting of his two complementary readings), the film is "a paramount laboratory for semiotic research into textual strategies . . . the first twenty minutes could be analyzed by a Russian Formalist and the rest by a Greimassian" (1986:197, 203). *Casablanca* as a whole, Eco thinks, "looks like a musical piece where every theme is exhibited according to a monodic line" (ibid:203). He apprehends an early hint of Arab music, which soon fades into the "Marseillaise." These themes are meant to, and do, evoke, on the one hand, the genre of adventure movies, and, on the other, of patriotic movies of the times. Later, the theme of the Barbarians, "Deutschland über Alles," is counterpoised. Although he validly identifies the cliché "They're Playing Our Song" as reflecting one of the film's several myths (Eco 1985:37), Sam reminds him of a brothel piano player from New Orleans (1986:204).

However, Eco nowhere mentions, let alone cites, the theme song (Ilsa: "Play it once, Sam, for old time's sake. . . . Play it, Sam. . . . Play, 'As Time Goes By.' . . . I'll hum it for you. Hm-hm, hm-hm, hm-hmmm— . . ." [Anobile 1974:94–95]) beyond noting that the tune is an "anticipated quotation" featured in the title of Woody Allen's parodic homage, "Play It Again Sam" (on prospective intertextuality, cf. Sebeok 1986:183).

A good measure of *Casablanca*'s enduring renown must surely correlate with the amazing number of heterogeneity of titles, mostly of books, which the lyrics of "As Time Goes By" have inspired and still keep enkindling. Universal recognition, at least by an Anglophone public, is taken for granted. That such books may directly relate to, or be about, *Casablanca*, as Charles Francisco's *You Must Remember This . . .*, is hardly surprising. And it is small wonder perhaps that Roger Ebert's *A Kiss Is Still a Kiss* (seventh line), which is about movies, is besotted with quotations from "As Time Goes By," except for the fact that his book makes no mention at all otherwise of *Casablanca*.

Ebert uses lines from the song for each of the chapter headings: ". . . no matter what the future brings" (twelfth line) for its Prologue; "A sigh is just a sigh" (eighth) for Chapter 1; "Hearts full of passion" (thirteenth) for Chapter 2; "Woman needs man—and man must have his mate" (fourteenth) for Chapter 3; "A fight for love and glory" (fifteenth) for Chapter 4; "It's still the same old story" (fourteenth) for Chapter 5; "A case of do or die" (fifteenth) for Chapter 6; "The fundamental things apply" (eighth) for Chapter 7; "The world will always welcome lovers" (seventeenth) for Chapter 8; and, finally, "As time goes by" (eighteenth) for Chapter 9.

The song's pertinence to other books in which it is cited is more remote, and, on occasion, neither spelled out nor clearly motivated. Thus Jeff Kisseloff chose to title his oral history of Manhattan from the 1890s to World War II *You Must Remember This* (seventh line). He characterizes his work as being "about listening" (1989:xvi). He mentions *King Kong*, the "Lullaby of Broadway," as well as Art Tatum, Fats Waller, and others at the piano, but leaves it to his readership to surmise his immediate wellspring.

More puzzling still, Norbert Hornstein titles—playfully, I guess—his rather technical treatise (1990) about universal grammar and the category of tense *As Time Goes By* (twelfth line). And the title of Diane K. Shah's crime story, of "murder in Hollywood's heyday" (1990), becomes, in an arch but unexplained variant, *As Crime Goes By*. Trivially, Linda Wells's article in the *Times*, "As Time Goes By" (1989), is about female cosmetics consumers who are growing "older."

There are also quite a few recent works of fiction infused by "As Time Goes By." The three which I found most intriguing among such, although very different one from another, are:

—Joyce Carol Oates's elaborate, powerful novel *You Must Remember This* (1987), the time frame, from the beginning of the 1950s, and preponderant mood of which amply justify the intertextual connotations and associations—of inexorable separations—aroused, at least in this spectator, by *Casablanca*. What must be remembered by Enid Stevick, the novel's central character, is her confusing affair, indeed the claustraphobic arena of her world, that she must leave behind.

—Robert Coover's astounding, funny flight of fancy—he calls it "ROMANCE! You Must Remember This" (1987:156–187)—which forms a part of a collection of "short fictions" under the umbrella title *A Night at the Movies; or, You Must Remember This*. Rick and Ilsa act out their obsessive sexual relationship so as to transmute *Casablanca*, in a witty trip of regretfulness, into a pornographic post-modernist homage—"A kiss is just a kiss is what the music is insinuating. A sigh . . . " (ibid.:165)—to the 1940s.

—In Hilary Bailey's *As Time Goes By* (1988), Polly, the mildly feminist protagonist, is beset by domestic predicaments of her large family as she struggles to finish a newly plotted, long-overdue screenplay for *Casablanca,* compared to which "rearranging the simple affairs of the denizens of Casablanca was no problem at all" (ibid.:38). The story's romanticism contrasts ironically with life in her house at Elgin Crescent. She wonders "why Ingrid hadn't sent a more effective message to Bogart at the railway station when her husband had suddenly turned up . . . Surely she could have made it a little bit plainer? What stopped her from going to the station and whispering the story in his ear? This lack of common sense had caused a lot of trouble and the making of the film . . ." (ibid.:37). But in the end, it is her script that solves the immediate problems, at least for the nonce.

"Well, everybody in Casablanca has problems," Rick says (Anobile 1974:168). That includes the Central European Victor Laszlo no less than the American Rick Blaine and his friends from all over, to say nothing of those rallied around either the Tricolor or the German flag. It's still the same old story. . . .

Just so, the toilsome pursuit of the doctrine of signs, whether in workshops in Bologna or Paris, Budapest or Tartu, and elsewhere in the Old World as much as over here, is beset with problems. There are riddles of belonging and identity, dilemmas of definition and terminology, conundrums of theory and application, disputes about its past and its future. In short, semiotics is happily brimming over with fascinating puzzles. These perplexities are precisely what make semiotics such an absorbing subject of study.

To date, since the first edition of my *Contributions to the Doctrine of Signs* (1976; 2d ed., 1985) appeared, I have published over half a dozen further essay collections—usually in English to begin with, but eventually in German, Italian, Japanese, and Spanish, in different combinations—variously addressing, or just chipping away at, facets of the sorts of problems mentioned, plus a congeries of related issues. In books such as those (see, for example, my Introduction to Sebeok 1981:1–16; Preface to Sebeok 1986:ix–xv; Foreword to Sebeok 1989:xv–xxi), or through interviews with young colleagues (for example, Skupien 1980; Marrone 1986; Switzer et al. 1990; Petrilli in Sebeok 1991:95–105; and so forth), I tried to emphasize the unity of thought underlying the manifestly patent diversity among these ventures and further to clarify points in contention. Two additional collections of mine are *Essays in Zoosemiotics* (1989–1990) and *American Signatures* (1991a).

Everybody's Welcome was the vehicle in which Frances Williams was originally to have introduced "As Time Goes By." Here, everybody is welcomed by way of the two complementary opening pieces, which are set out for the enjoyment of any reader who wishes first to engage with the world of modern semiotics. "The fundamental things apply" and they are exemplified in Chapter 1.

Following clues from George Herbert Mead (1934), Thure von Uexküll, in a landmark paper on biosemiotics (1991), clearly distinguishes among three types of semiosis: semiosis of information; semiosis of symptomatization (Mead's "unintelligent gestures"); and semiosis of communication (Mead's "intelligent gestures"). It is the third type that I emphasize in Chapter 2: the omnipresent interchange of signs among, and their lawful conversion within, organisms—a process too loosely and imprecisely called "communication"—which constitutes an inalienable contributory function, although one that is but subsidiary to the modeling property (discussed in Chapter 5), or the primary global representational, significative business of signs.

The following two companion pieces, "The Semiotic Self" and "The Semiotic Self Revisited" (Chapters 3 and 4), written about ten years apart, though very far from exhausting the topic, are especially meaningful to me because they reveal and manifest the decisive influence on my thinking about semiotic matters of two prodigious, but alas still insufficiently appreciated, contributors to the subject: the wonderously insightful and inventive Prussian theoretical biologist Jakob von Uexküll, especially as made plain, in present-day terms, by his eminent physician son, Thure; and the bold Swiss explorer Heini Hediger, who, over the past half-century, brought to light some of the most recondite enigmas of animal psychology.

The elder von Uexküll, who serendipitously reconfigured semiotics in his own image, and Hediger, whose questing passion for and strenuous erudition in all aspects of animal life in general and zoosemiosis in particular (see his summing up, 1990:415–439) are, each in his way, the sharpest observers of and profoundest thinkers about what Vernadsky came to call in 1926 the region of the "biosphere" (Bailes 1990:124, 190). They are indirectly responsible for the burgeoning, "with speed and new invention," of the copious province of "biosemiotics," believed to have been so baptized by Stepanov (1971: 27–32). Indeed, on the initiative of Thure von Uexküll—whose pioneering blueprint essay, "Biosemiotics," is in press (1991)—an International Biosemiotics Society was organized by some of us semioticians, leavened with a generous sprinkling of biologists, physicians, and allied health personnel. The foundation of the IBS took place in May 1990 and thereupon was formally incorporated under German law in Baden-Württemberg, with the new society beginning to function fully in May 1991.

I have already mentioned Chapter 5, in which I critically enlist in the daedal dance between the region of the biosphere and the semiosphere, as

Lotman, another contemporary giant of semiotics, evidently galvanized by Vernadsky, aptly dubbed this singular synchronic realm of humankind (1991, Part 2). I return to this perennial dialectic conversation, "things like third dimension," again in Chapter 15, but do so there in an appreciably wider frame.

When the question of the multifarious actual or possible rapports between semiotics and linguistics—superordinate, subordinate, coordinate, or merely of provincially pedantic attention—was put to me by the compiler of a "comprehensive" survey of current work in the latter field, I agreed to take a look. The resulting overview, which now constitutes Chapter 6 (see also Nöth 1990:231–234), was, however, catechized by the young man who first commissioned it. He opined that my article failed to take adequate account of the relationship between semiotics on the one hand and the challenge of Chomsky to "traditional" linguistics on the other. Admitting the deficiency of my sample in this regard, I tried to extenuate my neglect by pointing out that generative-transformational grammarians, no doubt being preoccupied with more important matters, had written next to nothing about semiotics. This, though admitted by my would-be editor, was countered with the grotesque demand that my article should set forth what Noam Chomsky's epigones *would* have said *if* they had considered the connection between the two fields. To this I said no—for I "get a trifle weary, with Mister Einstein's the-'ry. . . ."

What Chapters 7, 8, 10, and 9 have in common is the intromission of a temporal perspective: "As time goes by." All four convey the heavy freight of time. But whereas the first three contemplate sundry effects of the past, the last is a speculative excursus in extrapolation into what is yet to be ("No matter what the future brings . . .").

Chapter 7 was written as an article invited to assess several books beating a dead horse, which, poor beast, having been one of its pallbearers, I fancied had long been laid to rest. Chapter 11 examines some specific Elizabethan antecedents of the clever Hans phenomenon, from which it would appear that, where language games—*pace* Wittgenstein, I mean linguistic confidence games—are concerned, *plus ça change, plus c'est la même chose.*

Chapter 8 was commissioned to be a rundown of what some months ago I deemed to belong to "biosemiotics." But no state-of-the-art summation can be anything other than highly contingent. Advances, on many fronts, are all but impossible to keep up with. Take just two examples, themselves finally connected at their root:

—The implications of Sonea's magesterially sweeping portrayal of bacterial semiosis (1990) reach far beyond the prokaryotes (organisms lacking membrane-bounded nuclei and such membrane-bounded organelles as plastids or mitochondria). Prokaryotes not only constitute half or more of the living world, but these ancestors of ours also "invented" semiosis about two billion years before the eukaryotes—that is, protoctists, plants, animals, and fungi—collectively constituting all the rest of the living world, began to evolve. The ways of bacterial semiosis (alias "symbiosis") were indeed essential for the evolution of organisms like us, embodying the operations of the vertebrate central nervous system. Neither comparative semiotics nor diachronic semiotics will be possible any longer without a meticulous inventory and full comprehension of the bacterial sources of semiosis.

—Another case has to do with syntax-driven simplicity and complexity in nature. One way to picture syntax is as a set of instructions to go with a Lego kit, consisting of a few modules of different shapes and colors, with which, given a sufficient number of pieces and a few rules, a child can elaborate a potentially limitless number of aggregate structures. The periodic table devised by Mendeleev has, since 1869, been a familiar example of such a Tinkertoy-like set of elements out of which the entire known universe, inorganic as well as organic, is composed. Language is another, where universal phoneme constituents, called distinctive features, the number of which is astonishingly small, make up all higher-level sign components, that is, those having their own semantic referents (such as morphemes, words, phrases, clauses, and sentences). Together, these normalized units, their number being infinite, constitute the verbal semiotic hierarchy.

Comparably regulated semiotic hierarchies have been shown to govern sign processes (belonging to the domain called endosemiotics) involving communication between cells or cell complexes. These encompass, among others, the genetic code, the immune code, the metabolic code, the neural code. I mention them briefly in Chapter 8. However, the question "How many different exons were required to generate the current protein diversity?" has barely been unraveled. Now it is postulated that the basic pool is made up of only 1,000 to 7,000 exons, which are previously independent, short gene segments, separated by long introns, such modules naturally joining together to build up complex genetic information. Were no more than these needed to account for the staggering diversity of all terrestrial life? So it would appear. It is further believed that many of the core protein shapes, the fundamental elements of which have remained invariant, date back to four billion years ago, not long after life itself began. "The surprisingly small size of our estimate emphasizes the finite character of the underlying exon universe" (Dorit, Schoenbach, and Gilbert 1990:1381). While, so far, not all scientists accept the novel theory of Gilbert and his associates, "no matter that the progress, or what may yet be proved," their calculations are in good conformity with overall expectations and they have already galvanized further researches.

I define myself as a biologist *manqué,* as well as, concurrently, a "doctrinaire of signs" *malgré lui.* Some clinging filaments of my jejune, bottled-up fascination with the behavior of animals tie the knot ("when two lovers woo, they still say, 'I love you'"), in Chapter 10, with more seasoned semiotic reflections. To begin with, I captioned these cogitations, in the course of a private nostalgia trip, "What Is an Animal?" but was compelled to yield to *force majeure* when my editor adopted my query for the overall title of his book. This topic (see also Hoage 1989) led me to confront, or rather to nibble, with plenty of misgivings, at the edges of such issues as the distinction between inanimate matter and matter in a "living" state; the differences between scientific systematics and folk classification; the manifold but complementary codes to which an entity or object, such as an animal, must simultaneously belong, or how it straddles, by necessity, the unvarnished biosphere ("whale is a mammal") and the semiosphere ("the whale is a fish"), of which the mythic world is an informing part (Ahab's fathomless Moby Dick).

Any twentieth-century palimpsest on particular sign phases, whether by Charles Morris, Roman Jakobson, or any surviving commentators, myself among them, thus far turn out to be little else than more or less entertaining marginalia to Peirce's categories of Firstness, Secondness, and Thirdness: "tones or tints upon conceptions" (1.353), "thin skeletons of thought" (1.355). Each such reckoning is but another act of abduction, another "guess at the riddle," to cite a heading for one batch of notes for a book about the categories that Peirce conceived about 1890, but which—perhaps so arduous a feat exceeded even his own glorious powers—he never even came close to finishing. Yet we have to keep hacking away at the task. So I, too, have tried to pick away, if only to clarify them for my own benefit, and "at times relax, relieve the tension," at the Index (Chapter 13) and its sexy progeny, the Fetish (Chapter 12), enlarging upon some of my previous remarks about the Icon, the Symptom, the Symbol, and other identified sign facets.

"This day and age we're living in gives cause for apprehension" of the sort that troubled Francis Bacon, who labeled "Idols" bad habits in the mind of man. One irksome category of such fallacies he dubbed Idols of the forum. By this, Bacon meant to point to misunderstandings that can arise in the course of semiosic interactions, especially in the marketplace of ideas in human affairs. In Chapter 14 I discuss some troubling cases of fallacious discourse in the so-called concept industry and in the political arena.

In the final chapter, biology and semiotics are again conjoined. "The simple facts of life are such they cannot be removed." There I attempt once more to trace some consequences and corollaries of the view that terrestrial semiosis got its start in phylogeny with the emergence of the earliest cell and that, in mammalian embryogenesis, individual semiosis builds up step by step with the unfolding of the sense organs, such progression continuing throughout life. Among the ultimate interpretants that put a stop to this extended, concatenated spawning of representations are personal mortality and the extinction of species.

ONE

The Doctrine of Signs

> I am inclined to think the doctrine of signs a point of great importance and general extent, which, if duly considered, would cast no small light upon things, and afford a just and genuine solution of many difficulties.
>
> —George Berkeley (1732)

Consider what these ten little dramas have in common:

—A radiologist spots a silhouette on a chest X-ray photograph of a patient and diagnoses lung cancer.

—A meteorologist notes a rise in barometric pressure and delivers the next day's forecast taking that change into account.

—An anthropologist observes a complex of ceremonial exchanges practiced among members of a tribe; she draws analytical insights into the polity, economy, and social organization of the people she is studying.

—A French-language teacher holds up a picture of a horse. His American pupil says "horse." The teacher shakes his head and pronounces "cheval."

—A historian takes a look at the handwriting of a former President and therefrom gains insight into her subject's personality.

—A Kremlin watcher observes the proximity of a member of the Politburo to the Party Secretary on May Day and surmises the member's current status.

—A compromising fingerprint is introduced as evidence in a trial; the defendant is convicted on that evidence.

—A hunter notices in the snow sets of rectangular tracks of pointed hoofs with an impression of dew claws; the forefoot track is 15 cm. long and 13 cm. broad, and the corresponding measurements for the hind-foot track are 15 cm. and 11 cm. There are spherical droppings on the trail 20–30

This chapter is reprinted, with corrections, from the *Journal of Social and Biological Structures* 9 (1986):4.345–364. The two commentaries that accompanied the original, by Thure von Uexküll and Milton Singer, are omitted here. The article has also appeared, with minor variations, in French, German, Italian, and Norwegian.

mm. long and 15–20 mm. broad. The hunter surmises, with a high degree of probability, that a fully grown bull elk is trotting ahead of him.

—A man finds himself being stared at by a dog, growling, barking, head held high and neck arched, lips contracted vertically and teeth bared, ears erect and turned forward. The man concludes he is in danger of imminent attack and takes evasive action.

—A peacock displays to a susceptible peahen; she circles rapidly and squats. Coition ensues.

Those of us who practice semiotics tend to treat these happenings the same way despite their manifest substantive differences of setting, cast of human or speechless characters, and many other variables. What entitles us to do so is an abstractive operation which resolves each episode to an instance of *semiosis,* or sign action. In this view, semiotics is not about the "real" world at all, but about complementary or alternative actual models of it and—as Leibniz thought—about an infinite number of anthropologically conceivable possible worlds. Thus semiotics never reveals what the world is, but circumscribes what we can know about it; in other words, what a semiotic model depicts is not "reality" as such, but nature as unveiled by our method of questioning. It is the interplay between "the book of nature" and its human decipherer that is at issue. The distinction may be pictured by the simile of a fisherman casting his net; the size of the fish he can catch is limited by the morphology of the net, but this fact does not provide tutorage in ichthyology. A concept of "modeling systems" has been central to Soviet semiotics of the so-called Moscow-Tartu school since the 1960s, but, having been derived from a representation of language in structural linguistics, it has focused on culture to the exclusion of the rest of nature. In the age-old philosophical quest for reality, two alternative points of departure have been suggested: that the structure of being is reflected in semiotic structures, which thus constitute models, or maps, of reality; or that the reverse is the case, namely, that semiotic structures are independent variables so that reality becomes the dependent variable. Although both views are beset by many difficulties, a version of the second, proposed by the remarkably seminal German biologist Jakob von Uexküll (1864–1944), under the watchword *Umwelt-Forschung*—approximately translated as "research in subjective universes"—has proved to be in best conformity with modern semiotics (as well as with ethology). The same attitude was expressed by Niels Bohr when he answered an objection that reality is more fundamental than the language it underlies; Bohr replied: "We are suspended in language in such a way that we cannot say what is up and what is down" (French and Kennedy 1985:302). Signs have acquired their effectiveness through evolutionary adaptation to the vagaries of the sign wielder's *Unwelt*. When the *Unwelt* changes, these signs can become obstacles, and the signer, extinct.

According to the incomparable philosopher and polymath Charles Sanders Peirce (1839–1914), who has justly been called "the most original and the most versatile intellect that the Americas have so far produced" (Fisch 1980:1), and who uniquely reinvigorated semiotics, the antique doctrine of signs, semiosis involves an irreducibly triadic relation among a sign, its object, and its interpretant. This trio of terms and their next of kin have far-resounding philosophical overtones. Before rehearsing some of these, let me dwell on a common definition of semiotics and pause to consider its components and a few of its consequences. The subject matter of semiotics, it is often credited, is the exchange of any messages whatsoever—in a word, *communication*. To this must at once be added that semiotics is also focally concerned with the study of *signification*. Semiotics is therefore classifiable as that pivotal branch of an integrated science of communication to which its character as a methodical inquiry into the nature and constitution of codes provides an indispensable counterpoint.

A message is a sign or a string of signs transmitted from a sign producer, or source, to a sign receiver, or destination. Any source and any destination is a living entity or the product of a living entity, such as a computer, a robot, automata in general, or a postulated supernatural being, as when a boy (source), on bent knees (nonverbal message), beseeches his deity (destination) "I pray the Lord my soul to take" (verbal message). It is important to realize that only living things and their inanimate extensions undergo semiosis, which thereby becomes uplifted as a necessary, if not sufficient, criterial attribute of life. By "living things" are meant not just the organisms belonging to one of the five kingdoms, consisting of the Monera, Protoctista, Animalia, Plantae, and Fungi, but also their hierarchically developed choate component parts, beginning with a cell, the minimal semiosic unit, estimated to correspond to about fifty genes, or about one thousand billion (10^{12}) intricately organized atoms. (Viruses are omitted because they are neither cells nor aggregations of cells.) Our bodies are assemblages of cells, about one hundred thousand billion (10^{14}) of them, harmoniously attuned to one another by an incessant flux of vital messages. The origin of nucleated cells is a dimly apprehended story of the symbiotic and semiosic collaboration among single cells—populations of blue algae and bacteria without apparent internal components; they evolved less than one billion years after the formation of Earth (and ample traces of them were harvested in Greenland). Simple cells, it is thought, fused to form the complex confederations of cells composing each living being. They, in turn, are integrated into organs, organs into organisms, forming social systems of ever increasing complexity. Thus physics, biology, psychology, and sociology each embodies its own peculiar level of semiosis. The genetic code governs the exchange of messages on the cellular level; hormones and neurotransmitters mediate among organs and between one another (the immune defense system and the central nervous system are intimately interwreathed by a dense flow of two-way message traffic); and a variety of nonverbal and verbal messages conjoin organisms into a network of relations with each other as well as with the rest of their environment. As François Jacob picturesquely described (1974:320) the progression, "From family organization to modern state, from ethnic group to coalition of nations, a whole series of integrations is based on a variety of cultural, moral, social, political, economic, military and religious codes. The history of mankind is more or less the history of these integrons and the way they form and change." Semiosis on a superior level in the hierarchy of integrons is irreducible to that on a lower level, namely, ultimately to physics. (The reasons therefor are forcefully argued by Karl R. Popper, in his *The Self and Its Brain* [1977], with John C. Eccles.)

The semiosic comportment of even the major organismic groupings, with differing lifestyles, has been unevenly studied. In the web of nature, plants are, above all, producers; an examination of their communicative behavior, under the banner of "phytosemiotics," began only in 1981, when the German semiotician, Martin Krampen, published an insightful programmatic article under that title. The polar opposites of plants are the fungi, nature's decomposers; our knowledge of their peculiar brand of semiosis is even more rudimentary. Primary interest has hitherto focused on animals (zoosemiotics), the ingesters, which mediate between the other two and, according to what they consume, may be categorized either as herbivores or as predators; their nutritional mode may also mark the character of their respective reliance on sign use. (For a further discussion of this tripartition of plants, animals, and fungi, see Ch. 8, below.)

Note that message traffic in four out of the five kingdoms is exclusively nonverbal; verbal messages have been found only in animals and there surge solely in one extant subspecies, *Homo sapiens sapiens*. The most distinctive trait of humans is that only they, throughout terrestrial life, have two separate, although, of course, thoroughly commingled, repertoires of signs at their disposal: the nonverbal—demonstrably derived from their mammalian (especially primate) ancestry—and a uniquely human verbal overlay. The latter constitutes the subject matter of the most advanced and highly formalized branch of semiotics, general linguistics, the study of verbal commerce and its subjacent grammatical foundation. This essay, however, by and large concentrates on the nonverbal—as in most examples which opened this essay—or on issues concerning both, because the former are overwhelmingly more copious, not only in nature but even in human-to-human interchanges.

The definition advanced here presupposes a message producer, or source, and a message receiver, or destination. In the examples above, extant or formerly alive sources and destinations figure in such roles as those of patient and physician; ethnographic fieldworker and informants; teacher and pupil; historian and late public figure; remote foreign official and political scientist; elk and hunter; dog and potential victim; peacock and peahen. The barometer read by the weather forecaster is a man-made instrument of observation, one of a class of sense-enhancing devices, such as a bubble chamber, constructed to render ineffable messages effable; thus no physicist can really "see" subatomic particles, not even aided by the most powerful electron microscope (or accelerator-detector complex), but only (in the simple case) the tiny bubbles of hydrogen produced by them—the vaporous beads in the tank "stand for," that is, model, their interactions. As for the dermatoglyph presented to the court, this functions here as a probatively synecdochic message-by-contiguity about the guilt of a presumed criminal.

In any given transaction, a source is necessarily coupled by means of a channel to a destination; the variety of such passageways is constrained by the specific sensorium of each. This state of affairs was neatly summed up by George Dalgarno (the Scottish author of *Ars signorum,* a fascinating semiotic treatise from the mid-seventeenth century): "It is true," he wrote in 1680, "that all the Senses are Intelligencers to the Soul less or more; for tho they have their distinct limits, and proper Objects assigned them by nature; yet she is able to use their service even in the most abstracted Notions, and Arbitrary institution." Dalgarno adds that "Nature seems to have fitted two, Hearing and Seeing, more particularly for her service," but this is a superficial view. By far the most hoary messages are molecular, and the chemical channel is the most prevalent. Three of the hierarchical levels of basic endosemiotic control are regulated, respectively, by the genetic code, by humoral as well as cell-mediated immune reactions, and (since the appearance of the sponges) by the large number of peptides present in the central nervous system, functioning as neurotransmitters. The olfactory and gustatory senses are likewise semiochemical. Even in vision, the impact of photons on the retina differentially affects the capacity of the pigment rhodopsin, which fills the rods to absorb light of different wave lengths, the condition for the univariance principle. Acoustic and tactile vibrations, and impulses delivered via the thermal senses, are, as well, finally transformed into electrochemical messages. Humans and many other animals are routinely linked by several channels simultaneously or in succession. Parallel processing of messages introduces a degree of redundancy, by virtue of which it becomes more likely that errors in reception will be minimized; however, it is also possible for collimated messages to contradict one another—this is how a rhetorical figure such as irony performs in spoken or written discourse, as does the back-arch display of a house cat in zoosemiotics.

It is unknown how most sources generate—or, to use a less overburdened term, formulate—a message. Human beings are capable of launching an enormous number of novel messages appropriate to an indefinite variety of contexts, but the electrochemical intricacies of their initial entrainment by that cramped globe of tissue known as the brain remain an enigma. Plainly, however, the message-as-formulated must undergo a transductive operation to be externalized into serial strings appropriate to the channel, or channels, selected to link up with the destination. This neurobiological transmutation from one form of energy to another is called *encoding*. When the destination detects and extracts the encoded messages from the channel, another transduction, followed by a series of still further transformations, must be effected before interpretation can occur; this pivotal reconversion is called *decoding*. Encoding and decoding imply a code, a set of unambiguous rules whereby messages are convertible from one representation to another; the code is what the two parties in the message exchange are supposed to have, in fact or by assumption, totally or in part, in common. Using Joseph Weizenbaum's famous computer program, aptly named Eliza, human interlocutors tend to project sympathy, interest, and intelligence upon Eliza, as they would upon a psychotherapist. In fact, Eliza "knows" nothing. A similar fallacy about shared codes is the theme of Jerzy Kosinski's brilliant novelette *Being There* (and the faithful movie based on it), in which an illiterate, retarded gardener is ascribed supreme gnostic attributes because he—essentially a blank page—mimics, echoes, and reflects back the interactive codes of every one of his conversational partners, whatever their native speech community may be.

Receivers interpret messages as an amalgam of two separate but inextricably blended inputs: the physical triggering sign, or signal, itself, but as unavoidably shaped by context. The latter plays a cardinal role, yet the concept has eluded definition; too, it is generally unknown how destinations "take account of" context. In semiotics, the term is used both broadly and loosely to encompass preceding messages (anaphoric presuppositions), and probably succeeding messages (cataphoric implicatures), environmental and semantic noise, all filtered by short- and long-term memory, genetic and cultural.

These six key factors—message and code, source and destination, channel and context—separately and together make up the rich domain of semiotic researches. However, the pivotal notion remains the *sign*. This term has been defined in many different ways since its introduction in Ancient Greece. In medical semiotics, for example, sign has been used in conjunction with, or, rather, in opposition to, symptom since at least Alcmaeon, Hippocrates, and especially Galen (A.D. c. 130–c. 200). Clinical practitioners usually distinguish between "soft data," or subjective signs, dubbed symptoms, meaning by this whatever the patient relates verbally about his feelings ("I have a pain in my chest") or exhibits nonverbally (groans while pointing to the chest); and "hard data," or objective signs, which clinicians actually call "signs," meaning whatever the physician observes with his eyes and ears (bloody sputum, wheezing) or with his instruments (shadow on an X-ray photograph). Many philosophers also use the term "sign"; however, not a few contrast it with symbol rather than with symptom. The neo-Kantian, twentieth-century philosopher Ernst Cassirer (1874–1945), for instance, claimed that these two notions belonged to different universes of discourse, and that "a sign is a part of the physical world, a symbol is a part of the human world of meaning" (1944:32). Minimalist approaches such as these are far too imprecise and superficial to be serviceable, as Peirce painstakingly demonstrated throughout his voluminous writings. For Peirce, "sign" was a generic concept, of which there are a very large number of species, multiplying from a trichotomous base of icon, index, and symbol, each defined according to that sign category's relation to its object in a particular context.

To clarify what a sign is, it is useful to begin with the medieval formula *aliquid stat pro aliquo,* broadened by Peirce, about 1897, to "something which stands to somebody for something in some respect or capacity." To the classic notion of *substitution* featured in this famous phrase—the late Roman Jakobson called it *renvoi,* translatable as "referral"—Peirce here added the criterion of *interpretation.* At this point, let us take a closer look at the object-sign-interpretant trichotomous cycle alluded to earlier, and also pause to consider Peirce's "somebody": the destination or other receiver of the message.

The initial distinction between object (O) and sign (S) raises profound questions about the anatomy of reality, indeed about its very existence, but there is nothing approaching a consensus about these riddles among physicists, let alone philosophers. One obvious implication of this postulated duality is that semiosis requires at least two actants: the observer and the observed. Our intuition of reality is a consequence of a mutual interaction between the two, Jakob von Uexküll's private world of elementary sensations (*Merkzeichen,* or perceptual signs) coupled to their meaningful transforms into action impulses (*Wirkzeichen,* or operation signs); and the phenomenal world *(Umwelt),* that is, the subjective world each animal models out of its "true" environment (*Natur,* or reality), which reveals itself solely through signs. The rules and laws to which those sign processes—namely, semiosis—are subject are the only actual laws of nature. "As the activity of our mind is the only piece of nature known to us," he argued in his great work, *Theoretical Biology,* "its laws are the only ones that have the right to be called laws of Nature" (1973 [1928]:40). Any observer's version of his *Umwelt* will be one unique model of the world which is a system of signs made up of genetic factors plus a cocktail of experiences, including future expectations. A complicating fact of life is that the bare act of observation entails a residual juncture that disturbs the system being observed. The essential ingredient, or nutriment, of mind may well be information, but to acquire information about anything requires, via a long and complex chain of steps, the transmission of signs from the object of interest to the observer's central nervous system. Its attainment, moreover, takes place in such a manner that this influential action reacts back upon the object being observed so as to perturb its condition. In brief, the brain, or mind, which is itself a system of signs, is linked to the putative world of objects, not simply by perceptual selection, but by such a far-off remove from physical inputs—sensible stimuli—that we can safely assert that the only cognizance any animal can possess, "through a glass, darkly," as it were, is that of signs. Whether there is a reality behind signs—perhaps what Heraclitus called *logos*, the repeatable structure that secures for any object its ideal unity and stability, and which the French topologist René Thom and I have independently rendered as "form"—mankind can never be sure. As Heraclitus so eloquently put it, "You could not discover the limits of soul, even if you traveled every road to do so; such is the depth of its form." In sum, this reasoning entitles us to rewrite O as S_{o_n}, so that the initial twofold distinction is resolved to one between two sorts of signs.

What about the third correlate, Peirce's interpretant (I)? What did he mean by this much-discussed (and even more often misunderstood) concept? True, no single, canonical definition of it is to be found in his writings, but he does make it clear that every sign determines an interpretant "which is itself a sign, [so that] we have a sign overlying sign." He also points out that an interpretant can be either an equivalent sign or "perhaps a more developed sign," which is where novelty enters the system, enabling us to increase our understanding of the immediate object. To illustrate all this, ponder some interpretants of the English noun *horse*. They could be (partial) synonyms such as *colt, gee-gee, gelding, hinny, mare, pony, stallion, stud, thoroughbred*—to say nothing of *heroin*—and the like, or the interpretant could be a monolingual rewording, including standard dictionary definitions, as the *OED*'s beginning: "A solid-hoofed perissodactyl quadruped . . . having a flowing mane and tail, whose voice is a neigh." Another of its interpretants is the scientific name *Equus Przewalski caballus*, as are all (roughly) equivalent translations into verbal signs in other languages, such as *cheval, Pferd, losad, hevonen*, and so forth. Historical tokens, such as Bucephalus, Morocco, Clever Hans, and all the Lippizaners of the Spanish Riding School of Vienna belong here, as do such literary representations as Dean Swift's Houyhnhnms, Peter Shaffer's play *Equus*, Conan Doyle's saga *Silver Blaze*, Eco's creature Brunellus, and entire scientific treatises as different as Xenophon's disquisition *Treatise on Horsemanship*, Stefan von Maday's *Psychologie der Pferde und der Dressur*, and E. H. Gombrich's penetrating essay "Meditations on a Hobby Horse." Intersemiotic transmutations into nonverbal signs include innumerable and worldwide engravings and paintings of horses (notably from the

Magdalenian caves), sculptures (from the Neolithic period onward, including those of the Chinese tradition since Lung-shan), Scythian friezes, Greek centaurs as well as modern filmic portrayals such as *National Velvet* and *The Black Stallion*. Finally, of course, any "actual" horse I point to may become, by virtue of that gesture, which is an indexical sign, or an "object of direct experience so far as it directs attention to an object by which its presence is caused," an interpretant. There is no doubt that an intralingual synonym or paraphrase of, or extended discourse on, any sign will enrich comprehension of the object it represents, as will also its interlingual translations and intersemiotic transmutations. Each further interpretant tends to amplify intelligence and afford opportunity for a cascade of semantic innovation and therefore change. (Another, more technical way of putting this is that any metalanguage explicating an object language is always richer than the latter.)

In brief, it follows from Peirce's way of looking at the sign that the second distinction, as much as the first, resolves itself into two sorts of signs, to wit, S and S_{I_n}. Once more, here are his words: a sign is anything "which determines something else (its *interpretant*) to refer to an object to which itself refers (its *object*) in the same way, the sign becoming in turn a sign, and so on *ad infinitum*."

If objects are signs, in indefinite regression to a supposititious *logos*, and if interpretants are signs marching in progression toward the ultimate disintegration of mind, what is there left that is not a sign? What of the "somebody" mentioned by Peirce—the observer or the interpreter of the train after train of sign actions? In a celebrated article he published in 1868, Peirce anticipated and answered this question, contending "that the word or sign which man uses *is* the man himself," which is to claim that "the man and the external sign are identical, in the same sense in which the words *homo* and *man* are identical. Thus my language is the sum total of myself, for the man is the thought." (This man-sign analogy, and implications of the semiotics of identity more generally, constitute the central themes of *Man's Glassy Essence* [1984], an important book by the distinguished Chicago anthropologist, Milton Singer.) In short, the "somebody" is also a sign or a text. What of the human being's faculty of procreation, shared with all other life forms? Peirce showed that even this capacity is inherent in signs, a parellel that has been elaborated by Thom, in his pathbreaking article "From Icon to Symbol" (1973). *Omne symbolum de symbolo*—signs come into being only by development out of other signs.

The position adverted to in the foregoing paragraphs, according to which, at a certain point in the semiosic cycle, there are objects, included among them conscious observers or interpreters (which Charles Morris defined as organisms for which something is a sign)—such as people, porpoises, and perhaps Phobians—and there are, at another point in the cycle, interpretants, both being kinds of signs, is a familiar one in philosophical tradition. This position—one that surely follows from Peirce's wistful, throwaway remark (1905) about something he took to be a fact, "that the entire universe . . . is perfused with signs, if it is not composed exclusively of signs"—is known as Idealism, and that of a particular hue, sometimes called "conceptual idealism," which maintains that our view of reality, namely, our *Umwelt*, entails an essential reference to mind *(Gemüt)* in its constitution. As Kant insisted—and, of course, both Peirce and Jakob von Uexküll had thoroughly assimilated Kantian principles—"raw experience" is unattainable; experience, to be apprehended, must first be steeped in, strained through, and seasoned by a soup of signs. For this reason, this brand of Idealism can be called "semiotic idealism," in the apt designation put forward by the Toronto philosopher David Savan (1983). Furthermore, to paraphrase Savan, semiotic idealism comes in two flavors, strong or radical and mild or tolerant, between which he leans toward the latter, namely, "the thesis that any properties, attributes, or characteristics of whatever exists depend upon the system of signs, representations, or interpretations through which they are signified." Without necessarily committing oneself to this or that brand of idealism—only the realist positions are, I think, altogether devoid of interest—it is clear that what semiotics is finally all about is the role of mind in the creation of the world or of physical constructs out of a vast and diverse crush of sense impressions.

In 1984 I was an auditor at an international state-of-the-art conference, co-sponsored by Indiana University and the National Endowment for the Humanities. The topic debated was whether semiotics is a field or a discipline—a question Umberto Eco had suggested in a speech delivered ten years earlier on the Indiana campus. Most speakers were specialists in one or more of the complex historical sciences the French call *les sciences humaines*. The designated formal discussant was the illustrious and skeptical English social anthropologist Sir Edmund Leach, who had detected undue hubris in the presentations, pointing out to the speakers that "others were there before you." As to that, he was undoubtedly correct. Obsessive concern with signs dates from the appearance of the most dramatic of all steps in hominoid evolution, the emergence of verbal signs and the changes in information storage and transmission that accompanied that transition. The same preoccupation with signs is evident throughout infant and child development. When my five-year-old daughter asked me, a few weeks ago, "Daddy, just what does the Salivation Army do?" and, some time ago, when my seven-year-old wondered just how Dracula was killed by a "steak" driven into his heart, I knew I was not being led into the tangled thickets of philanthropy or Transylvania, but into that *locus classicus* of signs in action, paranomasia.

A few lines above I used the expression "historical sciences," but this, too, may well perpetuate an illusion. According to at least one version of quantum theory, John Archibald Wheeler's highly imaginative rendition of the so-called Copenhagen interpretation, the past is theory, or yet another system of signs; it "has no existence except in the records of the present." At a semiotic level we make the past as well as the present and the future.

TWO

Communication

All living things—whole organisms as well as their parts—are interlinked in a highly ordered fashion. Such order, or organization, is maintained by *communication.* Therefore, communication is that criterial attribute of life which retards the disorganizing effects of the Second Law of Thermodynamics; that is, communication tends to decrease entropy locally. In the broadest way, communication can be regarded as the transmission of any influence from one part of a living system to another part, thus producing change. It is *messages* that are being transmitted.

The constitution of messages forms the subject matter of semiotics: their ebb and flow, how they are organized and styled, how they get from here to there and back again, how they are formulated and packaged by the originating *source,* and how they are unwrapped and processed when received by the terminal *destination.* How does the *context* in which the entire transaction takes place control the makeup of messages, their generation and interpretation?

Semiotics is further concerned with two sets of interrelated historical problems: the course of development of appropriate mechanisms for processing messages by individual organisms in *ontogenesis;* and the evolution of such mechanisms in a species in *phylogenesis.* Finally, the *historiography* of communication studies has become a focus of attention in its own right.

The process of message exchanges, or *semiosis,* is an indispensable characteristic of all terrestrial life forms. It is this capacity for containing, replicating, and expressing messages, of extracting their signification, that, in fact, distinguishes them more from the nonliving—except for human agents, such as computers and robots, that can be programmed to simulate communication—than any other traits often cited. The study of the twin processes of communication and signification can be regarded as ultimately a branch of the life science, or as belonging in large part to nature, in some part to culture, which is, of course, also a part of nature. When dissolved into their elementary constituents, messages are found to perfuse the entire biosphere, the system of directed and responsive matter and energy flow which is the entirety of life on Earth.

This chapter, which has not previously been published in this form, was written in 1988, at the invitation of the editors of the *Enciclopedia Italiana: Enciclopedia della Scienze Sociali.*

An implication of this way of looking at communication is that the capacity for message generation and message consumption, which are commonly attributed only to humans, is here assumed to be present in the humblest forms of existence, whether bacteria, plants, animals, or fungi, and, moreover, in their component parts, such as subcellular units (for example, mitochondria), cells, organelles, organs, and so forth. The global genetic code, too, can (as it has been) quite fruitfully analyzed in communicational terms: the message originates in a molecule, the master blueprint called DNA, its end being marked by a protein. The intricate interplay of nucleic acid and protein, the essence of life on earth, provides a prototypical model for all forms of communication.

While thus widening its angle of vision to encompass a great deal more, attention here is focused on messages emitted and received by human beings. All human messages fall into two distinct categories: verbal messages and nonverbal messages. Language—as the array of verbal messages is collectively referred to—has, so far, been found only in the genus *Homo,* of which only our own subspecies, *Homo sapiens sapiens,* remains extant. Biologists would thus say that language is a "species-specific" trait. The study of this unique yet "species-universal" attribute of humanity, language, is the subject matter of linguistics, which is one of the most sophisticated, partially formalized branches of semiotics.

A message is a *sign,* or consists of a string of signs. According to a classic definition, a sign is something that stands for something else *(aliquid stat pro aliquo)* for some organism, and has two facets: a sensible *signifier*—or a perceptible impact on at least one of the sense organs of the interpreting organism—and something intelligible (the content) being *signified* by the former. The signified (also called the designatum) is capable of being translated, whereas the signifier (also called the sign vehicle) is not.

The human's rich repertoire of nonverbal messages—by sharp contrast with language—never constituted a unified field of study, and therefore lacks a positive integrative label. What all nonverbal messages have in common is merely that they are *not* linguistic. This negative delineation has led to terminological chaos in the sciences of communication, which is manifoldly compounded when the multifarious message systems employed by the millions of species of languageless creatures, as well the communicative processes inside organisms, are additionally taken into account.

Nonverbal messages can, however, be distinguished from one another according to several criteria of semiotic relevance. As further discussed below, this point can be illustrated by going back to a classic discussion found in the Hippocratic writings on medical communication, describing how the physician, relying on the patient's verbally and nonverbally reported "symptoms" combined with the "signs" observed by the physician, identifies a disease ("makes a diagnosis") and forecasts its eventual course ("makes a prognosis"). In other words, a symptom belongs to a category of signs the physician elicits from the patient (for example, the verbal string "I have a stomachache," or a moan accompanying a pained facial expression as the patient points to his abdomen, or both), whereas a "sign," as this term is used in a clinical context, belongs to a category which derives from the physician's own experience (for example, when the physician palpates the patient's abdomen and feels a tumor). A proper diagnosis is arrived at by a summation of both reported symptoms (or "subjective" signs) and observed ("objective") signs.

The binary classification of signs (in the generic sense) into subjective symptoms and objective signs (in the specific sense) is only one of many. Cassirer, for example, had a quite different binary classification, signs and symbols, the latter being a characteristic only of humans. The most widely accepted classification today, however, is not binary but one based on a trinary principle, established by Peirce. Peirce's classification is complex and has many far-reaching ramifications, but it is rooted in a three-way distinction between *icon* and *index,* with both opposed to *symbol,* all of which are really different facets of one generic sign.

The context determines the predominance of this or that facet. Thus the "Stars and Stripes" is a sign in which the iconic aspect is paramount when the interpreter focuses on the number of stars (representing the fifty states now composing the Union) or the number of stripes (representing the thirteen states that originally formed the Union). If the flag is used for signaling, for example, in a race, or to reflect the country in which a boat is registered, the indexical aspect becomes ascendant. If, however, the flag is ceremonially raised or lowered, say, at a funeral, we consider it to be primarily symbolic.

The standpoint of Hippocrates—whom medical historians have sometimes reverentially also labeled "the father and master of all semiotics"—hinges on an ancient but still widely prevalent distinction drawn between two types of messages: "conventional" and "natural." Conventional messages are those whose power to signify is thought to depend on some prior agreement, presumed to have been reached at some temporal juncture and thereafter accepted as a matter of custom. Such are, most importantly, messages cast in spoken or written utterances, but also frequently messages that are embodied in the shape of a parochial gesture, a tradition exercised and understood by one group of persons but not necessarily by its neighbors. The meaning of a conventional message, whether verbal or not, is invariably circumscribed by a time and a place.

So-called natural messages, on the other hand, have a power to signify the same things at all times and in all places precisely because their interpretation does not presuppose a familiarity with the conventions of a particular group. After describing certain nonverbal symptoms, Hippocrates went on to say that they "prove to have the same significance in

Lybia, in Delos, and in Scythia" (*Prognostic* XXV). Given the quasi universality of that class of nonverbal messages physicians call symptoms, he deems it evident "that one should be right in the vast majority of instances, if one learns them well and knows how to estimate and appreciate them properly."

By contrast, what is sometimes designated as a "multimessage," or conventional gesture, is one that has a number of totally distinct meanings, the choice of interpretation depending on the time and the place. Thus all Americans are familiar with the raised-hand gesture, such that the thumb and forefinger delineate a circle, which essentially signifies that something is OK. In other countries, however, the same configuration may mean something totally different: for example, "money" in Japan, "zero" or "worthless" in the South of France. In other places, the same configuration may convey an obscene comment or an insult, as it did in Greece more than two thousand years ago. Again, in yet other areas, it may suggest nothing at all.

These examples illustrate just one feature by which human nonverbal messages can be distinguished in terms of their temporal and spatial distribution. Other criteria will be mentioned below.

It is convenient to begin a a general preliminary consideration of messages where they are assumed to originate. Their inception can be pictured as in a box, designated the source. A message can now be provisionally defined as a selection out of a *code* by a source. The concept of a code will be explained later, but one should immediately note that many of the rules of probability governing this act of selection are unknown.

The source box is nothing more than a formal model used for facilitating the comprehension of hypothetical constructs: given a certain input, one must, more or less, guess at what takes place to account for the output. When psychologists speak of a "black box," they assume that nothing is known about what is inside the organism or about the functioning, say, of the central nervous system. However, correlations between input and output may enable certain inferences to be made, if not about the mechanism inside the box, about how it works.

The input process is usually referred to as the *formulation* (or, in a particular linguistics context, the *generation*) of the message. A source, we say, "formulates" a message, but precisely how a human does so is not known and will remain rather enigmatic until the electrochemical machinery of the brain/mind, in its immense complexity, is far better understood. The human being, it seems reasonable to postulate, follows, by and large, generative rules to create an enormous number of novel messages appropriate to an indefinite variety of contexts, but how the human being is able to accomplish this is still an utter mystery. Detailed charting of the highly intricate and continuously readapting pathways within the three-and-a-half-pound globe of tissue under the skull known as the human brain remains a task for the future.

The table shown here (Fig. 2.1) summarizes possible sign sources. Engineers sometimes speak of two kinds of sources: discrete and continuous. A discrete source produces messages ("letters") selected out on an enumerable set of possibilities (called an "alphabet"); such a source might produce, for example, a communication in written English. A continuous source is one that is not discrete—say, one that produces a communication in spoken English or as a piece of music.

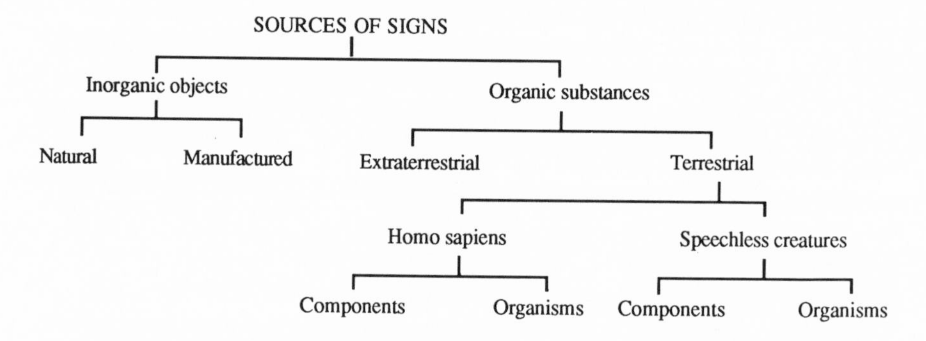

Fig. 2.1. Modified after Thomas A. Sebeok, *Contributions to the Doctrine of Signs*, 2d ed. (Lanham: University Press of America, 1985), p. 27, table 3.

In the communication disciplines, as throughout the life sciences, it is both legitimate and necessary to raise questions teleonomic in aspect. Accordingly, it is proper to ask: for what purposes do sources formulate messages? The functions of messages are various. They are end-directed in the same objective sense in which all animal behavior has a goal: an animal ingests food to gain materials and energy; its digestive apparatus and enzymes exist and operate as they do in order to promote that goal of survival. Messages embody information biologically or socially important for organisms; they are formulated, among other reasons, in order to be "transferred" to another entity, here named the *destination*.

The destination is the area at which the message flow initiated by the source terminates. Its workings can, once again, be roughly segmented into two temporally successive processes, but in reverse: an earlier one, whose characteristics are more or less understood, and an ultimate one—usually referred to as the *interpretation* of the message—the manner of which shades off into unfathomed dusk; in this case, the rightmost portion, or rear end, of the diagram (Fig. 2.3) would have to be darkened.

The source is normally incapable of launching its message in the electrochemical shape in which we surmise that it was initially formulated. The reason is that each source is linked with each destination via some sort of medium, or *channel,* a passageway through which the two are capable of establishing and sustaining their communicative exchange. An example of a channel is the link postulated between a pair of communicating Native Americans, such that one, the source, moves a blanket over a fire, while the other, the destination, observes the resulting message cast, or coded, in smoke (a form of electromagnetic energy). Any form of energy propagation can, in fact, be exploited for purposes of message transmission. Possible channels are displayed in Fig. 2.2.

The point to remember is that the message-as-formulated must next undergo successive transformations while progressing on its journey toward the destination. The transmissions are, as it were, handed on from one relay station to the next, and, before reaching the primary projection area, they need to be rearranged—filtered and variously adjusted—to suit the requirements of the chosen channel.

It is not known how, specifically, the messages are constructed and stacked in a hierarchy, or how their meanings are "agreed to" (that is, coded). Neurophysiologists surmise that, no matter what a message may correspond to in the external world, internally it is linked by chemical exchanges, probably functioning synchronously in various regions, which may be closely adjacent to or quite remote from one another on the two-dimensional cortical sheet of higher animals, including the human. The transformation from this unconscious parallel processing to an ex-

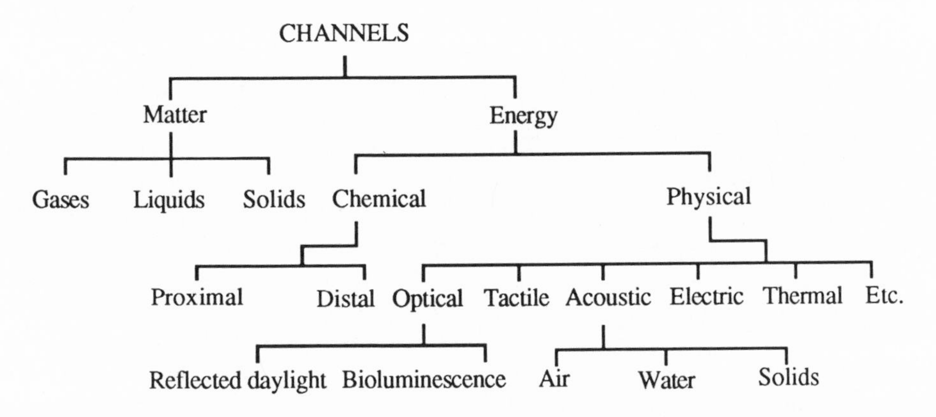

Fig. 2.2 Modified after Thomas A. Sebeok, *Contributions to the Doctrine of Signs,* 2d ed. (Lanham: University Press of America, 1985), p. 30, table 4.

ternalized serial string, as in speaking or writing or gesturing, must be effected by surface organ systems—in the human being, for example, the so-called organs of speech.

This crucial transduction is called *encoding*. Encoding happens at the interface between internal and external message systems, which, in a broad sense, stand in a specular relationship, in a homology of spatiotemporal transition probabilities.

When the destination receives the encoded message—which, because of entropy (the measure of disorder in the system), can never be identical with the message formulated and launched by the source—another transduction, followed by a series of further transformations, must be effected before this message can be interpreted. The pivotal reconversion is called *decoding*.

"Transduction" refers to the neurobiological transmutation from one form of energy to another, such as a photon undergoes when impinging on the vertebrate retina: we know that it entrains impulses in the optic nerve that change rhodopsin (a pigment in the retinal rods of the eyes), through four intermediate chemical stages, from one state to another. A message is said to be "coded" when the source and the destination are "in agreement" on a set of transformation rules used throughout the exchange.

The kind of code selected by the source depends crucially on the total sensory equipment at its disposal. Plainly, it would be abortive for an animal that is mute—as the great majority of them are—to broadcast acoustically coded messages to its fellows that may be deaf. A normal human being's sense organs are capable of registering only a small portion of ambient acoustic stimuli: thus we can generally cope only with frequencies between 16 and 22,000 hertz, and are, in this respect, surpassed by the smallest bat, every dog, rodents, and countless other animals.

The range of seeing likewise differs considerably in various animals: the human being, who is incapable (without mechanical enhancement) of perceiving ultraviolet, bordering on the X-ray region to about 100 angstroms, which is readily distinguishable by the honeybee and some other insects, will scarcely encode messages in the—to the human—invisible spectrum, which could be decoded by other humans only with special instrumentation. The same is true of infrared, which certain nocturnal mammals, possessing a special organ (the tapetum lucidum), causing reflected night eyeshine, can manage to communicate by "in the dark," as we cannot (save with the aid of recently developed devices). An excursion into the field of sense organs is necessary to understand the wide variety of codes utilized in nature, and by humans, to ensure that reciprocal understanding is achieved.

The very general diagram shown here (Fig. 2.3) aims to synopsize the main points made thus far. This model is not be be regarded as merely a piecemeal assemblage of constituents that can be represented as the sum of

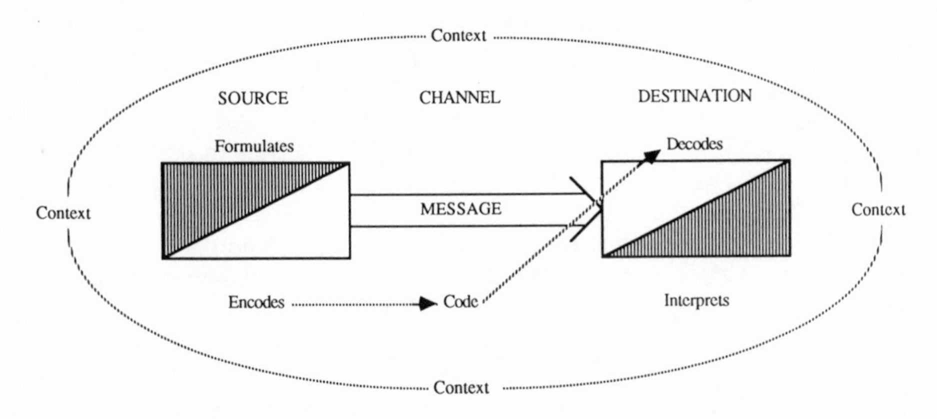

Fig. 2.3. Modified after Thomas A. Sebeok, *Contributions to the Doctrine of Signs,* 2d ed. (Lanham: University Press of America, 1985), p. 155, figure 1.

properties of its several parts; on the contrary, the communicational process indispensably requires that each constituent be conceived of as functioning in relation to every other.

One very important component is omitted from the flowchart model of the communication process depicted in Fig. 2.3. This is the *context* in which the entire transaction is embedded. The setting in which any message is emitted, transmitted, and admitted always decisively influences its interpretation, and vice versa: the context of transactions itself continually undergoes modifications by the messages being interpreted. Messages are, in brief, context-sensitive. That much is well recognized, but just *how* an organism takes its environment into account remains unclear. The notion of "context" has been employed differently by various investigators, but, broadly speaking, the term refers to the organism's cognizance of conditions and manner of appropriate and effective use of messages. Context includes the whole range of the animal's cognitive systems (that is, "mind"), messages flowing parallel, as well as the memory of prior messages that have been processed or experienced and, no doubt, the anticipation of future messages expected to be brought into play.

Some students of communication have consigned the study of contexts to a nebulous area of inquiry called "pragmatics," with complementing fields designated "syntactics" and "semantics," a three-way distinction proposed by Charles Morris (1971). In his usage, "syntactics" refers to the branch of semiotics that studies the way in which signs are combined to form strings of signs. "Semantics," which presupposes the former, refers to the branch that studies the way which sings signify (or "mean").

"Pragmatics," which presupposes both of the preceding, refers to the branch that studies the origin, uses, and effects of signs.

Context is often the crucial factor in resolving the significance of a message. Thus messages encoded in the chemicals isolaveric acid and methyl mercaptan are components, respectively, of human body malodor and halitosis. This notwithstanding, the same chemicals are responsible for some of the bouquet and flavor of cheese.

The context often determines whether the destination will believe or disbelieve the communication received. For instance, imagine a little boy running up to his mother, exclaiming: "Mummy, mummy, there is a tiger in the backyard!" More likely than not, his mother will reply: "Johnny, stop making up stories!" Suppose, however, that the family lives in Venice, Florida, practically next door to the winter quarters of a famous circus which, the mother is fully aware, features a "big cats" act. Her son's exclamation is more likely to be given credence than not.

Sometimes the actual form and content of the communication are ignored at the expense of the context. A distinguished psychologist, on a whim, once carried out the following informal "experiment." Each morning, as he entered the elevator in the office building where he worked, he was accustomed to greeting his co-workers, students, and employees with a cheerful "Good morning!" in a little ceremony that was echoed by a chorus of the same stereotyped salutation. One morning he said, equally cheerfully, with a broad smile, "Go to hell!" to which everyone responded with the wonted "Good morning!" The routine context sets up certain expectations about the probable range of messages likely to be received; even when the communication actually transmitted falls outside this range, as the speech signal in the foregoing situation did, the destinations tend to interpret it according to their expectations rather than by the triggering effect of what the exclamation actually signifies.

The diagram pictured in Fig. 2.3 might misleadingly suggest that the systems represented are static. All communication systems are, to the contrary, not just dynamic but adaptive; that is, they are self-regulated to suit both the external context (conditions of the environment) and the internal context (circumstances inherent within the system itself, such as the array of presuppositions and implicatures that characterize sentences). At successive points, intelligence mechanisms come into play to check the status of the system which can, accordingly, activate and shape coping responses; their flow is commonly described as a "feed process."

Feed processes typically move, in mutually complementary fashion, forward as well as backward, tending to form loops. Thus the source normally keeps checking whether the launched message stream reaches the destination according to expectations ("feedforward"), whereas the destination tends continually to confirm or to disconfirm this to the source ("feedback").

Feedforward is like a trend forecast that both biases perception and enables the source to adjust its performance in anticipation of changeful happenings. In the favorable case, it may facilitate the avoidance of mistakes. *Feedback* brings into the frame information about the efficacy of the system itself, information that is then "fed back" into the system, thus enabling fine-tuned adjustments on the basis of results accomplished.

Budgetary planning, in familiar organizational surroundings, is an example of feedforward: let's say that my dean (the source) tells me (the destination) by a memo (the message) how much money my academic unit may spend in the coming year, and that I then design, or reshape, my unit's activities based on this "foreknowledge." A different example: many a predator (the source) captures its prey (the destination) by a maneuver called "interception" (the message). This often means that the predator aims, not at where its quarry *is*, but where it is most likely to be later, at the moment of impact, that is, at a precise point ahead of the victim in its calculated trajectory.

A common example of feedback also comes from a habitual university setting. As I (the source) deliver a lecture (my message) to my class (the destination), I unintermittently monitor the students' fluctuating engrossment or tedium by way of their acoustic and optic messages broadcast back to me, wittingly or unwittingly, via a feedback loop; conscientiously, I endeavor to attune my presentation as guided by their expressions. A different example: my heartbeat (the source) is slowed or speeded up by a complex amalgam of humoral and neural factors (the message) by the vagal and sympathetic cardiac efferents (channels); changes from the normal rhythm are reported ("fed back") by sensitive interceptors (other channels) to my brain (the destination), specifying factors such as timing, volume, and pulse pressure (further messages). The feedback loop between heart and brain provides an oscillatory input to my central nervous system on the basis of which vital readjustments are then effected.

The message received (and at last interpreted) by the destination is, in practice, never identical to the message sent after having been formulated by the source. In other words, the output of the channel isn't at all tantamount to the input. This discrepancy may be due to random but persistent disturbances that variously intrude into the system and thus obscure the clarity or quality of the communication or, in extreme cases, obliterate its comprehension entirely. A channel might also, say, for secrecy, contain an interposed scrambling device. Such disarrangements, which render the output unpredictable even when the input is known, are collectively called *noise*.

A message always consists of an amalgam of signal and noise, which can be stated as a ratio of the two. If the signal (that portion of the message "intended" by the source) is greater than the noise (that portion of the message which intrudes in the course of its transmission to the destination), comprehension is, to a greater or lesser degree, ensured; if, however, the noise is greater than the signal, special techniques must be employed to restore a degree of accuracy in the reception.

To circumvent noise and thereby to decrease the probability of transmissions errors, the source habitually introjects *redundancy*. There are many kinds of noise and many techniques for overcoming them, but always at a price—such as slowing the source (and thereby the rate of the entire transaction). Imagine, for example, an airport traffic controller (the source) attempting to convey precise landing instructions (the message) to a pilot (the destination) by radio (the channel) during an electrical storm (noisy environmental context). One means—perhaps the simplest—whereby the controller can intromit redundancy to ensure reasonably error-free reception in such a high-risk situation is to reiterate all or parts of the original message, even at the expense of slowing him—and the process of landing—appreciably. After the delivery of every message instance, the controller might ask (feedforward): "Do you copy?" The pilot will repeat what he understands the instructions to be (feedback). If the pilot judges that a satisfactory consensus has been reached, he might so acknowledge with the code "Roger," and conclude with "out."

A different example: When I utter a sentence in the presence of a light source, I simultaneously engage in a wide array of other bodily movements, some of them audible ("paraphonetic"), most of them visible (nonvocal as well as nonverbal). These parallel communicational strands are always partially redundant to one another, a welcome fact which, under noisy conditions, reduces the degree of misunderstanding between the communicants. The force of this mundane example can be appreciated by turning off the sound on your television set or, alternatively, by leaving the sound on but masking the image.

Incidentally, geneticists have found that the relation between the (four-letter) nucleic acid code and the (twenty-letter) protein code—the genetic code—is replete with redundancy, since several groups of three nucleotides, or triplets, along the nuclei acid chain define the same amino acids along the protein chain (that is, these groups are synonymous).

Since the question whether there is life elsewhere in the universe remains as yet wide open, communication is assumed to be confined to the terrestrial biosphere, as well as to be a universal property of life on earth.

The first traces of life, hence the *phylogenesis* of communication, date from the Archaean Aeon, of 3,900 to 2,500 million years ago. The earliest living world consisted of prokaryotes, such as bacteria, made up of cells in which the genes are not packaged into a membrane-enclosed nucleus. These vastly multiform micro-organisms exclusively populated Earth until about 800 million years ago.

According to a current view of biologists, different species of microbes came to form symbiotic unions among one another, which subsequently co-evolved into wholly integrated and perduring collectives of higher life forms, composed of eukaryotic unicellular and multicellular organisms in which they live. Symbiotic alliances—subsuming concepts such as parasitism, mutualism, commensalism, and the like—depend crucially on communication between individual participants of two or more species for most of the life cycles of each; such alliances eventually become permanently interwoven communities, harmoniously coordinated by means of a steady ebb and flow of electrochemical signs.

Each of the three major groupings of eukaryotic organisms (in addition to a fourth, the unicellular protoctists) has evolved a particular type of communication, technically and respectively called phytosemiotic, zoosemiotic, and mycosemiotic. Animals form an intermediate superphylum, mediating between the plants (which they consume) and the fungi (by which they are ultimately dissolved). Because of their pivotal position as message transformers, their communicative processes are the most elaborate. They are also much better studied.

All animals, including ourselves, communicate by exchanging nonverbal signs. Verbal signs—that is, language—evolved uniquely in the genus *Homo* and seems first to have been present in a hominid species named *habilis* ("handy man") which flourished about 2.4 to 1.5 million years ago. This form was swiftly followed by *Homo erectus* ("upright man"), dated about 1.5 million years ago, and soon by at least two subspecies, of which solely a descendant of our own kind, *Homo sapiens* (about 100,000 years ago), survives. In the early hominids, language was not used for communication, but for "modeling," that is, a refined analysis of their surroundings: the advantages of the forerunners of language were not primarily social, but the individual advantages for survival appear to have been critical. However, our species eventually readapted language into a series of linear manifestations, first speech and later other means, such as script, which flourish as systems supplementary to the more ancient and fundamental ones by which the modern human too communicates. Human verbal and various nonverbal means of communication are now so thoroughly intermingled that they can be disentangled only by dint of careful scientific analysis.

As to *ontogenesis,* human infants are born with an array of nonverbal devices they can naturally use to communicate with adults in their immediate environment. They learn context many months before they learn linguistic devices, although the earlier forms (gaze, gesture, and so forth) don't get lost; they merely become contingent and optional. In senility and other circumstances of impairment, language is likewise attenuated and lost before the array of more ancient prelinguistic habits is dissolved.

Attention focused on communication studies, in the West, among the Greeks, in particular among those pioneering physicians who were concerned with describing interaction between themselves and their patients. Patients related verbally and displayed by nonverbal means their complaints (dubbed *symptoms,* which are kinds of indexical signs, that is, signs such as tracks, footprints, finger pointing, and, in language, pronouns) while reporting "I have a bellyache," or simply groaned while clutching their abdomen. The physicians asked searching questions about their patients' past ("took a case history") and examined them with hands ("palpation"), eyes, and ears, or with instruments measuring, for instance, such "vital signs" as blood pressure, temperature, and so forth. Summating their patients' symptoms, or subjective signs, with their own objective detection of other signs, they pronounced a *diagnosis* of the syndrome, and, evaluating that in the light of their overall experience, they made a *prognosis.* These notions and terms were known to Hippocrates and actually spelled out in a treatise by his follower, the prolific Galen.

Both Plato and Aristotle were concerned with problems of everyday communication and its specialized uses, for example, in poetics or the rhetoric of persuasion. For several Hellenistic schools of philosophy, notably the Stoics and the Epicureans, theories of language and of the sign, and of communication, were central preoccupations. The great Ancient rhetoricians, including Cicero and Quintilian, concentrated on the techniques of expression, a field which today focuses on the study of misunderstanding and ways to remedy it. The most outstanding thinker of antiquity on issues such as these was Saint Augustine, who also proposed the first coherent concept of the lie.

During the Middle Ages, studies of logic and language flourished and led to elaborate considerations of a philosophy of grammar and of principles of a "universal grammar." Locke's work of 1690 became enormously influential in examinations of the meaning of "meaning," and he can indeed be considered a forerunner of modern semiotics. Debates concerning universals and other aspects of communication were significantly advanced by Leibniz.

The nineteenth century, and the first decades of the twentieth, were marked by an explosive development of most of the basic communication technologies still in use: photography and telegraphy, the rotary press, the typewriter, the transoceanic cable, the telephone, motion pictures, wireless telegraphy, magnetic tape recording, radio, and television. These rapid changes in mass media and telecommunications (most recently, satellite) technologies, such as interactive TV as well as electronic mail and funds transfer, facsimile machines, and computer bulletin boards, are sometimes (for example, Beniger 1986) referred to as components of the "control revolution." Because the concept of communication is so central to our contemporary civilization, and because of the intensive social shaping of technology by governments and commercial interests, our age has increasingly come to be characterized as "the information society."

Communication studies have hitherto dealt predominantly with the past and the present, but speculative extrapolations toward the future have also been made. It is clear that such studies are inevitably linked to the biological fate of humankind. In 1980 the U.S. Department of Energy created a task force to investigate problems connected with the final marking of a filled nuclear-waste repository—to devise a method of warning future generations, up to 10,000 years hence, not to mine or drill at that site unless they are fully aware of the consequences of their actions. A significant component of this investigation was devoted to the question of how our generation can communicate with up to three hundred generations into the future. The report—which has become particularly relevant in view of the preliminary selection by the U.S. Congress, in 1987, of a site in Nevada—recommended, among other items, that a relay system of recoding messages be launched and that the messages to be actually displayed be imbued with the maximum possible redundancy.

In any event, in the future, communication will increasingly depend on developments in biotechnology and computer technology, which already provide humanity with an opportunity to redesign itself.

THREE

The Semiotic Self

Freud (1933:119) viewed anxiety in plainly semiotic terms when he defined it "as a signal indicating the presence of a danger-situation." His concept of anxiety as a sign, or string of signs, focused on a mechanism of defense which triggers the only kind of escape from an internal danger available to the organism, a flight from awareness. (Two of the most "significant" characteristics of signal anxiety may thus well be silence and invisibility.) Grinker (1966:131–132) developed some consequences of this way of analyzing the properties of anxiety states in declaring his belief "that anxiety is a signal to the self and others which indicates that organismic adjustments to present or expected situations are being made in dynamically related somatic, psychological and behavioral processes," and that, in mild form, "anxiety is of great significance as a signal of threat for it precedes or accompanies active preparation for adjustment." Paradoxically, anxiety may, in intense form, also produce serious kinds of self-inflicted (mental) illness (the heightened response being due to positive feedback).

What both Freud and Grinker loosely designated as a "signal," Peirce would have called an index—the kind which tends to be unwitting as opposed to the indices of fear and which, according to one of his approximations, "forces the attention to the particular object intended without describing it" (1.369); the relation between an index and the object signified may be a direct physical connection (1.372) or a correspondence in fact (1.558). Now, for Peirce, an emotion "is essentially the same thing as an hypothetic inference, and every hypothetic inference involves the formation of . . . an emotion" (2.643). He held, moreover, that "an emotion is always a simple predicate substituted by an operation of the mind for a highly complicated predicate" and gave this specific explanation for the arousal of anxiety: "The emotions . . . arise when our attention is strongly drawn to complex and inconceivable circumstances. Fear arises when we cannot predict our fate; joy, in the case of certain indescribable and pecu-

The first draft of this paper was prepared for presentation and discussion on December 8–17, 1977, at the Conference on the Semiotics of Anxiety, sponsored by the Werner-Reimers-Stiftung, in Bad Homburg, Germany. It was first published as Appendix I to my book, *The Sign & Its Masters* (Austin: University of Texas Press, 1979; 2d corrected and expanded edition, Lanham: University Press of America, 1989), 263–267.

liarly complex sensations. If there are some indications that something greatly for my interest, and which I have anticipated would happen, may not happen; and if, after weighing probabilities, and inventing safeguards, and straining for further information, I find myself unable to come to any fixed conclusion in reference to the future, in the place of that intellectual hypothetic inference which I seek, the feeling of *anxiety* arises" (5.293; italics in original).

The foregoing citations are intended to set the stage for a necessarily succinct consideration of some aspects of anxiety by the ancillary use of the tool kit of the sign science, and to serve as a convenient point of departure for the discussions to ensue. The model which immediately comes to mind is the one being developed to account for the vertebrate immunologic system in Darwinian terms (that is, based on random variation and selection), which may, moreover, be best posed in this context as a problem involving information flow.

The immune reaction has two fundamental components: recognition and response, or how an antigen—defined as any object that provides an antibody response—is recognized and how a structure exactly complementary to it is synthesized. Recognition is required for all positive responses and (very likely) for various refractory states, which is to say that tolerance is not simply tantamount to lack of recognition. The molecular basis of recognition is, of course, a set of immunoglobulins, or proteins in the blood that have antibody activity.

The immune system responds in two ways: there is a proliferation of recognition units; and there is a stimulation of reactions which can be broadly characterized as directed to antigen elimination. The diacritic trait of antibodies in general is their specificity, a matter of shape: "the business end of the antigen fits, in lock-and-key fashion, a receptor on the surface of the cell" (Schmeck 1974:44). The qualifying property of an antigen is its foreignness—its property of being non-Self. "The teleological rubric 'foreign = bad' has been pretty dependable, for immunological activity is now known to be essential for life" (Medawar and Medawar 1977:99). It is assumed that, in evolution, the earliest living entities "invented" the immunologic system in order to segregate themselves from the rest of the soup of surrounding organic material, in order to keep the Self distinct from the Other. The dilemma in assaying the native from the alien derives from the fact that all things are constituted of much the same chemistry. In solving this problem, the immunologic process became "our license to live in the sea of micro-organisms and as individuals everywhere" (Good, in Schmeck 1974:37). In brief, the immunologic system functions as a prime defense against infection and thus is pivotal in the maintenance of body integrity "by distinguishing between 'self' and 'nonself' " (ibid.:36); the triple pillars of the "new immunology," according to Medawar and Medawar (1977:98), are "a study of the biology of self-recognition, the molecular basis of specificity and the process of information transfer in biological systems."

Miscarriages of this immunologic process, like the aberrations of signal anxiety alluded to, are the consequences of faulty communication; allergies, hypersensitivity, autoimmune phenomena are responses of cells and tissues to misinformation or misinterpretations of signs emanating from the environment; this is "the price we must pay for possessing a response system attuned with the exquisite sensitivity necessary to discern and react upon non-Self components" (ibid.:111).

My thesis here is that this superb, although not flawless, gift of discrimination is, in fact, doubly expressed in man, by two parallel recognition systems and associated defense mechanisms: the immunologic memory, which consists of an array of cells whose surface receptors allow them to respond to particular types of molecules, supplemented by another, commonly called anxiety, which protects the Self in the sense that this is a continuous activity, or way of life, in a word, behavior. What is maintained by anxiety, another sort of memory, is not biological substance but the pattern of behavior that it operates. Both repair mechanisms are homeostatic, both ensure the continuity of the individual for a finite time, but the former is essentially provided by inherited instructions whereas the latter also has a large learned component. I am, by the way, in complete agreement with Heini Hediger's twin conclusions (1959:30) that the syndrome we label anxiety in humans has its roots (1) in our animal ancestry, "besonders der Säugetiere," as well as (2) "in der Normalpsychologie."

One consequence of Hediger's first conclusion—which he amply documents in his remarkable paper just cited—is that it suggests locating the sign processes together named anxiety on the borderline of the realm of endosemiotics with the continuum of zoosemiotics, i.e., what Thure von Uexküll (1978) proposes to call, respectively, the "level of vegetative life" and the field of "averbal or preverbal communication" (the second of which, he, by the way, explicitly notes, involves the notion of body image).

It may be necessary, at this point, to step for a moment beyond ancient anatomical schematism to the modern field of transducer physiology and to recall "the human problem of the greatest moment," as Shands (1976:303) quite correctly designated it, "of so relating the outer to the inner that the minimal information derivable from inner sources comes to be a reliable index of the external situation." This bifurcation, which was so powerfully foreseen by Leibniz and fascinatingly discussed by Bentley (1941), must finally be dealt with in a semiotic frame, as I had occasion to argue elsewhere (Sebeok 1977, Ch. 38). If they are to specialize, cells must communicate with each other, but, as Jacob (1974:308) has underlined, "evolution depends on setting up new systems of communication, just as much within the organism as between the organism and its surroundings."

Immunity must have arisen early in evolution; as exchanges multiplied, anxiety eventually emerged, a supplementary form of semiosis—an early warning system, so to speak—selected to favor reproduction, especially in the higher vertebrates, notably the mammals (cf. Hediger 1959). As the capacity to integrate becomes more sophisticated, the rigidity of the program of heredity attenuates, the brain grows more complex, the ability to learn, ever more refined. Learning consists of selectively attaching, in the *Innenwelt*, semiotic values to objects in the *Umwelt*. In the felicitous phrasing of Young (1977:15f.), "Images on the retina are not eatable or dangerous." What the senses can provide is "a tool by which, aided by a memory, the animal can learn the symbolic significance of events. The record of its past experiences then constitutes a program of behavior appropriate for the future." Anxiety, in this framework, constitutes a kind of induction device the special purpose of which is to increase the probability of continuance of the Self; this formulation accords equally well, I think, with Freud's as well as Peirce's view of the state of anxiety.

Anxiety, then, is activated when the Self is menaced by an event (a catastrophe, in Thom's parlance—see, for example, 1974a:239) deemed of sufficient importance by the endangered organism. The triggering index may take a quasi-biological shape, such as the olfactory trace of a leopard predator for a baboon prey, or be of a semantic character, such as some verbal assault whereby a stranger presses in upon the territories of the Self (for example, Goffman 1971:46). Note that the spatiotemporal nature of the tie between the sign and the interpretant (namely, anxiety) in animals tends to be superseded by a linkage perceived by humans as causal.

In other words, these are the outlines of a teleonomic conception of anxiety, in its beginnings as a regulatory mechanism based on indexical associations of a Pavlovian sort, gradually acquiring the symbolic attributes of causality of the kind intimated by Peirce. In animals (except, perhaps, in domestication) anxiety involves the great biological verities of alimentation, sexuality, and the like. In humans, however, this transitivity of the indexical relation is generalized to objects and concepts which may be biologically altogether indifferent.

In these brief notes, I could not dwell on the question where the "inner" Self begins and the "outer" Other begins, but the boundary is, clearly, beyond the skin. This basic problem was essentially solved, beginning in 1941, by Hediger's invaluable insights and demonstrations, and thereafter applied with varying degrees of success to humans by a host of followers (cf. the field of proxemics). Hediger's (1959:25) standpoint, with which I can but enthusiastically concur, is expressed in the following paragraph: "Fluchttendenz, Furcht vor Feinden, Angst vor allgemeiner Bedrohung oder wie immer wir dieses Phänomen nennen wollen, welches die gesamte körperliche Organisation und das gesamte Verhalten dominiert, ist also derjenige Affekt, dem im Tierreich die absolut überragende Bedeutung zukommt. Er bietet den wirksamsten Schutz, ist der stärkste Motor in der Ontogenese und Phylogenese. Sein Fehlen hat den Tod des Individuums und der Art zur Folge."

In conclusion, permit me to summarize the main propositions advanced here:

(1) There are at least two apprehensions of the Self:
(a) *immunologic,* or biochemical, with semiotic overtones;
(b) *semiotic,* or social, with biological anchoring.

(2) The arena of the immune reaction is contained within the skin; the arena for signal anxiety is normally between the perimeter of the Hediger "bubble" and the skin of the organism, the former containing the latter.

(3) Invasion of (a) is initially signified by the immune response, of (b) by anxiety, with the latter serving as an early warning system for the former.

(4) In evolution, (a) is very old, whereas (b) is relatively recent. There is a corresponding advance from a purely metonymic nexus to one perceived as causal efficacy.

(5) Communicational errors occur in both processes, and may have devastating effects on the Self.

FOUR

The Semiotic Self Revisited

In this insidiously sinuous sibilant celebration of Singer at seventy-six—punning *can* be infectious—the pivotal substantive is "self," specifically that manifestation of it localized as the "semiotic self." For this sentimental reader, the title, and some of the contents too, reverberate with the sound of another from a bygone age: *Symbols and Society* (1955), today an all too seldom revisited volume. Graced with a remarkable, lengthy paper, "Symbol, Reality and Society," contributed by the "Continental Phenomenologist" Alfred Schutz, his oral presentation was directly followed by a concise comment on the part of the "American Pragmatist" Charles Morris (Schutz 1955:202), who enthusiastically welcomed this "addition to the literature of contemporary semiotic," since, as he noted, "there are few basic discussions in this field written from the standpoint of phenomenology."

Singer cites Schutz's later, more developed phenomenological notion of "we-reality," that is, the notion of the priority of the We to the I, or, in common parlance, the overriding importance of human sociality. Schutz argued along two lines: first, that "I" is born into the world of others, who raised "me" and bequeathed to "me" patterns of signification ("knowing") and of communication ("behaving"); and second, that "I" is able to "stop and think"—the expression is John Dewey's—that is, to become conscious of "my" concealed individual self (Schutz 1962:169–172). This, of course, echoes what Coleridge—whose philosophy of *Ich-heit* Peirce himself cited circa 1902—called, as far back as 1817, in his *Biographia Literaria* (Ch. 13), "the primary Imagination." By this Coleridge meant "a repetition in the finite mind of the eternal act of creation in the infinite I AM," offering the means of escape from the prison house of the self by engagement with others, or the ability to distinguish subject ("I am") from object ("you are," "it is"). However, by 1908, as Peirce wrote (on December 14) to Victoria Lady Welby, he had come to realize that the putative contrast between Subject and Object—"in any of the varieties of German senses"—was

This companion piece to Chapter 3 was first published as the foreword to *Sign, Self, and Society*, ed. Benjamin Lee and Greg Urban (Berlin: Mouton de Gruyter, 1989), v–xiv. The book was dedicated to Milton Singer, of the University of Chicago, by a group of his students, colleagues, and friends. The contents of this chapter, together with those of Chapter 3, then formed the basis for further extensive discussions at two related colloquia held in Germany in 1990: Colloquium on Psycho-Neuro-Immunology (Tutzing, June 3–7); and Models and Methods of Biosemiotics (Glotterbad, June 7–9).

misleading and "led to a lot of bad philosophy . . .," these terms requiring a subtler sort of semiotic analysis than had been accorded them theretofore. (Further, some passages in Lee and Urban 1989 independently attempt to grapple with this unresolved issue.)

One can be sure that Morris would have embraced Singer's sympathetic, clarifying augmentation here of this perpetual, complicated dialectic, the synthesis of which was assigned in some circles to a hybrid field later dubbed "Social Phenomenology." (Cf. Morris 1970:149. He appears, however, to have been unaware of Schutz's ideas about sign systems, for *The Phenomenology of the Social World*, where Schutz faced such matters most candidly, came out in English only in 1967.)

Just how prodigious this dialectic interplay between *self* and *other* can become in its ramifications into countless categories and directions is beautifully exemplified, on a vast geopolitical canvas, by Todorov's (1982) insightful meditations on the discovery and conquest of America, or the encounter between "us," the European colonizers, and "them," the colonized Native Americans.

The closest link of the self in nature as well as in culture is with memory, both as a feature of a physical repository and as a social construct. The reasons are quite straightforward: each organism requires information—I use "information" casually here to mean the representation of sets of prior events embodied in a code—about certain experiences in its past to enable that individual to steer with reasonable certitude of survival in its specific current *Umwelt*.

Memory in "man, proud man" makes up, as it were, a multisensory private documentary archive, severally composed of nonverbal signs with a verbal overlay. It is the *articulatio secunda*, or the syntactic aspect of language, which provides the machinery whereby memory organizes, continually remodels as a child playing with a tinkertoy, and finally imposes a coherent and personal narrative schema upon each of us. Since writing tends to conserve the semiotic self far beyond any oral tradition, literate peoples have invented the diary or intimate journal (and, later, the family photo album, home movies, and comparable technological accoutrements) to delineate for themselves, in the form of supplementary *aides-mémoire*, a kind of dramatic "I" to furnish, in Peirce's memorable phrase (MS 318–355, 1907), their "theater of consciousness."

This blueprint, too, is what Jacob envisioned when, in the concrete titular and key metaphor of his recent autobiography, he fantasized carrying within himself a kind of *statue intérieure*, "sculpted since childhood, that gives my life a continuity and is the most intimate part of me, the hardest kernel of my character. I have been shaping this statue all my life. I have been constantly retouching, polishing, refining it. . . . Not a gesture, not a word, but has been imposed by the statue within" (1988:19).

Along with Popper and Eccles (1977:129), we may say of the self that, "like any living organism, it extends through a stretch of time, from birth to death." The semiotic self is by no means identical with "the consciousness that binds our life together" (Peirce 1935–1966:1.381). While even the consciousness of synthesis is interrupted by periods of sleep, continuity of our semiotic persona (presumably even by those claiming to have been Born Again) is normally taken for granted. Again, Jacob's question (1988:14) is stirring: "Why doesn't the system slip so that, after sleep has disassembled the mind, its memory and will, the mechanism is not reassembled somewhat differently, to form a different person, a different me?"

Memory agglutinates man's glassy essence into a unitary configuration and—as Lecky insists in his theory of personality, *Self-Consistency* (1945)—an enduring, more or less singularly consolidated autobiographical identity (excepting, arguably, in that one percent or so of the population designated, for that very reason, as "schizophrenic"). Memory also creates the illusion—"most ignorant of what he's most assured"—that all our acts are performed by the selfsame person, labeling the array of "fantastic tricks" that happened to us in our past as incidents which, notwithstanding that they may "make the angels weep," do compose a coherent sequence of experiences. Memory itself is, of course, continually refigured to ensure the maintainance of positive self-esteem.

The twin functions of memory in our lives—the archival and the amalgamative—have two coupled sources: genetic and semiotic. There are, as well, as I have argued elsewhere, two intertwined notions of individuation: the immunologic, or biochemical, "with semiotic overtones," and the semiotic, or social, "with biological anchoring" (Sebeok 1988:263–267; also above, p. 40). An apprehension of how the immune system creates the capacity for distinguishing between self and nonself by the immunoglobulin molecules expressed in B cells and antigen-specific receptors expressed in T cells is a fascinating problem at the very frontiers of research, with momentous implications for the diagnosis and treatment of critical human ailments.

So also the human self is passed on by a fusion of two means of inheritance, which may—though imprecisely—be termed the "Darwinian" and the superimposed "Lamarckian" avenue (Sebeok 1989a).

The notion "semiotic self" registers and emphasizes the fact that an animate is capable of absorbing information from its environment if, and only if, it possesses the corresponding key, or code. There must exist an internalized system of signposts to provide a map to the actual configuration of events. Therefore, "self" can be adequately grasped only with the concepts and terminology of the doctrine of signs. Another way of formulating this fact is that while living entities are, in one commonly recognized sense, open systems, their permeable boundaries permitting certain sorts of energy-matter flow or information transmissions to penetrate them, they are at the same time closed systems, in the sense that they make choices and evaluate inputs, that is to say, in their semantic aspect. For this reason, a Turing Machine necessarily lacks a "semiotic self"—its *Umwelt* forever being merely specular to its creators' *Innenwelt* (cf. Uexküll and Wesiack 1988:188, 196).

It would be instructive to reflect at leisure (not afforded here) on three predominant styles of ethnographic discourse. It is the hallmark of great (or near-great) bourgeois ethnographies that they depict and interpret the semiotic self of their subjects by their possessions rather than, as was the custom in other works, by their actions. In the bygone era of "culture-and-personality" studies, dramas of imaginary inner conflicts were juxtaposed as sharply at odds with the outer milieu; in other words, the "unconscious" was enthroned as the "other" within "one-self."

Ethnography melds with the fruits of bioanthropology when the focus of inquiry is narrowed from its looser accessories and belongings to the human body *(L'Homme nu)* in the strict sense. This body has—or rather consists of—a veritable armamentarium of more or less palpable indexical markers of unique selfhood (save perhaps for identical twins).

Fingerprints, and what Alphonse Bertillon in such protosemiotic works of his as *Service de signalements* (1888) and *Identification anthropométrique: Instructions signalétiques* (1893) called "the professional signs" (cf. Rhodes 1956:143), and later biometric refinements in Sir Francis ("When you can, count") Galton's anthropological contributions in the field of measurement, exhibit one such array. Ginzburg's brilliant essay (1983) on the interpretation of a variety of phenotypic clues musters other striking manifestations—by art historians (Morelli), psychoanalysts (Freud), and detectives (Sherlock Holmes)—of this same epistemological model. On the genotypic plane, "DNA fingerprinting" can in fact now identify, with absolute certainty, on a level of discrimination far above anything available before, every person (again excepting an identical twin), even by a single hair root, on a small piece of film displaying his or her unique sequence of DNA molecules.

The odors—of which Peirce remarked (1935–1966:1.313) that they "are signs in more than one way," especially by contiguous association—and the subjacent chemical composition of every human being differ from those of every other. Some consequences of these stark facts were horrifyingly depicted in Patrick Süskind's gripping and (in John Updike's words) "beautifully researched" 1985 novel, *Das Parfum* (Ch. 31): "*the* odor of human being did not exist, any more than *the* human countenance. Every human being smelled different, no one knew better than [the book's antihero] Grenouille, who recognized thousands upon thousands of individual odors and could sniff out the difference of each human being from birth on." Above the basic theme of human odor, "each individual's aura [hovers] as a small cloud of more refined particularity," the highly complex, unmistakable semiotic code of a *personal* odor.

The study of the distinctive pheromonal function, subsumed under the new scientific rubric "semiochemistry," of human chemical signatures is in fact comparable to that of individual fingerprints (for example, Albone 1984; on the comparison to fingerprints, see p. 65). It is, by the way, well known that human infants can sort out their mother's peculiar odor, and possibly even her idiosyncratic breast odor, from those of all other women.

The immune system utilizes approximately as large a number of cells dispersed throughout our bodies as the number of cells that composes our brains. The mammalian nervous system, consisting of an endosymbiotic (better: endo*semiotic*) aggregation of spirochetal remnants, provides the hardware for the functioning of the no less important but even less clearly understood self, the semiosic capacity of which is based on electrochemical signing function and kindred processes begun already to be utilized by bacteria some 3,400 million years ago. Half a century ago, Jakob von Uexküll introduced a musical metaphor of "*Zell-Subjecten*" being endowed each with a quasi-melodic specific "*Ich-ton.*" Concrete applications from brain research may be found in, for instance, Vernon B. Mountcastle's and John C. Eccles's important series of studies of neuronal impulses (Uexküll and Wesiack 1988:217f.).

Some geneticists have argued (for example, Waddington 1961:121), that even self-awareness "evolved from simple forms which are experienced by non-human [comprehending inanimate] things." Wherever this line of reasoning, which smacks of panpsychism but which was once very influential all the same, may lead, it is certain that sexually reproducing organisms, "since complex animals undergo a complex program of development from their conception in the form of a fused egg and sperm cell, . . . have special aptitudes for identity and death" (Margulis and Sagan 1986:162).

Are all speechless creatures capable of internal self-representation? This is an empirical question, though not an easy one to investigate. The "special aptitude for identity" in animals, their semiotic selfhood, has been most fruitfully examined so far by that *nonpareil* explorer of animal behavior, Heini Hediger (for example, 1980:38–62). Does an animal's self-appraisal include an awareness of its detachable appendages (such as spontaneous tail amputation in the course of evasive maneuvers of many Sauria)? Of its exclusive body odor? Of its image reflected in water? Of its shadow upon the ground? Hediger affirms, for instance, that there is evidence to show that animals evolved relatively early an ability to recognize their own shadow, impermanent as this may be, as a spatial extension of, or image isomorphic to, their self (the model). The genesis of the image, the nature of the physical processes which come into play in such examples, was newly analyzed in a pathbreaking (though Peirce-inspired) study by René Thom (1973).

In the identification of the semiotic self, as in all domains of semiosis, context is determining: a live snail's shell is a part of that mollusk's integumentary self, whereas the hermit crab's shell, its temporary dwelling, equally vital though it may be in securing that creature's survival, remains but a foreign object.

What of body size? As long as sixty years ago, R. Oeser (cf. Hediger 1980:42) propounded this intriguing and empirically testable principle: that an animal tends to know the dimensions of its own body (although not, say, that it is white). Such knowledge, both logical and biological, must be unambiguous. (It incidentally concerns zoo planners directly, as, for example, in the design of enclosures for Bovids and Cervids of both sexes and different ages.)

Singular proper names (in whatever channel, inclusive of chemical pheromones) tend inherently to be found in those vertebrates which form personal societies. One's name is therefore deeply conjoined with one's self (Hediger 1980:63–84; Sebeok 1986a, Ch. 7). The self assumes its corporeality through the semiosic act of denomination; one's name becomes thereby a quasi-iconic index which denotes it. It is the "within" that motivates the "without" in baptism.

Some people, such as Alice when she passed into the wood "where things have no names" *(Through the Looking-Glass)*, feel that their name should embody the exceptional status of their semiotic self. So Todorov (1982), relying on contemporaries, such as the Dominican "Apostle of the Indians" Bartolomé de las Casas, showed that the obsessive preoccupation of Christopher Columbus with both his name (specifically, his signature) and his emblematic siglum indeed bordered on the fetishistic. Dante's formula, *Nomina sunt consequentia rerum,* does appear to find application at least in this limited, privy domain of our vocabulary.

And what of social position? "The self," it has been suggested (Chance and Larsen 1976:205), "is intimately tied to primate social dominance. . . ." The salience of this link in human affairs—the iconic spatial expression of social hierarchy—is generally clear (Sebeok 1988:118), but let me adduce one familial example.

In my father's household, in interwar Hungary, he, the "head" of the family, was seated during meals, as you would expect, at the "head" of table. On Sundays and most other holidays, the midday (main, often extended) family meal of the day began almost invariably with chicken soup. Cooked in the broth, there floated the severed head of a rooster, cockscomb prominently displayed. The maid always served my father first, ladling out of the tureen the rooster's head into his bowl, beak facing my father. After he had finished his soup, he would pick up the head, munch on the comb, then, with a special instrument, trephine the skull and suck out the brain. When my father was absent, protocol demanded that the elder son, myself, be served the head, with the same tasty rite ensuing.

Leaving aside the psychoanalytic innuendos (if any) of this recurrently observed ceremony of my youth, it will be observed that status in our domestic establishment was being reinforced by the manner in which we all behaved around the table. Iconic signs were used both to remind of and fortify status, in order to warrant the perpetuation of the prevailing system of distinctions (cf. Sommer 1969:17). When guests were present, as was often the case, they learned at a glance who was the alpha and who the beta male, and all the servants knew as well who had maximum access to amenities and information. The mechanisms at work here were incorporated, indeed, drummed into my *self,* which, as Peirce however wisely observed (1935–1966:5.462), "is only inferred," for "your neighbors are, in a measure, yourself, and in far greater measure than . . . you would believe" (7.571), and because "the Self of the man is . . . included within a larger Self of the community" (8.123), as if these Selves formed a continuum.

Some of the topics touched on in Lee and Urban 1959, notably those that consider aspects of personal identity, were substantially refined by the late Erving Goffman, especially in *Stigma* (1963), the most semiotic among all of his writings. He was one of the first explicitly to recognize positive indexical marks of personal identity, which he named "identity pegs" (roughly corresponding to Morris's family of signs called "identifiors"; cf. Sebeok 1985a:138–139). Goffman, moreover, duly credited (1963:57) the role of memory, in the idea of "the unique combination of life history items that comes to be attached to the individual with the help of these pegs for his identity." The trope he used, in its way every bit as homely yet as original as Jacob's statue, was that of candy floss, which he envisioned as a sticky substance to which the "facts" of one's biography gradually adhere.

According to Buddhist precepts (as who among us knows them better than Milton Singer?), the "self" is an illusion, or, more accurately, an infinity of interlocking illusions—in fact, a set of *dharmas* and relations among *dharmas*. From this it follows that the "other" must likewise be an illusion. Neither exists. But this being so, the semiotic self cannot, in that tradition, ever be understood: what is understood is that there is nothing and that there is no one to understand it (cf. Holm 1982, Ch. 23). But in Western ontology, we prefer to heed the admonition inscribed upon the Delphic oracle: *Gnothi seauton*—Know thy*self!*

As the contributors to Lee and Urban 1959, inspired by Singer, grapple, each in his way, with the oracle's injunction, they all do so within a social science frame. During the same decade, in the domain of the neurosciences, by connecting Darwinian selection, that most basic of biological principles, with events in the brain, Gerald M. Edelman (1987) has, perhaps even more provocatively and decisively, moved individuality back to center stage, convincingly showing that the semiotic self, far from being an epiphenomenon, plays *the* starring role. Such events, which eventually result in behavior, thought, and memory (Rosenfeld 1988) all argue for the supreme importance of individuality. The standard human-computer (or human-machine) analogies, by leaving novelty out of the equation that links the *Innenwelt* with the *Umwelt*, are incapable of coping with novelty. The beauty of Edelman's theory of Neural Darwinism derives precisely from its *in*ability to predict how the brain will evolve. Each human brain develops, in the course of a ceaseless progression of sign interpretation, its own distinct way of ordering reality; or, as we might say in semiotic parlance, every mind has an inherent capacity to launch ever more developed, enriched interpretants in its three Peircean varieties (corresponding respectively to sense, meaning, and signification) on their journey toward infinity.

FIVE

In What Sense Is Language a "Primary Modeling System"?

The expression "primary modeling system"—coupled, as a rule, with the contrastive concept "secondary modeling system," which emphasizes its derivational character in relation to natural language—has been central to Soviet semiotics of the Moscow-Tartu school since 1962, when it was proposed by A. A. Zaliznjak, V. V. Ivanov, and V. N. Toporov (in English in Lucid 1977:47–58; see also Rudy 1986, and Shukman in Sebeok 1986b:I.166–168, 558–560).

In 1974 (Sebeok 1985:23n38), I interpreted the inferred concept—having checked my provisional understanding, when I gave a lecture at the University of Tartu in August 1970, with Ivanov—as follows:

> The notion of a secondary modeling system, in the broad sense, refers to an ideological model of the world where the environment stands in reciprocal relationship with some other system, such as an individual organism, a collectivity, a computer, or the like, and where its reflection functions as a control of this system's total mode of communication. A model of the world thus constitutes a program for the behavior of the individual, the collectivity, the machine, etc., since it defines its choice of operations, as well as the rules and motivations underlying them. A model of the world can be actualized in the various forms of human behavior and its products, including linguistic texts—hence the emphasis on the verbal arts—social institutions, movements of civilization, and so forth.

Although Ivanov graciously acquiesced at the time in my *ad hoc* formulation, this, in retrospect, seems to me to require still further elucidation. Accordingly, the purpose of the remarks that follow is to provide amplification and clarification.

The canonical delineation of modeling systems was framed by Ju. M. Lotman in 1967 (rendered in English in Lucid 1977:7) as "a structure of

This chapter was originally prepared for the Proceedings of the 25th Symposium of the Moscow-Tartu School of Semiotics (Imatra, Finland, July 27–29, 1987). It first appeared in the Proceedings volume, *Semiotics of Culture*, ed. Henri Broms and Rebecca Kaufmann (Helsinki: Arator, 1988). Versions later appeared in the People's Republic of China (in Chinese), Hungary (in Hungarian), and Portugal (in French).

elements and of rules for combining them that is in a state of fixed analogy to the entire sphere of an object of knowledge, insight or regulation. Therefore a modeling system can be regarded as a language. Systems that have a natural language as their basis and that acquire supplementary superstructures, thus creating languages of a second level, can appropriately be called secondary modeling systems." Natural language, in brief, is thus posited as the primary, or basic, infrastructure for all other (human) sign systems; and the latter—such as myth or religion—are held to be resultant superstructures constructed upon the former. In 1971, Lotman and Uspensky (in English, 1978) elaborated their view of the semiotic study of culture, noting that, in their scheme, language is viewed as carrying out a specific communicative function by providing the collective with a presumption of communicability.

An underlying question concerns, more generally, the concept of "model"—which is essentially a reductive analogy, and therefore ultimately a kind of icon—and its applications, if any, as a technical term in semiotics of the nonverbal and of the verbal in particular. Certainly, it is a fashionable appellation in the literature and philosophy of science, where it has, however, acquired many different connotations. Some of the more important of these—notably in logic, mathematics, and physics (but not in biology, more of which below)—are stimulatingly discussed by Hesse (1967).

The only recorded discussion of models in linguistics that I am aware of took place at the 1960 International Congress for Logic, Methodology and Philosophy of Science, with the participation (among others) of Bar-Hillel and Chomsky. The proceedings include a highly useful, although neglected, paper by Yuen Ren Chao, who correctly notes that, while "the term 'model' is relatively new in linguistics . . . the use of what may reasonably be regarded as models is as old as the study of language" (Chao 1962:558; for later references, see Welte 1974:1.386–387, and Stewart 1976; also cf. Koch 1986). Chao claims that the earliest mention of models in (American?) linguistics was in 1944 by Z. S. Harris. However this may have been, the term was thereafter used with increasing frequency, yet in a bewildering variety of senses: Chao lists no less than thirty synonyms or more or less equivalent phrases of "model" for the fourteen years he had surveyed. But none of these seems to conform to, or possess the scope of, the uses of "model" in the Soviet tradition.

Some twentieth-century pre-Chao and post-Chao models of semiosis—or aspects of semiosis—are illustrated by the graphic displays shown here, a modest sample chosen almost at random from a far larger number (cf. Fiske 1982, Ch. 2, for Gerbner's, Newcomb's, and Westley and MacLean's models, among others). It should also be noted that these models are all, more or less, linked intertextually among one another, namely, their framers were aware of earlier models and their interpretations of these models were repositioned in the light of each later model.

The "convenient diagram of Symbol, Reference and Referent" (Fig. 5.1) was contrived, in the 1920s, by Ogden and Richards (1938:11). In Europe, the "organon model" of language (Fig. 5.2) by Bühler (1965:28) became widely influential after the mid-1930s. Shannon and Weaver's (1949:5) schematic flowchart (Fig. 5.3), representing a general communication system, has become a classic that keeps being copied, since the early 1950s, with all sorts of variations, since it is heuristically so valuable and because it suggests ways of expanding the theory embedded in it. In the early 1960s, Sebeok (1972:14) tried to depict by way of a Morley Triangle the relationships between Bühler's model and Jakobson's (orginally, 1960:253, 257) more comprehensive information-theoretical schema of six constitutive factors, each of which is posited to determine a different function of language; this was, in turn, actuated by the Shannon and Weaver model (Fig. 5.4).

Chao does not press his own views, but it is clear that, had he developed them, they would have mirrored common semiotic principles by changing their parity. What he does say (1962:564) is that, in his model of models, "there are things and models of things, the latter being also things but used in a special way." One would now rather say that there are objects and signs of objects, the former also being signs but used in a special way (cf. Ch. 1, above).

Chao then gives this example: "If we take any two things, say cabbages and kings, and make, say, a cabbage the model of a king, there is not likely to be much that is true of one that is also true of the other, though usually not zero, e.g. both are living things or can be, etc., but the modelity of cabbages with respect to kings is fairly low" (1962:564).

This can be rephrased in standard semiotic idiom in this way: a cabbage *(aliquid)* stands for *(stat pro)* a king *(aliquo)*. If it is likely that much of what is true of one (that is, of the sign "cabbage") is also true of the other (that is, of the object "king"), then perhaps one might amplify, with Peirce (1935–1966:2.257), that the cabbage tends to be a Dicent Sinsign, involving both "an Iconic Sinsign to embody the information and a Rhematic Indexical Sinsign to indicate the Object to which the information refers." However, if very little is true of one that is also true of the other (even though it isn't entirely zero), one might say, again with Peirce (ibid.:2.261), that the cabbage tends to be a Rhematic Symbol or a Symbolic Rheme, such as a common noun. In Jakobson's much simplified version of semiosis (1980:11, 22), a model M, a cabbage, could be said to function as a *renvoi* to the thing T, a king, and this referral could, by virtue of an effective similarity, be iconic (after all, as Morris [1971:273] taught us, "Iconicity is . . . a matter of degree"). On the other hand, by virtue of an imputed, conventional,

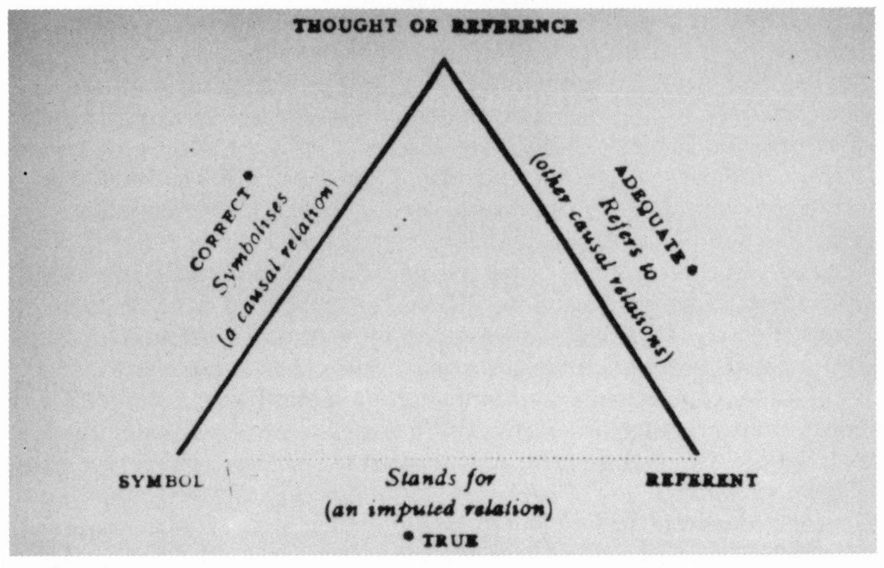
THOUGHT OR REFERENCE
CORRECT*
Symbolises
(a causal relation)
ADEQUATE*
Refers to
(other causal relations)
SYMBOL
Stands for
(an imputed relation)
* TRUE
REFERENT

Fig. 5.1

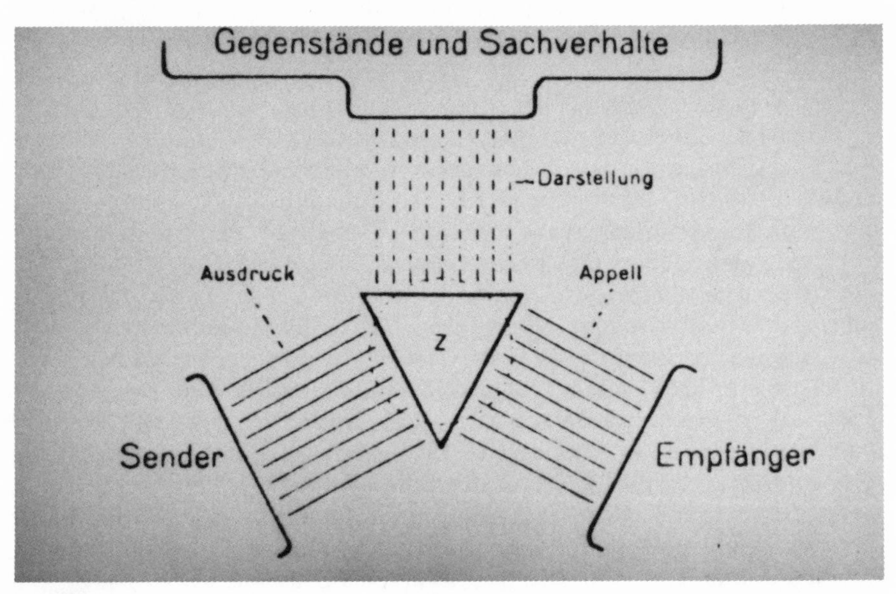
Gegenstände und Sachverhalte
Darstellung
Ausdruck
Appell
Z
Sender
Empfänger

Fig. 5.2

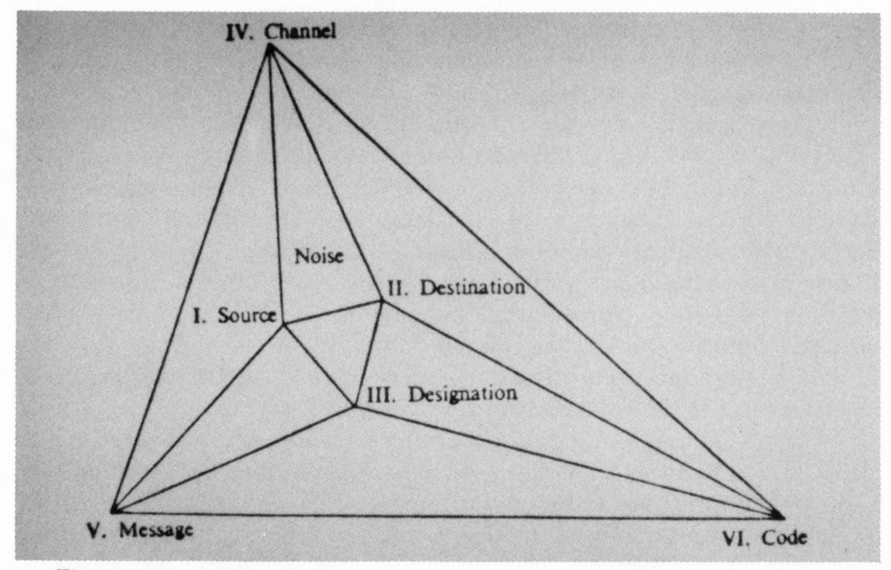

Fig. 5.3

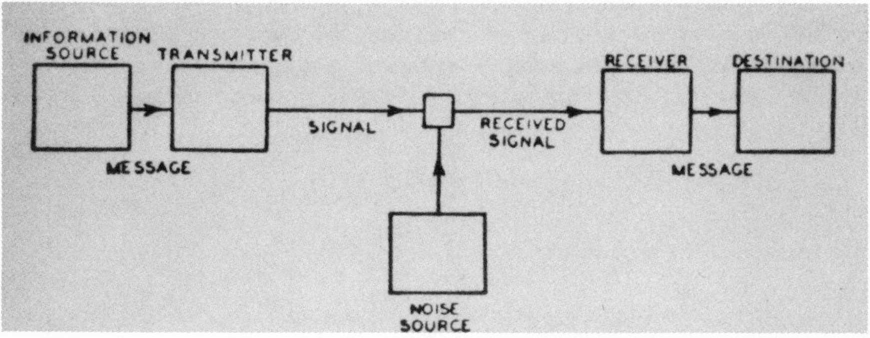

Fig. 5.4

habitual contiguity, the referral could be symbolic, much as, for the experimental dog in the Pavlovian paradigm, the sound of a metronome became an arbitrarily paired symbol (that is, a conditioned reflex) for dry food.

Soviet conceptions of models and modeling systems clearly owe much to Jakob von Uexküll's theory of meaning (1982; cf. Gipper 1963, Ch. 6, and Sebeok 1979a, Ch. 10), developed, in Hamburg during the first four decades of this century, by this great biologist in a series of sagacious, if quirky, contributions to semiotics. Stepanov (1971:27–32), for instance, singles him out for extended mention in the course of his sketch of (then) current trends in modern (bio)semiotics.

Jakob von Uexküll's highly original *Umwelt-Forschung*—which its creator viewed as a scientific theory anchored in Kant's *a priori* intuitions—is truly a fundamental theory, as much of sign processes (or semiosis) as of vital functions. Moreover, his conception at once *utilizes* a pivotal model—the famous "functional cycle," this simple, albeit not linear, diagram (Fig. 5.5) by which, as Lorenz (1971:274) noted, "a vast programme of research is implied"—and in itself *constitutes* a cybernetic theory of modeling so fundamental that the evolotion of language, as I have argued elsewhere (Sebeok 1985c, 1986c), cannot be grasped without it.

The term *Umwelt* has proved notoriously recalcitrant to translation, although "subjective universe," "phenomenal world," and "self-world" variously approximate Jakob von Uexküll's intent. However, "model" renders it more incisively, especially in view of his credo (1982:87) that "every subject is the constructor of its Umwelt."

As Jacob (1982:55) later explained with utmost clarity: "Every organism is so equipped as to obtain a certain perception of the outer world. Each species thus lives in its own unique sensory world, to which other species may be partially or totally blind. . . . What an organism detects in its environment is always but a part of what is around. And this part differs according to the organism." The-world-as-perceived depends crucially on each organism's total sensorium and on the way its brain integrates sensory with motor events. But the inclusive behavioral resources of any organism must be reasonably aligned with its model of "reality" *(Natur)*, that is, the system of signs its nervous system is capable

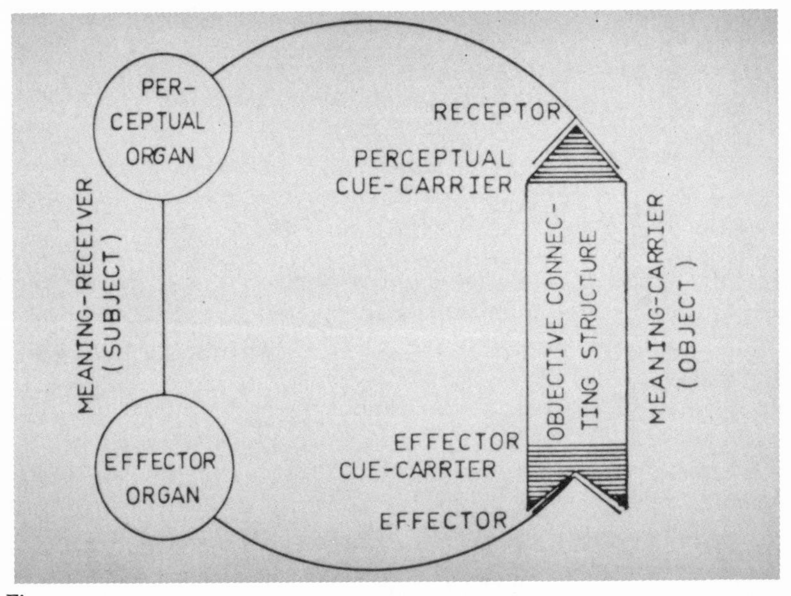

Fig. 5.5

of assembling—or it will surely be doomed, by natural selection, to extinction.

Schneirla's biphasic approach-withdawal theory (1965) furnishes a *minimal model* that must have been crucial for the survival of all animal types, from protozoans to primates (including humans). Such a miniature model—or "modelita," in Chao's (1962:565) sobriquet—evidently requires much the same organs but is played out in two functionally opposed systems, one for the reaching of food and mates, the other for the evasion of noxious situations. A key postulate of this holistic oppositive A-W theory, allowing as it does for plasticity through experience, is that it cyclically relates every organism's *Innenwelt* (or inner world, "comprising" as Lorenz explains [1971:275], "the whole of its bodily structures and/or functions") to its charactistic habitat (*Umgebung*, or observer's *Umwelt;* after Jakob von Uexküll 1909).

The *Innenwelt* of every animal comprises a model—whether of a minimal A-W type or of a more eleborate kind—that is made up of an elementary array of several types of nonverbal signs (variously elaborated by Jakob von Uexküll [1982:10–11] under such labels as *Ordnungszeichen, Inhaltszeichen, Lokalzeichen, Richtungsqzeichen, Wirkzeichen,* and the like, none of which can be discussed here). Solely in the genus *Homo* have verbal signs emerged. To put it in another way, only hominids possess two mutually sustaining repertoires of signs, the zoosemiotic nonverbal, plus, superimposed, the anthroposemiotic verbal. The latter is the modeling system the Soviet scholars call primary but which, in truth, is phylogenetically as well as ontogenetically secondary to the nonverbal; and, therefore, what they call "secondary" is actually a further, tertiary augmentation of the former. The congruity of this expanded paradigm with Karl R. Popper's famous Worlds 1-2-3 model (Eccles 1979, Lecture 6; Sebeok 1979a:204–205) is unmistakable: his World 3 is the World of Culture; his World 2, "the other uniquely human world" (Eccles 1979:115–116), explicitly encompasses language and develops together with the former "in some kind of symbiotic interaction"; and his World 1 is the whole material world of the cosmos, both inorganic and organic, including machines all of biololgy.

The earliest known species in the genus *Homo* is the form Louis Leakey named *habilis,* first described in 1964 and now usually regarded as a short-lived, transitional African form of some two million years ago, ancestral to all later hominid species. With a brain capacity of 600–800 cubic centimeters (cc), this ancestral creature must have had a mute verbal modeling device lodged in its brain (Sebeok 1986c), but it could not yet encode it in articulate, linear speech. Language is, in fact, among its quintessential taxonomic markers (in conjunction with chipped pebbles and clusters of animal bone that evince deliberate cutting and breaking).

The evolutionary success of *habilis* is corrobrated by the very swift appearance, a mere half-million years later, of the succeeding species, *H. erectus,* with a brain volume of 800–1,200 cc; this speedy attainment is undoubtedly due to the species' linguistic competence, also indirectly manifested by its possession of tool kits exhibiting standardized design, the use of fire, and its rapid global dispersion.

Starting about 300,000 years ago, an archaic form of *H. sapiens* evolved out of the *erectus* species, with a growth of skull capacity up to 1,400 cc, and many concurrent novelties. It is reasonable to conclude that this pre-modern human already had the capacity to encode language into speech and the concomitant ability to decode it at the other end of the communication loop. *H. sapiens sapiens* appeared a mere 40,000 years ago, with our brains averaging 1,500 cc.

The cardinal points in this brief scenario are twofold: *language evolved as an adaptation;* whereas *speech developed out of language as a derivative exaptation* over a succeeding period of approximately two million years. These twin propositions need to be made plain with reference to a suggestion by Gould and Vrba (1982). These authors emphasize the distinction between historical genesis and current utility, suggesting that characters that evolved for other usages (or none) may later come to be co-opted for their current role. The former operation is customarily called *adaptation;* for the latter, they propose a new designation, *exaptation.*

Accordingly, language—consisting of a set of features that promotes fitness—had best be thought of as having been built by selection for the cognitive function of modeling, and, as the philosopher Popper and the linguist Chomsky have likewise insisted (see also Ch. 7, below), not at all for the message-swapping function of communication. The latter was routinely carried on by nonverbal means, as in all animals, and as it continues to be in the context of most human interactions today.

Several million years later, language, however, came to be "exapted" for communication, first in the form of speech (and later of script, and so forth). This relatively brief elapsed time was required for a plausible mutual adjustment of the encoding with the decoding capacity, but, since absolute mutual comprehension remains a distant goal, the system continues to be fine-tuned and tinkered with still. Gould and Vrba give many interesting examples of comparable biological processes, stressing that current utility carries no automatic implication about historical origin, and concluding with the empirical observation that "most of what the brain now does to enhance our survival lies in the domain of exaptation" (1982:13). The common flaw in much evolutionary reasoning—"the inference of historical genesis from current utility"—has egregiously contaminated virtually all researches, in the nineteenth century and even quite recently, into the problem of the origin of language, which researches have therefore proved intractable to most probes based on such unbiological principles.

It is interesting that in the other universal domain of human modeling (which cannot be discussed here) where nonverbal—or, as Bullowa (1979:9–10) termed it, "extra-verbal"—communication clearly has exclusive primacy over language, to wit, in ontogenesis, the identical marring feature "has delayed the study of the earliest human communication," namely, "our habit of thinking of communication consisting mainly of language."

As Peirce (1935–1966:1.538) taught us, "Every thought is a sign," but as he also wrote (ibid.:5.551), "Not only is thought in the organic world, but it develops there." Every mental model is, of course, also a sign; and not only is modeling an indispensable characteristic of the human world, but also it permeates the entire organic world, where, indeed, it developed. The animals' *milieu extérieur* and *milieu intérieur*, as well as the feedback links between them, are created and sustained by such models. A model in this general sense is a semiotic production with carefully stated assumptions and rules for biological and logical operations.

This is as true of bees (Peirce 1935–1966:5.551) as it is, on a far vaster scale, of Isaac Newton's and Albert Einstein's grand models of the universe. Einstein, for one, it will be recalled, constructed his model from nonverbal signs, "of visual and some of muscular type," and labored long and hard "only in a secondary stage" to transmute this creation into "conventional words and other signs," so that he could communicate it to others. "The words or the language, as they are written or spoken," Einstein wrote in a letter to Hadamard (1945:142–143), "do not seem to play any role in my mechanism of thought. The psychical entities which seem to serve as elements in thought are certain signs and more or less clear images which can be 'voluntarily' reproduced and combined."

The relatively simple, nonverbal models that animals live by and that normal human infants likewise employ are more or less pliable representations that, as we saw, must fit "reality" sufficiently to tend to secure their survival in their ecological niche (an ethological expression that in semiotic parlance, refers to the *Umwelt* as viewed by an observer of the subject under scrutiny). Such "top-down" modeling (to use a current jargon borrowed from the cognitive sciences) can persist, and become very sophisticated indeed in the adult life of exceptionally gifted individuals, as borne out by Einstein's testimonial or by what we know about Mozart's or Picasso's ability to model intricate auditory or visual compositions in their heads in anticipation of transcribing this onto paper or canvas. This kind of nonverbal modeling is indeed primary, in both a phylogenetic and an ontogenetic sense.

Language itself is, properly speaking, a secondary modeling system, by virtue of the all-but-singular fact that it incorporates a syntactic component (for there are, so far as we know, no other in zoosemiotic systems, although this feature does abound in endosemiotic systems, such as the genetic code, the immune code, the metabolic code, and the neural code). Syntax makes it possible for hominids not only to represent immediate "reality" (in the sense discussed above) but also, uniquely among animals, to frame an indefinite number of possible worlds (in the sense of Leibniz).

Thus is the human being able to fabricate tertiary modeling systems of the sort Bonner (1980:186), for instance, calls "true culture," requiring "a system of representing all the subtleties of language," in contrast to "nonhuman culture," and thereby produce what the Moscow-Tartu group has traditionally been calling a "secondary modeling system." It is on this level, redefined now as tertiary, that nonverbal and verbal sign assemblages blend together in the most creative modeling that nature has thus far evolved.

SIX

Linguistics and Semiotics

The relationship between semiotics and linguistics is to be conceived of as either coordinate or hierarchical. If the relationship is hierarchical, there are two possibilities: either linguistics is superordinate, that is, it subsumes semiotics; or semiotics is superordinate, that is, it subsumes linguistics. Each of these three conjunctions has been variously put forward, but only the third has enjoyed sustained support. The first two can thus be disposed of briefly.

The view that semiotics and linguistics are coequal is maintained on utilitarian rather than abstract grounds. As Metz (1974:60), for instance, has expostulated, "In theory, linguistics is only a branch of semiotics, but in fact semiotics was created from linguistics. . . . For the most part semiotics remains to be done, whereas linguistics is already well advanced. Nevertheless there is a slight reversal. The post-Saussurians . . . have taken the semiotics he foresaw and are squarely making it into a translinguistic discipline. And this is very good, for the older brother must help the younger, and not the other way around." Unfortunately, Metz's argument is riddled with fallacies, the most serious among them being the historical one: semiotics was not at all created from linguistics, but, most likely, from medicine (Sebeok 1985a:181), and also has far deeper roots in the annals of humankind. Sometimes, however, the fraternal metaphor enjoys administrative sanction; thus Rice University, in 1982, created its Department of Linguistics and Semiotics (Copeland 1984:x).

Roland Barthes may have been unique in his advocacy of the radical stand that semiology (alias semiotics) is but "a part of linguistics: to be precise, it is that part covering the *great signifying unities* of discourse. By this inversion [of Saussure's celebrated dictum, more of which below], we may expect to bring to light the unity of the research at present being done in anthropology, sociology, psychoanalysis and stylistics round the concept of signification" (1967:11). Of this passage, one of Barthes's memorialists remarked: "Even if language were the only evidence semiologists had,

This chapter is based on my keynote address delivered at the 37th Georgetown University Round Table on Languages and Linguistics (1986), and then published in the Proceedings volume, *Developments in Linguistics and Semiotics, Language Teaching, and Learning Communication across Cultures*, ed. Simon P. X. Battestini (Washington: Georgetown University Press, 1987), 1–18. A version has also appeared in German.

this would not make semiology part of linguistics any more than the historians' reliance on written documents makes history a part of linguistics. But semiologists cannot rely on language alone; they cannot assume that everything named is significant and everything unnamed insignificant" (Culler 1983:73–74). Prieto's opinion (1975:133), that "[m]algré l'attrait que peut exercer ce point de vue [that is, Barthes's], je considère qu'il est insoutenable," is shared by most semioticians and others.

The subject matter of semiotics is often said to be "the communication of any messages whatever" (Jakobson 1974:32) or "the exchange of any messages whatever and of the system of signs which underlie them" (Sebeok 1985a:1). Its concerns include considerations of how messages are, successively, generated, encoded, transmitted, decoded, and interpreted, and how this entire transaction ("semiosis") is worked upon by the context. Further questions revolve around problems of coding, phylogenesis and history, ontogenesis, loss of semiosic capacity ("asemasia"; cf. Sebeok 1979a:71), and the like. A message is equivalent to a string of signs. Signs, defined by whatever rhetorical sleight-of-tongue—and, as Nietzsche observed, only what doesn't have a history can be defined, and surely semiotics has a very long history—are classifiable according to many (often partially overlapping) criteria; common oppositions may comprehend subjective signs, or symptoms, versus objective signs (Sebeok 1984a; Thure von Uexküll 1986); "wanted" signs, or signals, versus "unwanted" signs, or noise (cf. Ch. 2, above); signs versus symbols (Maritain 1943; Cassirer 1944:31; Alston 1967b); icons versus indexes, and both against symbols (involving one of many Peircean trichotomies; cf. 2.274–307); and so forth. The distinction which is most immediately pertinent here, however, is the one between nonverbal signs (the unmarked category) and verbal signs (the marked category). This differentiation—which places semiotics in a superordinate position over both linguistics and the putative discipline, with, as yet, no universally agreed upon global designation, which studies nonverbal signs—enjoys a most respectable tradition among both philosophers and linguists.

The early development of the notion "verbal signs" out of its Stoic beginnings has been expertly tracked by Telegdi (1976:267–305), but for the continuation of the story since the seventeenth century we must begin anew with Locke. In the two-page concluding chapter of his *Essay* (1690:720–721), where he deals with the division of the sciences, Locke abruptly introduces the term semiotics (with a minor variation in spelling), briefly defining it as *the Doctrine of Signs*, and explaining that its business "is to consider the Nature of Signs, the Mind makes use of for the understanding of Things, or conveying its Knowledge to others." A bit further in the same paragraph, he goes on to observe: "to communicate our Thoughts to one another, as well as record them for our own use, Signs of our *Ideas* are also necessary. Those which men have found most convenient, and therefore generally make use of, are articulate Sounds. The Consideration then of *Ideas* and *Words,* as the great Instruments of Knowledge, makes no despicable part of their Contemplation, who would take a view of humane Knowledge in the whole Extent of it." Locke's epistemological classification here is based, as Armstrong (1965:380) rightly points out, "upon the special theory of relations between *thing, idea,* and *word.*" And, as Deely (1985:309–310) says, these key terms, "words and ideas," are here used by Locke synecdochically, that is, by the former Locke means verbal signs, in the ordinary sense of any and all units of language, whereas he equates (1690:47) the latter with objects. At any rate, in these short passages, Locke establishes two points: first, that "words," or the verbal, constitute only one class of signs but that, second, for humans, this class is a privileged one.

The Alsatian philosopher Lambert, who was strongly influenced by Locke, published his workmanlike *Semiotik* some three-quarters of a century later, devoting the first of its ten chapters to types of signs other than verbal, while the rest of his monograph deals with language ("die Untersuchung der Nothwedigkeit der symbolischen Erkenntnis überhaupt, und der Sprache besonders" [1764:8]). By this proportion, he implies his concurrence with Locke.

The importance Peirce attached to his doctrine of signs is vividly illustrated by a famous quotation from a letter he wrote to Lady Welby, on December 23, 1908: "Know that from the day when at the age of 12 or 13 I took up, in my elder brother's room a copy of Whately's *Logic,* and asked him what Logic was, and getting some simple answer, flung myself on the floor and buried myself in it, it has never been in my power to study anything—mathematics, ethics, metaphysics, gravitation, thermodynamics, optics, chemistry, comparative anatomy, psychology, phonetics, economic, the history of science, whist, men and women, wine, metrology, except as a study of semeiotic" (Hardwick 1977:85–86). We can confidently take "phonetics" in this catalogue as a *pars pro toto* for linguistics, which Peirce elsewhere (1935–1966:1.271) certifies as "the vast and splendidly developed science of linguistics."

Among philosophers, Charles Morris (1946:220–223, 1964:60–62) appears to have been the most circumspect about the links between semiotics and linguistics. The suggestion he made in 1946 (221), and that I well remember from seminars of his that I had attended six years before that, is that semiotics was to provide "the metalanguage of linguistics," and thus that the terminology of linguistics would be defined in semiotic terms. "The carrying out of this program consistently and in detail would mean the emergence of a semiotically grounded science of linguistics." Oddly enough, Morris's wish came true, in a way, four years after his death, when Shapiro made an earnest "attempt to found a Peircean linguistics . . . along lines suggested by Peirce's semiotic in the context of his entire philosophy" (1983:ix). This shot seems, however, to have misfired, for it was either ignored by workers in the mainstream of linguistics or condemned by other experts on Peirce; for instance, one of these wrote: "Die Gefahr besteht, dass dieses Buch [that is, Shapiro's] als Vorwand dafür dienen Könnte, dass andere Linguisten ihre Ausführungen ebenfalls mit semiotischen Begriffen dekorieren und ihre Publikationen dann als semiotische Analysen ausgeben. Eine Grundlagenwissenschaft wie die Semiotik darf nicht zum Dekor degradiert werden" (Walther 1984:117). (Actually, Shapiro's approach was anticipated by several other linguists, notably including Uriel Weinreich and Raimo Anttila, but these treatments of linguistic data within a strongly semioitic framework, as Irmengard Rauch occasionally reminds us with characteristic understatement, have not provoked a revolution in linguistic method either.)

Linguistics, Carnap (1942:13) specified, "is the descriptive, empirical part of semiotic (of spoken or written languages). . . ." Charles Morris expanded on Carnap's proposition by introducing the very general notion of a *lansign-system,* applicable not only to spoken and written languages but also to mathematics and symbolic logic, "and perhaps to the arts" (Morris 1964:60), noting that it is commonly admitted (he mentions, however, only Hjelmslev, L. Bloomfield, and Greenberg) "[t]at linguistics is part of semiotic" (ibid.:62). His proposal to replace the word "language" with "lansign-system" (1946:36), and associated terminological innovations, proved stillborn; but he was right in observing that most linguists who have given the matter any thought at all did view their discipline as a part of semiotics. Among linguists of this persuasion, Saussure is customarily discussed first.

Saussure, who used the word semiology rather than semiotics—and sometimes the more apt, yet never espoused, French synonym *signologie*—seems to have devoted very little time in his lectures to thus situating linguistics. A compact, but revered and influential, passage reads as follows:

> A language . . . is a social institution. But it is in various respects distinct from political, juridical and other institutions. Its special nature emerges when we bring into consideration a different order of facts. . . . A language is a system of signs expressing ideas [cf. Locke!], and hence comparable to writing, the deaf-and-dumb alphabet, symbolic rites, forms of politeness, military signals, and so on. It is simply the most important of such systems. . . . It is therefore possible to conceive of a science *which studies the role of signs as part of social life.* It would form part of social psychology, and hence of general psychology. We shall call it *semiology* (from the Greek *semeion,* "sign"). It would investigate the nature of signs and the laws governing them. Since it does not yet exist, one cannot say for certain that it will exist. But it has the right to exist, a place ready for it in advance. Linguistics is only one branch of this general science. The laws which

semiology will discover will be the laws applicable in linguistics, and linguistics will thus be assigned to a clearly defined place in the field of human knowledge [Saussure 1983:15–16].

Several essays were subsequently fashioned to carry out the implications of Saussure's program, the first among them being the thoughtful—and too long neglected—attempt of Buyssens, who took it as given that "[s]eul le point de vue sémiologique permet de déterminer scientifiquement l'objet de la linguistique" (1943:31). To the principle articulated here, according to which linguistic problems are "first and foremost semiological," and the "need will be felt to consider them as semiological phenomena and to explain them in terms of the laws of semiology" (Saussure 1983:16–17), another has to be juxtaposed, namely, that linguistics, in Saussure's view, was to serve as the model *("le patron général")* for semiology (or semiotics). (This formula, by the way, turned out to have been thoroughly mistaken, and fatally misleading for research endeavors, for instance, in such adjacent areas as "kinesics.")

Sapir (1929:211) also viewed linguistic facts as "specialized forms of symbolic behavior," and he mentions among "the primary communicative processes of society . . . language; gesture in its widest sense; the imitation of overt behavior; and a large and ill-defined group of implicit processes which grow out of overt behavior and which may be rather vaguely referred to as 'social suggestion.' " He then adds that "[l]anguage is the communicative process par excellence in every known society" (Sapir 1931:78–79). He did not, however, as far as I know, use any term of the "semiotics" family.

Gardiner (1932:85) remarks about the "student of linguistic theory" that he "treats utterances solely as instruments of communication, as significant signs. His interest is, in fact, what has been variously called semasiology, significs, or semantics. It is a wide field, and when rightly understood, embraces the entire domain of both grammar and lexicography" (cf. Sebeok 1985a:47–58 as to the terminological confusion inherent in the foregoing).

Here should be mentioned, as well, Bloomfield's dictum (1939:55), that "linguistics is the chief contributor to semiotic"; and Weinreich's (1968:164), that "specialized research into natural human [*sic*] language—the semiotic phenomenon par excellence—constitutes linguistics." To round out such aphoristic dicta, one might finally cite Greimas and Courtés's (1982:177) interpretation of what linguistics is: this, they claim, "may be defined as a scientific study of language as semiotic system." (See further Mounin 1970.)

The contributions of two major figures of twentieth-century linguistics need to be singled out: those of Hjelmslev—who was thoroughly influenced by Saussure—and of Jakobson—who was equally permeated by

Saussure but far more persuaded by Peirce. Of Hjelmslev, Trabant (1981:169n10) observes: "Zusammen mit Saussures vorbereitenden Bemerkungen zu einer allgemeinen Wissenschaft von den Zeichen stellt die Glossematik den eigentlich europäischen Beitrag zur allgemeinen Semiotik dar, der auch gleichzeitig der Betrag der Sprachwissenschaft zur Semiotik ist." Greimas and Courtés (1982:288), ignoring history altogether, proclaim that Hjelmslev "was the first to propose a coherent semiotic theory," a reckless exaggeration by which they seem to mean merely that he considered semiotics "to be a hierarchy . . . endowed with a double mode of existence, paradigmatic and syntagmatic . . . and provided with at least two articulation planes—expression and content." Natural semiotic systems, then, in Hjelmslev's conception, comprehend natural languages. As Eco (1984:14) says, Hjelmslev's definition can indeed be taken "as a more rigorous development of the Saussurean concept," but it is also the case that his program for semiotics "so confidently advertised has never been carried out successfully in any domain of science" (Sebeok 1985b:13). Even Trabant (1981:149) concedes that "Hjelmslev hat selber die theoretisch radikale Konzeption seiner Theorie nicht konsequent durchgehalten," even while he tries to show Hjelmslev's originality in the development of modern linguistics in his only partially successful feat of having commingled it with general semiotics.

Turning now to Jakobson, whose input into the doctrine of signs is every bit as pervasive as Hjelmslev's, yet remains less readily identifiable (it is presented cogently and comprehensively in Eco 1977), the point most pertinent to the matter under discussion here is that, while Jakobson (1974:32) concurs with other linguists that "of these two sciences of man," to wit, semiotics and linguistics, "the latter has a narrower scope," being confined to the communication of verbal messages, "yet, on the other hand, any human communication of non-verbal messages presupposes a circuit of verbal messages, without a reverse implication," he unfurls a more all-embracing multilayered hierarchy of the "communication disciplines." (In doing so, he is actually fine-tuning a scheme originally put forward by Lévi-Strauss; cf. 1958:95.) According to this wider conception, in any (human) society communication operates on three levels: "exchange of messages, exchange of commodities (namely goods and services), and exchange of women (or, perhaps, in a more generalizing formulation, exchange of mates). Therefore, linguistics (jointly with the other semiotic disciplines), economics, and finally kinship and marriage studies 'approach the same kinds of problems on different strategic levels and really pertain to the same field. . . .' All these levels of communication assign a fundamental role to language."

In my view, what vitiates this design is that it is not catholic enough by far; in particular, it fails to take into account the several fundamental divisions of biosemiotics or biocommunication (Tembrock 1971), such as endosemiotics (Thure von Uexküll 1980:291), zoosemiotics (Sebeok 1963), phytosemiotics (Krampen 1981), and so forth, in none of which does language—an exclusively genus-specific propensity of *Homo*—play any role whatsoever. In short, while elegantly disposing of the chief departments in the "semiotics of culture," this scheme fails to account for those of the much broader domains in the "semiotics of nature" within which all of the foregoing rest embedded. If semiotics is indeed to remain "the science of communicative sign systems," its immense responsibility for synthesizing linguistics with "research on animal behavior, particularly signaling systems, and much more" (Lekomcev 1977:39) is forfeited.

At the end of the fourth paragraph of this chapter, I alluded to the fact that, while the study of verbal signs is everywhere called linguistics, the correlative province of nonverbal signs—the unmarked member of the pair—lacks a commonly accepted denomination. Since I have discussed the whys and wherefores of this state of affairs before (see Sebeok 1985:158–162), let me merely cross-refer interested readers to that survey, with the assurance that none of the facts has changed.

A sweeping study of signs and systems of signs, whether verbal or nonverbal, demands both synchronic approaches (structural as well as functional) and an application of diachronic perspectives (developmental, or ontogenetic, and evolutionary, or phylogenetic) (cf. Sebeok 1979a:27–34, 57–60, and Sebeok 1985a:26–45). The following concluding remarks are intended to round out arguments previously introduced by reflecting on their historical dimensions.

As to the ontogeny of semiosis in our species, it is perfectly clear that manifold nonverbal sign systems are "wired into" the behavior of every normal neonate; this initial semiosic endowment enables children to survive and both to acquire and to compose a working knowledge of their world *(Umwelt)* before they acquire verbal signs (in general, see, for example, Bullowa 1979 and Bruner 1983). The point to keep in mind is that nonverbal sign systems by no means atrophy (though they may, of course, become impaired; cf. Sebeok 1979:69–73) in the course of one's reaching adulthood and old age. In other words, the two repertoires—the chronologically prior and the younger—become and remain profoundly interwoven, both to complement and to supplement one another throughout each individual's life. This reliance on two independent but subtly intertwined semiotic modes—sometimes dubbed zoosemiotic and anthroposemiotic—is what is distinctively human, rather than the mere language propensity characteristic of our species.

When it comes to questions of phylogeny, I have previously contended (Sebeok 1985c) that the emergence of life on earth, some 3.5 billion years ago, was tantamount to the advent of semiosis. The life science and the sign science thus imply one another. I also argued that the derivation of language from any animal communication system is an exercise in total futility, because language did not evolve to subserve human communicative exigencies. It evolved, to the contrary, as an exceedingly sophisticated modeling device (in the sense of Jakob von Uexküll's *Umweltlehre,* as presented, for example, in 1982; cf. Lotman 1977), surely present—that is, language-as-a-modeling-system, *not* speech-as-a-communicative-tool—in *Homo habilis.* This ancestral member of our genus appeared, rather abruptly, only about two million years ago. Language, which was an evolutionary adaptation in the genus, had become "exapted" (Gould and Vrba 1982) in the species by a mere 300,000 years ago in the form of speech. It took that long for the encoding abilities of *Homo sapiens* to become fine-tuned with our species' corresponding decoding abilities. Note that, as in human ontogeny, verbal semiosis has by no means replaced the much, much hoarier diversiform nonverbal manifestations, for reasons that are spelled out and elucidated by Bateson:

> [The] decay of organs and skills under evolutionary replacement is a necessary and inevitable systemic phenomenon. If, therefore, verbal language were in any sense an evolutionary replacement of communication by [nonverbal] means . . . we would expect the old . . . systems to have undergone conspicuous decay. Clearly they have not. Rather, the [nonverbal sign uses] of men have become richer and more complex, and [nonverbal communication] has blossomed side by side with the evolution of verbal language [1968:614].

In sum, a preponderance of expert opinion persuades that linguistics is a structurally rather than functionally autonomous branch of semiotics, the rest of which encompasses a wide variety of nonverbal systems of signification and communication which, in humans, flourish side by side with the former, related in reciprocity. In the longitudinal time section, whether in the life of organisms or in the lives of men and women, nonverbal semiosis has substantial primacy. Studies of precisely how verbal and nonverbal signs intermingle with and modify each other in the multiform speech communities of human beings must be further considered conjointly by linguists and other semioticians.

All living beings interact by means of nonverbal message exchanges. Normal adult human beings interact by *both* nonverbal *and* verbal message exchanges. Although the latter, namely, language, is a semi-autonomous structure, it lies embedded in a labyrinthine matrix of other varieties of semiotic patterns used among us and variously inherited from our animal ancestry. "Since," as Jakobson (1974:39) emphasizes, "verbal messages analyzed by linguists are linked with communication of nonverbal messages," and since, as Benveniste (1971:14) insists, "language is also human: it is the point of interaction between the mental and cultural life in man," efficacious language teaching should be regarded as endeavor in what Morris (1946:353–354) has called "applied semiotic [which] utilizes knowledge about signs for the accomplishment of various purposes." The question that I would like to repeat here (from Sebeok 1985a:179, but first raised in 1975) is this: "if, as is the case, we lavish incalculable amounts of energy, time, and money to instill in children and adults a range of foreign-language competencies, why are the indissolubly parallel foreign gesticulatory skills all but universally neglected, especially considering that even linguists are fully aware that what has been called the total communication package, 'best likened to a coaxial cable carrying many messages at the same time . . .,' is hardly an exaggerated simile?"

When I first asked this question, over a decade ago, very sparse materials existed for training in foreign gesticulatory skills; those that did were restricted to French and Spanish (Iberian, Colombian). Today, the situation has ameliorated, but not by much. The impact of nonverbal behavior on foreign-language teaching was reviewed by Ward and von Raffler-Engel (1980:287–304), but they describe the results of a very modest experiment. In the late 1970s, our Research Center for Language and Semiotic Studies began to give this manifest lack of material some preliminary attention (the project is described by Johnson, in her 1979 dissertation, "Nonverbal Communication in the Teaching of Foreign Languages"; and in Wintsch 1979). Johnson also completed handbooks on nonverbal communication for teachers of Japanese, which were accompanied by a widely used half-hour film in which native Japanese perform specific gestures as well as situational interactions, and for teachers of Gulf Arabic. Later, Harrison (1983) published a parallel handbook comparing Brazilian and North American social behavior. All this, however, can only be deemed a mere beginning in what needs to be accomplished worldwide, especially in the production of indispensable visual aids.

SEVEN

Toward a Natural History of Language

> Two coeds met a frog on the campus. "Kiss me," the frog said, "and I'll turn into a psychologist." One of the girls picked him up and tucked him in her jeans. "Aren't you going to kiss it?" the other asked. "No. A *talking* animal is really *worth* something."
>
> —Anonymous

1. SETTING THE SCENE

Konrad Lorenz, who, in 1973, was awarded the Nobel Prize for his studies of animal behavior, concluded his book *The Foundations of Ethology,* published five years later and translated into English in 1981, with an appendix concerning *Homo sapiens.* He professes there to "share Noam Chomsky's opinion that syntactic language is based on a phylogenetic program evolved exclusively by humans."[1] Some of his terms require notice.

First of all, by "humans" Lorenz does not mean only members of the species *Homo sapiens sapiens,* to which we—the writer and his readers, and Professor Lorenz too—belong. He intends to include all our predecessors in the genus *Homo,* beginning—so far as paleontologists now know—with a species the late Louis Leakey had dubbed *Homo habilis,* a creature which seems to have emerged from the australopithecine line, in East Africa, about 2 million years ago, and rather abruptly at that. This advanced ape was endowed with a substantial increment in brain weight over its ancestors, having a skull capacity of about 750 cc. The number of tool types that these archaic hominids employed in this period, which is called the Oldowan, amounted to perhaps a half-dozen or so. A recent close look at their stone artefacts reveals that these hominids "habitually transported materials, presumably for future use,"[2] a circumstance which implies that they operated with considerable—and ever increasing—advance planning. The point here is that long-range foresight presupposes language,

This chapter first appeared as an illustrated review article commissioned by the editors of *The World & I* (October 1986, pp. 462–469). It was loosely constructed around four books: Linden (1986), Premack, (1986), Savage-Rumbaugh (1986), and Terrace (1986 [1979]). An expanded version then appeared in *Semiotica* 65 (1987):343–358.

so that, judging by the technological complexity of *Homo habilis*, we can safely assume that language must have evolved prior to two million years ago.

This assumption is reinforced by the fact that a critical lateralization of the hominid brain had occurred by 1.9 to 1.4 million years ago, and that the unique hominid preference for right-handedness must have been allied to language, "since both traits appear to be strongly controlled by the left hemisphere of the brain in most modern humans."[3] Language, moreover, is believed to have been selected for first, followed by a neurological "field effect" in the left hemisphere, and that it was in consequence of this that right-handedness developed in most modern humans.[4]

The appearance, in an era called the Acheulian, a mere half-million years later—which is amazingly swift in evolutionary terms—of another hominid form, *Homo erectus*, with a skull capacity of up to 1,300 cc, hence endowed with far more advanced cognitive skills, argues strongly for the survival value of this new aptitude we call language. Then, in an even more impressive evolutionary acceleration, an early form of *Homo sapiens* emerged, a mere 200,000 to 300,000 years ago. This fellow, of the Mousterian era, had a 1,400 cc brain capacity. And, by 40,000 years back, in an age known as the Upper Paleolithic, the modern human being, *Homo sapiens sapiens* (you and me, in short) materialized, with our brains averaging 1,500 cc. It was during this period of, roughly, 2 million years of overall hominid development that, as I shall argue, yet another unique human propensity—which must by no means be confused with language, although it habitually is—ultimately evolved. We call it speech.

Further questions raised by Lorenz's observation are these: Just what does he mean by a "syntactic language"? And, more generally, what does the term "language" denote—or, more accurately, does *not* convey—in this context? Most laymen (and perhaps some scientists, too) might argue that the essential purpose of language is to enable people to communicate with one another. However, the same Chomsky, this eminent contemporary linguist Lorenz opted to associate his opinion with in his cited statement, has also pointed out "that either we must deprive the notion 'communication' of all significance, or else we must reject the view that the purpose of language is communication."[5] This provocative statement needs to be considered from several points of view: how *did* ancient men and women communicate among themselves; and, if language did not emerge as an adaptation for purposes of communication, what could its true function have been to merit such undeniable evolutionary success?

Ancient men and women communicated—that is, exchanged messages—within and between their societies very much as all other species of animals do and have always done: by means of nonverbal signs. Each and every member of each and every species alive or ever existing has come into the world with its unique repertoire of nonverbal signs which decidedly promotes its survival.[6] This holds for modern human beings no less than for our ancestors: that is, we ourselves communicate with other human beings, as well as with the other forms of animal life we share an ecological niche and regularly interact with, most of the time by a means of a large variety of nonverbal messages.

It was Gregory Bateson, one of the great thinkers of our age, who pointed out that the coding devices characteristic of language differ profoundly from those of the many nonverbal devices prevalent throughout the animal world (ourselves, of course, included) and that the general belief that "language replaced the cruder systems of the other animals" is totally wrong. Were language in any sense an evolutionary replacement for nonverbal communication, we would expect the older devices "to have undergone conspicuous decay." Clearly, they not only have not done that, but also have in history become even more intricately elaborated in humans, so much so, indeed, that our skills in this respect exceed by far anything that any other animal is capable of displaying. This surely means, Bateson then goes on to argue, that language, on the one hand, and our repertoire of nonverbal communicative contrivances, on the other, must serve totally different functions.[7]

To appreciate the true function of language at this early age, we must sharply distinguish between two pivotal concepts of evolutionary theory: historical genesis and current utility.[8] As was emphasized by Gould and Vrba in their attempt to clarify the confusion surrounding this issue, "Most of what the [human] brain now does to enhance our survival lies in the domain of exaptation" (a term they coined to account for characters that have evolved for other usages but were later "co-opted" for their current role).[9]

In that sense, it can be argued that, whereas language was a primary evolutionary *adaptation*, speech—which appeared, with *Homo sapiens*, not more than about 300,000 years ago—is but a recent secondary *exaptation*. This means that this vocal-auditory, temporal (hence linear) expression of *language* has acquired, in its manifestation as *speech*, an important incremental function, namely, to serve the current utility of a communicative function, thus supplementing, in a subtle and intricate fashion, the entire human repertoire of nonverbal devices inherited from our primate ancestry.

It is reasonable to suppose that the adjustment, or fine-tuning, of the encoding capacity required by speaking to the decoding capacity required to understand speech, and vice versa, took about two million years to achieve at least partially. (Full understanding is a rare commodity; most of the time most of us don't quite grasp what another human being is trying to tell us.) Even today, humans have no special organ for speech, which is formed by a tract orginally designed for two entirely different biological functions: the alimentary and the respiratory. Speech is then received, as any other sound, by the ear, which has still another phylogenetic source and is a rather newly acquired sensory receptor.

But if language was not, in its origins, a character selected for its current role to supplement, or to enhance, communication, what *did* it evolve for?

The answer to this cardinal question is inherent in the life's work of one of the most original—although, for reasons that can't be discussed here, persistently misunderstood—geniuses of theoretical biology, Jakob von Uexküll.[10] Briefly, Uexküll founded a special method of inquiry he called *Umwelt-Forschung,* a term notoriously difficult to render into English. It means research into the worlds surrounding all animals, as they themselves perceive their own subjective universes.

These phenomenal worlds, which diverge from species to species, can be visualized as if they were bubbles within which each creature is imprisoned, as it were, by virtue of its total and unique stock of particular sensory instruments. (Phenomenal worlds differ not only among species but even among members of the same species. An elementary example: most of us humans see our surroundings in color; however, an occasional individual who chances to be totally color-blind sees the identical surroundings in black and white.)

Every animal comes alive equipped with its distinctive *Umwelt,* which some can modify to a degree by learning. Let's call this self-world a *model.* Obviously, a reasonably accurate correspondence must obtain between reality and the model of it in every animal's mind, or else the species will become extinct. The reasons for this were vividly protrayed by another Nobel Laureate (1965), the French geneticist François Jacob: "No matter how an organism investigates its environment, the perception it gets must necessarily reflect so-called 'reality' and, more specifically, those aspects of reality which are directly related to its own behavior. If the image that a bird gets of the insects it needs to feed its progeny does not reflect at least some aspects of reality, then there are no more progeny. If the representation that a monkey builds of the branch it wants to leap to has nothing to do with reality, then there is no more monkey. And if this did not apply to ourselves, we would not be here to discuss this point."[11]

The term "model" is here intended to convey (1) an intellective construct, together with (2) rules for logical operations. The models at the disposal of other animals are relatively rigid, with only a few simple rules necessary to ensure, or at least to tend to improve, their chances for survival. The human model, by contrast, includes not only the objects of everyday life ("reality") but also an extremely elaborate and powerful set of rules capable of working radical transformations to suit human purposes and goals. Such a set of rules is called a *syntax.*

Fasten, if you will, on Jacob's last phrase, where he switches to a human example, and let us at last return to Lorenz's expression, "syntactic language." A *language,* as the term is used here, refers, in its evolutionary beginnings, not to an external communication system at all, but rather to a *modeling system.* (In passing, it might be worth noting that Soviet scholars, independently, came to this same conclusion in the early 1970s.)[12]

While all speechless creatures, as Jacob emphasizes, must model their universe, in order to survive, in fair conformity to "what is really out there"—this is, in the end, the deep meaning of the notion of an *Umwelt*—humans have evolved a way of modeling *their* universe in a way that not merely echoes "what is out there" but can, additionally, dream up a potentially infinite number of *possible worlds* (the phrase and idea hark back to Leibniz).

This kind of capability is achievable solely by means of a language, such that sentences in that language can be decomposed and recomposed in an indefinite number of ways (given a sufficient number of pieces to start out with); we can do this because all our natural languages possess (as do the genetic code, which is the language of life, and the immune code, which we now know constitutes the biological language of the self) a *syntactic component*.

By means of such a syntax, we can construct numberless novel narratives, imagine many versions of the past and construct as many future scenarios (including those of our death and afterlife), lie, frame scientific hypotheses (such are Newton's and Einstein's great models of the universe), including hypotheses about language itself, create poetry—in short, build a civilization. (It was Niels Bohr who first emphasized the doctrine that scientists have no concern with "reality"; their job has to do with model building.) Putting the matter somewhat more technically, in addition to making declarative sentences, we can construct as many conditionals ("what ifs") as may be called for by an infinite variety of circumstances. No other animal, so far as we know, has language in this sense.

There are two points in the foregoing that are not currently controversial (save perhaps at the lunatic fringes of science), and then there is a third one that is passionately so. The first two are that (1) all living creatures, therefore all animals, can and do communicate; and that (2) no animal other than *Homo sapiens* is endowed with speech. (Although everybody agrees now that the latter is so, such was not the case earlier in the century: in 1916 William H. Furness III of Philadelphia tried, but dismally failed, to teach an orangutan to speak; and even as late as the 1950s Keith and Cathy Hayes of Florida lavished six fruitless years trying to coax a chimp to speak.)[13]

The hotly contested issue—the one which each of the four books under review must come to grips with and take a stand on—is the question whether language (in the sense used above, not, of course, metaphorically) does or does not occur in any species outside the genus *Homo*.

2. THE CAST OF CHARACTERS

The search for talking animals is ancient and ubiquitous. It pervades our myths and our literature, down to Dr. Dolittle and one of the late Bernard

Malamud's last fantasies, *God's Grace* (1982). As Calvin Cohn, the sole human survivor of a thermonuclear war, trying to fashion the island on which he has survived only in the company of baboons, chimps, and one gorilla into a functioning social community, with himself as advisor and protector, daydreams in this novel: "You are not the chimps your fathers were—you can talk. Yours, therefore, is the obligation to communicate, speak as equals, work and together build, evolve into concerned, altruistic living beings."[14]

Allegedly language-endowed or calculating animals and the like have also long figured as living props in exhibitions by fairground entertainers and miscellaneous con artists, demonstrating over and over again—in the words of Joseph Jastrow (who, by the way, seems to have held the first Ph.D. granted in psychology in America)—"how a simple humanizing error in observation under a prepossession can compromise rationality."[15]

Before the 1950s, this sort of generally amiable con was played out typically using domestic animals, such as dogs and cats, horses and pigs, geese or other birds, and sometimes even fleas, as stage props.[16] The famous case of Clever Hans—solidly enshrined in standard textbooks of psychology—was perhaps the most notable episode in the annals of such illusions, or errors (technically ascribed to "experimenter bias"), that offered an explanation of the phenomenon, not as one caused by deliberate deception, but rather as one due to mere innocent self-deception.

Hans was a stallion (in Berlin, around the turn of the century) that answered by stomping the correct number of times when asked even very complicated arithmetical, spelling, or other kinds of questions. The investigator of the phenomenon, a farseeing German psychologist named Oskar Pfungst, found that Hans responded to subtle, unwitting visual cues provided unknowingly by his owner or by the audience participants present at the demonstrations.[17] Alas, a confession by Hans's groom has just been uncovered; this rascal is quoted in an interview as having blurted out: "Clever Hans, he is really myself. When I lower my eyes, then the horse stomps until I raise my eyes again."[18]

Beginning about 1960, the playing stakes were significantly raised, as a result of the abrupt infusion of government funding required to support a new habit. This unprecedented financial support, largely on the part of the taxpayers, accompanied a shift from domestic animals as targets of language-instillation experiments to those involving remote, hitherto alien—therefore extremely expensive—creatures in our midst. At first, these were marine mammals, notably the bottlenosed dolphin, *Tursiops truncatus*, soon followed by other kinds of whales (and, eventually, by the California sea lion, which is a pinniped).

In the next heady decade and a half, four species of apes became the objects of such studies: two sorts of chimpanzees, the gorilla, and the orangutan.[19] Here only ape language games can be discussed, as these

Bartholomew Fair.

SIGNOR CAPPELLI

(Previous to his leaving London) begs leave most respectfully to inform the Visitors and Inhabitants of the Metropolis, that having met the most flattering encouragement while in Regent-street, London, Brighton, Bath, Cheltenham, Manchester, Liverpool, Dublin, Edinburgh, &c. &c. where he has been patronised by the Nobility and Gentry, will now exhibit his WONDERFUL AMUSEMENTS,

Performed by Cats,

At 19, GILTSPUR STREET,

EVERY DAY

DURING THE FAIR.

The Entertainment will commence with an Exhibition of some extraordinary manœuvres or

SLEIGHT of HAND

By Signor Cappelli, the Inimitable Tuscan;

Executed in a style the most remarkable and unknown in the country. The Cats will then be introduced, and their performance will be, ts beat a drum, turn a spit, grind knives, play music, strike upon an anvil, roast coffee, ring bells, set a piece of machinery in motion to grind rice in the Italian manner, with many other astonishing exercises. One of the Cats, the cleverest of the company, will draw Water out of a Well, at her Msster's command, without any other signal being given than the sound of the voice; this command being pronounced both in French and Italian. All who have witnessed her prompt obedience, have expressed themselves at once astonished and delighted at the prodigy.

The Wonderful Dog

WILL PLAY ANY GENTLEMAN AT DOMINOES THAT WILL PLAY WITH HIM

Gentleman 4d.——Working People 2d.

Printed at the Literary Saloon, 14, Holywell-street, Strand.

form the subject matter of the books under review. However, while the tacit claim which underlies all of the latter is the truism that efforts to inculcate quasi-linguistic skills in the great apes, being "Our Closest Living Kindred Species" (Savage-Rumbaugh, p. 4), somehow sanctifies the lavish funding required to assist in the discovery of human origins, no such profession will hold water (as it were) when it comes to studies of off-shore and pelagic animals distantly related to us, that is, related only by virtue of their being fellow mammals. Consequently, a sharp shift in the justification for working with such creatures becomes necessary; now attention is focused on the sensory modalities rather than on the cognitive preadaptations, as, for instance, in the following: "The human and the dolphin share the capability of communication by means of sounds. The chimpanzee and the gorilla cannot do this with any degree of complexity whatsoever."[20] This is also a truism, of course, but two truisms don't add up to a single truth.

As Linden plaintively remarks (p. 86), "from roughly 1976 onward, the 'market,' in the sense of financial and academic support for the work [with primates] began to contract." By now, it has all but dried up. The reasons for this decline (apart from the scarcity of federal research funding overall) are twofold: first, the investigations were producing virtually nothing but negative results; and, second, all the best talent, having sensed this total lack of success before others did, nimbly faced up to it and wisely turned to more amenable scientific problems.

It might be worth noting, by the way, that ape language games were, and are, played out all but exclusively in the United States, presumably the only nation whose citizens could afford the price tag and thus tolerate them. One such project was begun at the University of Kyoto, but rapidly came to naught. An ape is, after all, the Cadillac among experimental animals; the French, on the other hand, opted for a *deux-chevaux* model, incarnated as a woodpecker, yet whose trainer claimed results "analogous to that found by the Gardners and Premack" with their exorbitant chimpanzees.[21]

Of the authors represented here, three are professional psychologists, and the fourth, Eugene Linden, is a journalist. After his two earlier efforts in this area, *Apes, Men and Language* (1974, 1981) and *The Education of Koko* (with Francine Patterson, 1981),[22] Linden's new book—which might perhaps have been titled more appropriately *The Education of Eugene*—comes as a distinct and pleasant surprise. In his first publication, written in his early twenties, he displayed a deplorable gullibility, one that seems to seize not only the media-enthralled public at large, but also most scribblers when they contemplate and then are moved to write about this subject.

It is easy to see why this should be so. As a well-known publicist once explained (speaking of another sensational topic), when a UFO descends in your backyard, that's news; but when a UFO *doesn't* land there, that's no news at all. Similarly, when Koko the gorilla is reported "to tell stories, escape blame, make jokes, tell fibs," and the like (p. 121), that's news; but when Koko merely imitates the gestures of her keeper, Ms. Patterson—"all of Koko's . . . utterances . . . were prompted," Terrace repeatedly tells us (for example, p. 221)—that's simply another illustration of the adage "Monkey see, monkey do." It is hardly worth sounding off about so commonplace an event. Notwithstanding these obvious facts, Linden had collaborated with Patterson on what is surely one of the silliest books in the age-old literature about "talking" animals.

It is to Linden's credit, however, that in this new book, which "involved a painful reexamination of events" he had written about before (p. xi), he retreats, on a broad front, from his previous positions. He now confesses (pp. 124–127) that Patterson's (and, of course, his own previous) claims were "catastrophic in terms of credibility . . . because the context of the scientific debate is so far removed from the sophisticated behaviors" attributed to this pathetically sequestered pet gorilla; and then he goes on to admit (doubtless still too charitably) that this "impression is compounded by the fact" that Koko's trainer "has on occasion stretched her interpretations of Koko's gestures."

Little wonder, then, that Patterson "has had a procession of assistants who have arrived starry-eyed with anticipation and have left more or less disillusioned." This last point must, alas, be generalized: the field is littered with disenchanted "former assistants" from this and several of the other major projects. A most reprehensible consequence seems to have escaped Linden: namely, that the senior investigators supposed to provide for the training of their successors have in fact abdicated this common academic responsibility. This explains why this game is played by fading stars: there are no promising starlets, with novel ideas or improved research designs, anywhere in the visible firmament.

In writing this book, Linden has exhibited courage of a sort Kipling called "grace under pressure." But while it is encouraging to be able to report that his education has become more sophisticated, it is, all the same, troubling to reflect on the length of the maturation process. After all, the strictures he recognizes only now—not just about his former coauthor's labors, but also about many other aspects of the ape-language illusion—were foreseen at least six years ago by others.[23] (Of course, in the interval, he did busy himself with the preparation of two well-selling books.)

Unsaying is the hallmark which stamps not only Eugene Linden but also the scientists whose work he recounts. Take only the three psychologists under review here:

David Premack: "As early as 1970, I essentially quit concentrating on the attempt to operationally analyze some aspects of human language, develop training procedures for them and instill them in the ape, because it was clear to me that the accomplishments of which the ape was capable with regard to human-type language were very slight. . . ."

E. Sue Savage-Rumbaugh: "Frankly, we are not interested in whether or not language is the exclusive domain of man. That question leads all who address it into a quagmire of confusion, despair, and impatience. We want none of that!"

Herbert S. Terrace: "When I began my study with a male chimp called Nim Chimpsky, I hoped to demonstrate that apes can, indeed, form sentences. I wanted to . . . show that grammatical rules are needed to describe many of an ape's utterances. . . . I discovered that the sequences of words that looked like sentences were subtle imitations of teacher's sequences. I could find no evidence confirming an ape's grammatical competence, either in my own data or those of others, that could not be explained by simpler processes."[24]

Terrace has been severely chastised by the faithful for his recantation, as Linden, for one, reports (pp. 65–69, 236). Nevertheless, the proper method of science *is* to formulate falsifiable hypotheses, and then to search vigorously for negative instances. This is precisely what Terrace has done: he has posited a hypothesis—one that, to be sure, was truly preposterous, albeit not wholly impossible (to wit, that apes are capable of forming sentences, that is, that they do possess language propensity); found, in the course of his empirical researches (described in *Nim*), essentially only negative instances (data from his own subject as well as those of his from fellow investigators, including B. T. Gardner and R. A. Gardner, Patterson, Lyn Miles, and Savage-Rumbaugh), thereby refuting his prediction; and finally proposed a much simpler explanation. As Popper emphasized, "*It is through the falsification of our suppositions that we actually get in touch with 'reality.'*"[25]

So far, so good. But now the plot takes on an unexpected, not to say Byzantine, twist. The selfsame Terrace, the man who had insisted, as late as 1981, that the study of syntax in apes be abandoned on the grounds that "multiple sign combinations are unlikely to provide meaningful evidence of syntax," since the signs made by chimpanzees known to him "were simply repetitions made shortly before by the animal's trainer,"[26] turns up reincarnated as a scientific consultant for the selfsame "we-want-none-of-that" Rumbaughs, who, with renewed and generous public funding, are happily back in the language business. (Even the innocent Linden sniffs at this turn of events [pp. 70–71]!)

With this news, we have, however, reached merely the threshold of a brand new chapter in the seemingly never ending saga about animal language. In 1986, the Columbia University Press announced the start of a new series, edited by Herbert S. Terrace, devoted to the subject of "animal intelligence." Yet the first volume in this series is on the subject of ape *language* and written by—you guessed it—E. Sue Savage-Rumbaugh, whose "discoveries," Terrace confidently trumpets as he relentlessly draws us back to the very "quagmire" out of which we have just barely escaped, "should add significantly to our understanding of the origin and nature of language" (p. xix). The question therefore arises: what is meant by intelligence, especially in a zoological context, and what is the relation of that to language?

According to the classic accounts of Lenneberg, "The definition and measurement of intelligence is difficult enough in our own species. When it comes to comparing different species, it is no longer permissible to talk about intelligence as if it were a single, clear-cut property that can be measured by a single objective instrument so as to yield quantities that are commensurable across species. . . . I would like to propose . . . that the ability to acquire language is a biological development that is relatively independent of that elusive property called intelligence."[27]

In 1983, Howard Gardner went much further still, suggesting that "intelligence" is but an indeterminate concept of common sense which may well not refer to "a genuine tangible, measurable entity," but rather be "a convenient way of labeling some phenomena that may (but may well not) exist." In fact, Gardner, in his tour de force synthesis, posits a set of up to seven human intellectual potentials, "of which all individuals are capable by virtue of their membership in the human species."[28]

As if this kind of vagueness weren't damaging enough, Terrace, in introducing his new series, scarcely mentions "intelligence," dwelling instead on the currently faddish topic of animal *thinking*, and the continuity or discontinuity thereof with human thinking, and on the putative "linguistic competence of animals with highly developed brains." He thus so thoroughly confounds apples ("intelligence") and oranges ("thinking") and bananas ("language") with one another that his entire discussion becomes impossibly vacuous.

If this kind of hodge-podge is what Linden refers to in his remark (p. 236) that today "there is a veritable renaissance in the study of cognitive behavior of all types of animals" and what Terrace has in mind when he predicts that "the coming decades may prove to be the beginning of an era of psychology that will parallel the era of the blossoming of biology" ("Foreword," in Savage-Rumbaugh 1986:xii), both writers are bound to be gravely disappointed. It would be far wiser to heed John Stuart Mill's admonition (in his 1867 inaugural address at the University of St. Andrews) "To question all things . . . , letting no fallacy, or incoherence, or confusion of thought, step by unperceived; above all, to insist upon having the meaning of a word clearly understood before using it, and the meaning of a proposition before assenting to it."

But there is more. Although the Savage-Rumbaugh volume inaugurates a series about "animal intelligence" and features the noun "language" in its title, it compounds the terminological inexactness already alluded to by throwing in—although never defining—an arguably even more heavily freighted word: "symbol" (throughout, but esp. Ch. 11). Savage-Rumbaugh seems to think that the teaching of symbols to an ape constitutes some sort of a breakthrough. In point of fact, instances of the sign category that philosophers (especially since Peirce) routinely call "symbols" occur naturally not only throughout the animal kingdom,[29] but, as the late Gordon M. Tomkins brilliantly revealed, unique states of the environment can also be represented by symbols in the metabolic code that governs processes *inside* animal bodies.[30]

A desperate hunger for priority, coupled with acute anxiety over research funding and a generally insatiable craving for favorable publicity (Terrace cites "public opinion," p. xv), is doubtless responsible for the exceptionally venomous and unforgiving nature of the discourse among the handful of psychologists still extant in the field of animal-language research. Threats of legal action resound. These men and women can't quite succeed, it seems, without also constantly castigating, or putting down, their peers; even the (early) Terrace is ritually criticized, until his "colleagueship"—presumably coincidentally with his consultantship—is welcomed (pp. 375–379) by Savage-Rumbaugh and other members of her team. (Likewise, by the way, Premack excoriated what I take to be Savage-Rumbaugh's core project, which claims to have established "symbolic communication" between two her subjects and to which Chs. 7–11 of her book are mainly devoted.)

This palpably rancorous, politically charged atmosphere "has taught us," the Rumbaugh team importunes (p. 383), "that scientists need to work harder both to establish and to retain a sense of community," for "efforts on the part of some researchers to preempt or to preclude the entry of others into the field of ape-language research was misguided and unfortunate in that they put at severe risk the probability that 'community' and the exchange of data between laboratories might ever be attained."

It is certainly true, as Gerald Holton reminds us, that "the first principle of integrity is that you must submit yourself to the dialogue with others to find out whether you are right. New science starts in the head of an individual, but it does not survive if it does not become part of the consensus of the community."[31] Unfortunately, as became apparent, for instance, to the organizers who tried to assemble a reasonably representative cast of characters for a conference held under the auspices of the New York Academy of Sciences (see note 23), most of the invited ape-language investigators either refused to confront their colleagues or accepted an invitation but failed to show; and those who did show (for example, Duane and Sue Savage-Rumbaugh) had their say but left before their colleagues had an opportunity to respond.

It should further be pointed out that the criticisms of this or that project are typically directed at the underlying logical design of the experiments and the results announced. Personal inspections in working laboratories—except by spectators known in advance to be sympathetic—are not tolerated, and the most outlandish excuses for such exclusions are invented. (One famous animal psychologist once reported, with much amusement, that he was forbidden to visit one of the best-known ongoing experiments on the grounds that he might infect the chimpanzee with viral hepatitis, which the man had never had and which is not, in any case, aerobically transmissible.)

The title *Gavagai!* echoes a coinage by Willard Van Orman Quine,[32] which has to do with subtle arguments by that eminent philosopher about the indeterminacy of translation from one language into another. Given the insuperable problems raised by such interlingual operations, Premack asks, what problems might be raised by (to use a more sophisticated terminology) intersemiotic transmutations, that is, when decoding "the chimpanzee's would-be words or sentences"? His answer: none other than "we do with our language peers" (p. 8).

Premack's own "linguistic" work with Sarah and his other chimpanzees has been severely censured. As noted above, and as he himself announced, he had abandoned his initial goals sixteen years earlier. One of the points at issue had been his lack of proper measures against social cueing, that is, the intrusion of the Clever Hans phenomenon, but which he considers "a red herring," not "a legitimate scientific issue." He feels that his critics should have pointed out "what a proper clever-Hans control would look like" (p. 12).

Unfortunately, Premack either does not know the huge literature on the subject or he chooses to ignore it. Admittedly, the pioneering work of Oskar Pfungst, in the first decade of this century, was flawed, but Premack never mentions the subsequent voluminous writings of Heini Hediger, or the book of Ernst Timaeus; worst of all, he disregards the far-reaching researches of Harvard's Robert Rosenthal on the very nature of experimentation itself.[33]

Premack concludes his essay with the finding—and, as to this, one must surely concur with him, for it brings us round precisely to where we started our own protracted journey—of "not only a discontinuity between human and nonhuman" but also "the lack of any degree of language among nonhumans" (p. 149). The last sentence of his paper then reads, in part: "To get on with an understanding of our species, we shall have to relinquish our infatuation with language" (p. 155). Ape-language researchers, above all others, please take his admonition to heart! And please remember one other, the sage advice of P. B. Medawar to scientists of any age: *"The intensity of the conviction that a hypothesis is true has no bearing on whether it is true or not."*[34]

Before ending this perhaps overlong chapter, a possible misunderstanding needs to be anticipated: the more or less simultaneous appearance of several books devoted to a similar topic must not be taken to mark a resurgence of animal "language" studies. Terrace's *Nim* is a reprint of a book already seven years old; Savage-Rumbaugh's *Ape Language* mostly brings together materials already published elsewhere, although here rhetorically refurbished; Linden's apostasy tidies up others' works; and Premack's piece is but a slightly altered (and, in the book, unacknowledged) version of an earlier magazine piece bearing the same title.[35]

Notes

1. Konrad Z. Lorenz, *The Foundations of Ethology* (New York: Springer, 1981), 342.

2. Nicholas Toth, "The Oldowan Reassessed: A Close Look at Early Stone Artefacts," *Journal of Archaeological Science* 12(1985):114.

3. Nicholas Toth, "Archaelogical Evidence for Preferential Right-handedness in the Lower and Middle Pleistocene, and Its Possible Implications," *Journal of Human Evolution* 14(1985):612.

4. Dean Falk, "Language, Handedness, and Primitive Brains: Did the Australopithecines Sign?" *American Anthropologist* 82(1980):72–78.

5. Noam Chomsky, *Rules and Representations* (New York: Columbia University Press, 1980), p. 230. The philosopher Karl K. Popper makes a similar point when he speaks of the "futility of all theories of human language that focus on . . . *communication*"; see his *Objective Knowledge: An Evolutionary Approach* (Oxford: Clarendon Press, 1972), 121.

6. A large variety of such repertoires is described in, for instance, Thomas A. Sebeok, *How Animals Communicate* (Bloomington: Indiana University Press, 1977).

7. Gregory Bateson, "Redundancy and Coding," in Thomas A. Sebeok, *Animal Communication* (Bloomington: Indiana University Press, 1968), 614.

8. These are discussed by G. C. Williams, in his classic book, *Adaptation and Natural Selection* (Princeton: Princeton University Press, 1966).

9. Stephen Jay Gould and Elisabeth S. Vrba, "Exaptation—A Missing Term in the Science of Form," *Paleobiology* 8(1982):13.

10. See especially his *The Theory of Meaning*, republished from the German original (1940) in *Semiotica* 42:1.1–87 (Special Issue).

11. François Jacob, *The Possible and the Actual* (Seattle: University of Washington Press, 1982), 56.

12. This concept is discussed, for instance, by Ju. M. Lotman, in his "Primary and Secondary Communication-Modeling Systems," originally published in Russian in 1974, but available in English in Daniel P. Lucid's anthology, *Soviet Semiotics* (Baltimore: The Johns Hopkins University Press, 1977, 1988), 95–98.

13. For details, see the entertaining book by Adrian J. Desmond, *The Ape's Reflexion* (New York: Dial Press/James Wade, 1979).

14. *God's Grace* (New York: Farrar Straus Giroux, 1982), 127.

15. *Wish and Wisdom: Episodes in the Vagaries of Belief* (New York: D. Appleton-Century, 1935), 213.

16. Such scams are well documented since Elizabethan times. See the excellent account by the outstanding magician, Milbourne Christopher, *ESP, Seers & Psychics* (New York: Thomas Y. Crowell, 1970), 39–54.

17. See Dodge Fernald, *The Hans Legacy: A Story of Science* (Hilldale: Lawrence Erlbaum, 1984).

18. See Thomas A. Sebeok, "A Scientific Quibble," *Semiotica* 57(1985):123.

19. Known in the zoological literature, respectively, as *Pan troglodytes, Pan paniscus* (the pigmy chimp), *Gorilla gorilla*, and *Pongo pongo.*

20. So says John C. Lilly, in his *Communication between Man and Dolphin: The Possibilities of Talking with Other Species* (New York: Crown, 1978), 78.

21. On the Gallic Greater Spotted Woodpecker, see Bernadette Chauvin-Muckensturm, "Y a-t-il utilisation de signaux appris comme moyen de communication chez le pic epeiche?" *Revue du comportment animal* 9:185–207. There are also reports of experiments, in this country, with parrots and pigeons, showing, by and large, embarrassingly comparable results to those accomplished with the primates.

22. Reviewed by Thomas A. Sebeok under the title "The Not So Sedulous Ape," *Times Literary Supplement* (September 10, 1982). The fuller, original version is to be found in Thomas A. Sebeok, *I Think I Am a Verb* (New York: Plenum Press, 1986), 205–208.

23. For example, see Thomas A. Sebeok and Jean Umiker-Sebeok, *Speaking of Apes: A Critical Anthology of Two-Way Communication with Man* (New York: Plenum Press, 1980), esp. 1–59; and, afterward, many of Terrace's publications, such as "A Report to an Academy, 1980," in Thomas A. Sebeok and Robert Rosenthal, *The Clever Hans Phenomenon: Communication with Horses, Whales, Apes, and People* (New York: The New York Academy of Sciences, 1981), vol. 364, pp. 94–114.

24. Premack, in a debate with Noam Chomsky, "Species of Intelligence," *The Sciences* 19(9):8. Savage-Rumbaugh, with Duane Rumbaugh, writing in 1979, quoted by Linden, p. 58. Terrace, in a characteristically titled piece, "How Nim Chimpsky Changed My Mind," *Psychology Today* 13(6):65, 76.

25. Popper, *Objective Knowledge: An Evolutionary Approach*, 360.

26. In D. R. Griffin, ed., *Animal Mind—Human Mind* (Berlin: Springer Verlag, 1982), 402.

27. Eric H. Lenneberg, ed., *New Directions in the Study of Language* (Cambridge: MIT Press, 1964), 77–78. Lenneberg greatly elaborated on these statements in his very influential book, *Biological Foundations of Language* (New York: Wiley, 1967), esp. 228–230.

28. *Frames of Mind: The Theory of Multiple Intelligences* (New York: Basic Books, 1983), 69, 278.

29. For further discussion, definitions, and examples, see Thomas A. Sebeok, *Contribution to the Doctrine of Signs* (Lanham: University Press of America, 1985), 134–138.

30. "The Metabolic Code," *Science* 189:760–763.

31. "Niels Bohr and the Integrity of Science," *American Scientist* 74(3):240.

32. *Word & Object* (Cambridge: MIT Press, 1960), Ch. 2.

33. Among the extensive writings of Heini Hediger on this general subject, but including ape language research as well, see, most recently, his *Tiere Verstehen: Erkenntnisse eines Tierpsychologen* (Munich: Kindler, 1980), esp. the chapter "The Return of Clever Hans," 112–160. One of the few psychologists who tried to replicate (partially) the original experiments with Clever Hans was Ernst Timaeus; see *Experiment und Psychologie: Zur Sozialpsychologie psychologischen Experimentierens* (Göttingen: Hogrefe, 1974). Robert Rosenthal's books and papers are too numerous to list here, but see esp. his *Experimenter Effects in Behavioral Research* (New York: Irvington, 1976). For one review of the Premacks' *The Mind of an Ape*, see the *Times Literary Supplement*, June 29, 1984.

34. *Advice to a Young Scientist* (New York: Harper & Row, 1979), p. 39.

35. This will be found in *Cognition* 19:207–296. At least three errors need to be corrected in the 1986 version: the article by Miles, referred to on p. 29, was published already in 1983, by Springer. "Petitio," named on p. 33, is actually Laura A. Petitto. And the "Menzle," who appears twice on p. 141, is in fact the primatologist E. W. Menzel.

EIGHT

The Evolution of Semiosis

1. WHAT IS "SEMIOSIS"?

In Peirce's usage (1935–1966:5.473), semiosis, or "action of a sign," is an irreducibly triadic process, comprising a relation among (1) a sign, (2) its object, and (3) its actual or potential interpretant. It particularly focuses upon the way that the interpretant is produced, and thus concerns what is involved in understanding or teleonomic (that is, goal-directed) interpretation of the sign. Similarly, Charles Morris (1946:253) defined semiosis as "a sign-process, that is, a process in which something is a sign to some organism." These definitions imply, effectively and ineluctably, that at least one link in the loop must be a living entity (although, as we shall see, this may be only a portion of an organism, or an artifactual extension fabricated by a hominid). It follows, then, that there could not have been semiosis prior to the evolution of life. For this reason, one must, for example, assume that the report, in the King James version of the Bible (Genesis 1.3), quoting God as having said "Let there be light," must be a misrepresentation; what God probably said was "let there be photons," because the sensation of perception of electromagnetic radiation in the form of optical signals (Hailman 1977:56–58), that is, luminance, requires a living interpreter, and the animation of matter did not come to pass much earlier than about 3,900 million years ago.

2. THE COSMOS BEFORE SEMIOSIS

The regnant paradigm of modern cosmology is the Big Bang theory of the origin and evolution of the Universe (for example, Silk 1980; and Barrow and Silk 1983). The genesis of the cosmos, in a singularity (that is, the point at which something peculiar happens to a physical process represented by an equation when one or more variables have certain values), is though to have occurred about 15 billion years ago. Of prior to Planck time 10^{-43}, we know nothing. What ensued afterward is a bit clearer: from the time that the Universe was three minutes old until about a million years after its

A somewhat different version of this chapter appears in *Semiotik: Ein Handbuch zu den zeichentheoretischen Grundlagen von Natur und Kultur*, ed. Roland Posner, Thomas A. Sebeok, and Klaus Robering (Berlin: Walter de Gruyter, in press).

apparent beginning, it was dominated by the influence of photons (heat and light). The elementary particles multiplied, matter became ordered, and the Universe organized itself into ever more complex systems. The quasi-semiotic phenomena of nonbiological atomic interactions and, later, those of inorganic molecules, were consigned by the late oncologist Prodi (1977) to "protosemiotics," but this must surely be read as a metaphorical expression. Prodi's term is to be distinguished from the notion "primitive communication," which refers to the transfer of information-containing endoparticles, such as exists in neuron assemblies, where it is managed in modern cells by protein particles (see, for example, Fox 1988:91). The age of the Earth is about 4.5 billion years, while the solar system is deemed to be a little older (4.6 billion).

It becomes useful to allude briefly, at this point, to the conjoined ideas of information and entropy, which is a measure of disorder (Brooks and Wiley 1986; Wicken 1987:17–28; Wright 1988:87–91). These are mutually implicative technical terms which arguably belong on the margins of semiotics. Cosmic expansion is accompanied by a departure from a state of maximum entropy, and information (as a measure of the nonuniform, orderly properties of physical systems) evolved out of that initial state of utter chaos. Eventually, "information" came to be viewed as a measure of the number of alternative messages (Shannon 1948), and then the biophysicist Gatlin (1972) came to apply Shannon's elegant, highly abstract, and therefore powerful theorems to a theory of living organisms. She showed that, since information in the living system is transmitted from DNA to protein along a channel of biochemical processes in the cell, it can be subjected to Shannon's equations.

On the other hand, Yates and Kugler (1984), eschewing such terms as "information" and "communication," because in them lies embedded the elusive property of "intentionality," recently proposed a quite different and very promising scenario for the transition from a physical (kinetic) system to a semiotic (kinematic) system, that is, one incorporating significance.

"Meaning," which is indeed a pivotal term in semiotics, played a crucial part in Niels Bohr's model of a participatory universe, and significance has moved to center stage in the work of such contemporary theoretical physicists as Wheeler (for example, 1984, 1986). Wheeler's subtle "meaning model" of nature posits a circuit whereby particles owe their definition and existence to fields, fields owe theirs to phases, phases to distinguishability and complementarity, "and these features of nature going back for their origin to the demand for meaning. . . ." Hence his dictum: "The past is theory." In this model, meaning before the advent of life must, of course, be founded on construction: "Only by [life's] agency is it even possible to construct the universe of existence or what we call reality" (1986:314). In sum, in Wheeler's grand conception, physics is the offspring of semiosis, "even as meaning is the child of physics" (1984:123).

3. THE ORIGIN OF LIFE AND THE ORIGIN OF SEMIOSIS ON THE EARTH

The question of whether there is life/semiosis elsewhere in our galaxy, let alone in deep space, is wide open; since there is not a single example, one can but hold exobiology and extraterrestrial semiotics to be twin sciences that so far remain without a subject matter.

On the other hand, research into the origin and evolution of our terrestrial biosphere has made encouraging progress, although, of course, untold unresolved problems require multidisciplinary analysis in the future (Schopf 1983). The first traces of life date from the so-called Archaean Aeon, from 3,900 to 2,500 million years ago. The story of the quest for the origins of life is detailed in Margulis and Sagan (1986a, Ch. 2), and the molecular biological revolution is then deftly spelled out by them in the next chapter, tellingly titled "The Language of Nature" (1986:59–67). Cairns-Smith has recently shown, especially in his chapter titled "Messages, Messages" (1985, Ch. 2), that *semiosis* is at the heart of life, since messages provide "the only connection between life now and life a million or a billion years ago" (ibid.:28). Messages are obviously the most important inheritance, since only they can persist over the vast reaches of time. All living systems are composed of carbon, nitrogen, and hydrogen compounds in water; are bounded by lipid membrane; are autopoietic systems, that is, they self-maintain their organization and function by a ceaseless exchange of matter, energy, and messages, or, as Maturana (1980:53) put it, "through their interactions recursively generate the network of productions that produced them, and . . . realize this network as a unity by constituting and specifying its boundaries in the space in which they exist."

3.1. "The Language of Life"

The Language of Life is the title of a book by Nobel Laureate George Beadle and Muriel Beadle (1966; the same tag was also used by Berlinski 1986). During the years following its publication, much fruitless debate ensued about whether the genetic code is (like) a language or not. Thus Jakobson (1970:437) asserted that the Beadle and Beadle title was "not a mere figurative expression," and then went on to stress the close similarities in the structure of these "two informational systems" (ibid.:438), that is, the genetic and the linguistic. By contrast, Lees (1980), for example, argued that, although there is a very abstract and deep connection between the two, the similarities usually noted are superficial. "I advocate," said Lees (ibid.:226), "that linguistic competence be viewed analogously to the genetic code as a mechanism invented by minds to serve as a scratch pad."

There were also somewhat parallel discussions of this issue among some molecular biologists of that time. The question of an analogy between the two codes, the endosemiotic (molecular) and the anthroposemiotic (including a verbal component) seems, however, a secondary one. What matters is that both are productive semiotic systems. This is made possible by the principle of double articulation, referred to by the Schoolmen, in linguistic contexts, as *articulatio prima et secunda*. In language, this concept refers (roughly) to the dichotomy between merely distinctive, or phonemic, units and significative, or grammatical, units (such as morphemes or words). Duality can of course be expressed in radically different substances: say, polymeric molecules (the four nucleotides, which can generate the proteins that manufacture everything else alive) in the one; and sound waves in the other. (Double articulation, however, by no means presupposes animation of matter; on the contrary, its fundamental realization is embodied in Mendeleev's periodic table of elements with related electronic configurations).

3.2. ON ENDOSEMIOTIC SYSTEMS AND BEHAVIOR

The substantive "endosemiotics" was coined by Sebeok (1985a:3). As a consequence of Jakob von Uexküll's consistent and elaborate doctrine of signs (Jerison 1986:143–144; Sebeok 1988, Ch. 10), nothing exists for any organism outside its bubble-like private *Umwelt* in which, although impalpably to any outside observer, it remains, as it were, inextricably sealed. The behavior of an organism—"behavior" being definable as the commerce by means of signs among different *Umwelten*—has as its basic function the production of nonverbal signs for communication, first of all for communication of that organism with itself. It follows that the primal universal sign relation in the ontogeny of an organism is realized as an opposition between the self (ego) and the other (alter) (see also Ch. 4, above). This elementary binary split subsequently brings to pass the second semiosic dimension, that of inside versus outside. It is this secondary opposition that enables an organism to "behave," that is, to enter into relations to link up with other living systems in its surrounding ecosystem.

3.2.1. Variety in Endosemiosis

Thure von Uexküll wrote (1986:204): "The overwhelming majority of objective evidence of a disease belongs to those types of processes taking place within the body, which, in turn, are subdivided into subsystems (organ systems, organs, tissue, cells, cellular organelles). . . . The participants in the exchange of signs that takes place on the biological level are thus given," and this fact is described by the adjective endosemiotic. He continued:

> The sign processes use chemical, thermal, mechanical and electrical processes as sign carriers. They make up an incredible number. If one reflects upon the fact that the human body consists of 25 trillion cells, which is more than 2,000 times the number of people living on earth, and that these cells have direct or indirect contact with each other through sign processes, one gets an impression of the amount. Only a fraction are known to us. Yet this fraction alone is hardly comprehensible. . . . The messages that are transmitted include information about the meaning of processes in one system of the body (cells, tissues, organs, or organ systems) for other systems as well as for the integrative regulation systems (especially the brain) and the control systems (such as the immune system).

3.2.2. *The Immune System*

Semiosis being at the pivot of the immune system, terms such as "semioimmunology" and "immunosemiotics" are finding increasing application. Considering that the human immune system consists of about 1,012 cells, dissipated over the entire body, the problem immediately arises how these cells form an orderly, finely regulated functional network operating via signs consisting of chemical substances. Moreover, the immune system (units of which, the lymphocytes, although they circulate among most other cells of the body, seem to be excluded from the brain) and the nervous system are known to influence one another by means of signs. Niels Jerne, in his 1984 Nobel address, not only proposed a far-reaching model of the vertebrate immune system as exhibiting the properties of any semiotic system, but also described it as one that functions as an "open-ended" generative grammar: "The immense repertoire of the immune system . . . becomes a vocabulary comprised not of words but of sentences that is capable of responding to any sentence expressed by the multitude of antigens which the immune system may encounter" (1985:1058). The context for this approach was provided by Jerne's idiotype network theory fifteen years ago, suggested by a remarkable feature of the immune system, namely, that its receptors and specific secreted products, or antibodies, not only recognize the exosemiotic world of antigenic determinants (epitopes), but also recognize antigenic determinants on the immune receptors themselves (the endosemiotic idiotopes). Jerne's theory postulated that within the reflective symmetry of idiotopes, and so forth, formed within the organism's immune system would be found representations, or indexical icons, of most of the epitomes of the external universe. Internal imaging, a fascinating type of biochemical mimicry performed by the immune system, is now of paramount interest to semiotics.

3.2.3. *Metabolic Code*

"Metabolic code" is an expression coined by Gordon M. Tomkins (1975) in the course of his discussion of biological symbolism and the origin of intracellular communication. Tomkins distinguished between simple and complex modes of regulation, both present in modern organisms. By the former, he meant a direct chemical relationship between regulatory molecules and their effects (equivalent to Peirce's secondness). Complex regulation, on the other hand, involves metabolic symbols and their domains (or Peirce's thirdness). By symbol Tomkins meant a specific intracellular effector molecule, cyclic APM, which accumulates when a cell is exposed to a particular environment (or context). This symbol stands for a shortage of carbon; and the live organism, "upon processing the symbol, behaves so as to reconcile its well-being with that environmental condition (by heading elsewhere)" (Wright 1988:104). The term is appropriate because "metabolic symbols need bear no structural relationship to the molecules which promote their accumulation"; and, since a particular environmental condition is correlated with a corresponding intracellular symbol, "the relationship between the extra- and intracellular events may be considered as a 'metabolic code' in which a specific symbol represents a unique state of the environment" (Tomkins 1975:761). Tomkins also pointed out that, in most multicellular organisms (that is, the eukaryotes), only certain cells are stimulated directly by the environment; but that, in higher organisms, these in turn secrete specific effector molecules (the hormones), which signal other cells, presumably sequestered from the *milieu extérieur*, to respond metabolically, via a high number of intermediate steps, to the initial sign. "Specifically, the metabolic state of the sensor cell, represented by the levels of its intracellular symbol, is 'encoded' by the synthesis and secretion of corresponding levels of hormones. When the hormones reach responder cells, the metabolic message is 'decoded' into corresponding primary intracellular symbols" (1975:762). It should finally be emphasized that, in many organisms, the endocrine and the nervous systems are intimately connected; thus hormone release is often a function of neural stimulation (for example, Janković et al. 1987, *passim*).

3.2.4. Neural Code

As Prosser (1985:118) rightly observes, "Communication is what neurobiology is about. The modes of communication include membrane conductances, patterns of neuronal spikes and graded potentials, electric coupling between cells, electrical and chemical transmission at synapses, secretion, and modification of neural function." Moreover, over the past three decades, neurobiology has moved increasingly into the orbit of semiotics, in the guise of a distinct discipline, named Neurocommunications, regarded by its practitioners, who draw on many basic sciences, as a "meta-subject" (see Whitfield 1984:4). In brief, this new field is apt to represent the (human) mind (the "software" level) and its underlying mechanism, the brain (the "hardware" level of the biological organ which allows cognition), as a pair of semiotic engines, or computational devices for processing verbal-and-nonverbal signs. However, there remains sharp disagreement about the representation of language and nonverbal systems, ranging from Chomsky's theory, that we are born with genetically determined "mental organs," requiring that the rules be in some sense innate for generalization to be possible from impoverished samples, a view which received considerable support from the work of David Hubel and Torsten Wiesel, who discovered just such innate connections in the visual system, as well as from the distinguished researches of Colwyn Trevarthen on the prenatal growth of brain parts in infants, to Gerald Edelman's and his colleagues' researches on cell adhesion molecules (CAMs); this view accepts that the general patterns of neural connections are shaped by gene action, but suggests that the exact connections of individual cells are not genetically determined. At any rate, the critical questions—how rules are programmed genetically and how they are carried out by the intricate circuitry of the brain (let alone represented in the mind)—remain unanswered at this time. Cook uses the phrase "brain code" to describe the set of fundamental rules concerning how signs are stored and transmitted from site to site within the brain, to distinguish this from "neuron code," which is reserved for the manner in which the mechanisms by which large groups of neurons transmit "images, thoughts and feelings which we suspect are the fundamental units of our psychological lives" (1986:xiii, 2–4). Although the decipherment of the brain code remains the ultimate goal of most research in the neurosciences and psychology, in practice this often proceeds by clarification of aspects of the neural code.

4. SEMIOSIS IN THE SUPERKINGDOMS

According to one standard scheme for the broad classification of organisms (after R. H. Whittaker, also discussed elsewhere in this book, passim; cf. Margulis and Schwartz 1988), five Superkingdoms are now distinguished: protists (including microbes composed of nucleated cells); bacteria; plants; animals; and fungi. In each group, distinct but intertwined modes of semiosis have evolved, some of which are better understood than others. Brief indications of general principles are given below, but no detailed discussion is possible in this chapter.

4.1. The Microcosmos

Microcosmos is the title of a superb book (Margulis and Sagan 1986a) portraying four billion years of microbial evolution which, of course, is still in progress, both around, within, and, indeed, *as* us—human bodies, for instance, are composed of one hundred quadrillion (100,000,000,000,000,000) bacterial cells, and our endosemiotic systems, including the nervous system, are all derived from intercommunicating aggregations of bacteria. The microcosmos began to evolve four billion years ago, in the Hadean Aeon, out of debris of supernova explosions, spread to land 1.3 billion years ago (in the Protozoic Aeon) as composite organisms, and these microcosmic collectives evolved into our plant and animal ancestors a mere 0.8 billion years ago (in the Proterozoic Aeon). According to the modern view of semiosis in the microcosmos, or bacterial semiosis, all bacteria on Earth constitute the communications network of a single superorganism whose continually shifting components are dispersed across the surface of the planet. Sonea and Panisset (1983:85) liken in extent the bacterial world to a global computerized communications network, possessing an enormous data base—more than the brain of any mammal—which functions in a manner reminiscent of human intelligence. Bacterial social life takes three forms: localized teams, the global ensemble itself, and a body interacting with eukaryotes (Sonea 1988:42–43; 1990:639–662). Each of these types of associations is characterized by its appropriate form of semiosis, a rapid and continuous shuffling, which seems unrestricted by physical, chemical, or geographic boundaries of energy, matter, and signs.

4.1.1. Symbiosis

The quintessentially semiotic concept of symbiosis (Füller 1958; Margulis 1981; Margulis and Sagan 1986a, esp. Chs. 8, 9)—together with such subsumed concepts as parasitism, mutualism, commensalism, and the like—is the key to semiosis in the microcosmos. The term refers to the living together of individuals of two or more species for most of the life cycle of each, and this cohabitation is clearly "often [in fact, invariably] facilitated by simple [?] forms of COMMUNICATION [*sic*] between the participants" (McFarland 1982:540). Symbiotic alliances, in due course, became permanent, converting organisms (namely, prokaryotes, which share a kind of immortality, but at the expense of lacking individuality) into new, lasting collectives (namely, eukaryotes, which, on the contrary, pursue individuality, but at the expense of an existence between the two poles of sex and death) that are more than simply the sum of their symbiotic parts. In brief, all visible organisms evolved through symbiotic unions between different microbes, which subsequently co-evolved as wholly integrated communities, enduring sharing of cells and bodies; such mergers of diverse organisms can be regarded as thoroughly interwoven living "corporations" (Margulis and Sagan 1986a:127), harmoniously coordinated by means of nonverbal (and, in the case of hominids, also verbal) signs. These authors believe that "the concepts and signals of thought are based on chemical and physical abilities already latent in bacteria," and are then moved to ask: "Could the true language of the nervous system . . . be spirochetal remnants, a combination of autocatalyzing RNA and tubulin proteins symbiotically integrated in the network of hormones, neurohormones, cells, and their wastes we call the human body? Is individual thought itself superorganismic, a collective phenomenon?" (ibid.:150–151). Although their hypothesis is not proven, it is most congenial with modern semiotic thinking, as is their additional extrapolation, that perhaps "groups of humans, sedentary and packed together in communities, cities, and webs of electromagnetic communication, are already beginning to form a network as far beyond thought as thought is from the concerted swimming of spirochetes" (ibid.:153). It is fascinating that as semiotically informed a student of the "information society" as Beniger suggests the same kind of "integrative machinery we might build from the spare parts amassed by our various disciplines" (1986:105; semiotics and semiosis are discussed on pp. 89–90), and traces the beginnings of what he calls "the control revolution" to the DNA as a three-dimensional control model (ibid.:112–118).

4.2. Overview of the Plant-Animal-Fungus Trichotomy

These three categories—plants, animals, and fungi—distinguished by taxonomers according to the nutritional patterns of each class, that is, three different ways in which information (negentropy) is maintained by extracting order out of their environment, are complementary. Plants are the producers, which derive their food from inorganic sources by means of photosynthesis; animals, or ingesters, are the transformers, deriving their food, preformed organic compounds, from other organisms; fungi are the decomposers, which break their food down externally and then absorb the resulting small molecules from solution. On this macroscopic scale, we have two polar-opposite life forms: the composer plants, or the organisms that build up, and the decomposer fungi, or the organisms that break down; animals, which became supreme experts at semiosis in interactions among their many cells, among themselves, and with members of other life forms, can be seen as intermediate transforming agents midway between the other two. In passing, the remarkable parallelism between this systematists' P-A-F model and the classic semioticians' O-S-I model should be noted (but cannot be here explored).

4.2.1. Phytosemiotics

The semiosic principles of the vegetative world were most thoroughly discussed, under the designation "phytosemiotics," by Krampen (1981; cf. Thure von Uexküll 1986:211–212). He argues that these are different from those of the animal world, "in that the absence of effectors and receptors does not allow for the constitution of [Jakob von Uexküll's] functional cycle [see p. 54 above], of object signs and sign objects, or of an Umwelt," but that the vegetative world "is nevertheless structured according to a base semiotics which cuts across all living beings, plants, animals, and humans alike" (Krampen 1981:203). Although plants are able to distinguish "self" from "nonself," they are otherwise brainless solipsistic systems.

However, plants "don't really need brains," for, as Margulis and Sagan (1986a:174–175) picturesquely point out, "they borrow ours. They have a strategic intelligence that resides more in the chemistry of photosynthesis and the ploys of the genes than in the tactics of the cerebral cortex; we behave for them." Plant semiosis, as a matter of fact, incorporates the ancient microcosmos, a circumstance that accounts in part for botanical success. A "unifying theory of intercellular communication" has recently been developed (Roth and LeRoith 1987), which aims to explain at a single stroke the many coincidences involving plant molecules and animal (including human) cells, by showing that both the endocrine system and the nervous system descended from a common, more generalized evolutionary ancestor. This theory provides the explanation, as well, for scores of coincidences in cellular communication in plants and in animals, for instance, accounting for the efficacy of various medicinal herbs and modern plant-derived drugs, and such circumstances as the presence of an insulin-like substance in spinach and that truffles produce molecules identical to a steroid in boars, and the fact that sows detect and seek out even deeply buried truffles. Plants also have significant interactions with fungi as well as with animals (Krampen also described some conspicuous examples of the latter.) There is, however, a great deal of curious folklore about plant communication, the scientific basis of which remains to be investigated (see, for example, Montalverne 1984).

4.2.2. Mycosemiotics

The general features of fungi are presented by Burnett (1968). Mycologists agree that all fungi are heterotrophic organisms, the vast majority of which are constructed of more or less microscopic, cylindrical filaments (hyphae), with well-designed cell walls; but they disagree as to their taxonomic limits. Semiosis in fungi is not yet well understood, but the interactions of fungi with other organisms are basically known (ibid., Ch. 12): these can occur without actual contact, by secretion or leakage, and by other means as well. Fungi communicate with green plants (especially their roots), with algae, in particularly dense engagements (which have produced up to about 20,000 species of lichens), with warm-blooded animals (to which they are pathogenic), and with insects; "the essential steps in the establishment of any interaction appear to be governed by contact reactions and/or nutritional relationships" (ibid.:359), and competition among them is fierce. One of the most fascinating forms of semiosis was found in an excitingly relevant model species called Dictyostelium discoidium (which many, although not all, taxonomers class with the fungi). This was described in a classic paper by Bonner (1963):

> Slime-mold cells [join to form an organism] in each life cycle. At first they are single amebocytes swimming around, eating bacteria, aloof from each other,

> untouching, voting straight Republican. Then, a bell sounds, and acrasin is released by special cells toward which the others converge in stellate ranks, touch, fuse together, and construct the slug, solid as a trout. A splendid stalk is raised, with a fruiting body on top, and out of this comes the next generation of amebocytes, ready to swim across the same moist ground, solitary and ambitious.

The sign carrier is cAMP (the ubiquitous molecule adenosine monophosphate), identical with the one Tomkins (1975) described in his article on the metabolic code and which has assumed the twin functions of (physiological) epinephrine action and (semiotic) mediation of the intracellular actions of almost all those hormones that interreact with the cell membrane or, in the case in point, signify starvation. The aggregation of the slime molds in single-cell form is coordinated by a sign system involving the cAMP receptor, the structure and activity of which is now clear (Klein et al. 1988). Significant homologies link the cAMP to sensory processes in higher organisms. The latest findings support the possibility that this relatively simple eukaryotic chemotactic semiosic system and various vertebrate sign systems evolved from a common ancestor. (For fuller details of this remarkable story of cell-cell semiosis by cAMP, the earliest symbolic vehicle uncovered thus far, and the implications thereof for eukaryotic chemotaxis in general, see Devreotes 1982; and, in layman's terms, Wright 1988:196.) The same molecule is at work as a "second messenger" secreted by human liver cells as soon as epinephrin molecules ("first messengers") bind to them. Second messengers of this sort are common in humans, mean different things in different contexts, but their basic *Grundbedeutung* (in Jakobson's sense) is always "emergency."

4.2.3. Zoosemiotics

The term "zoosemiotics" dates from 1963 and is discussed, in some detail, in Sebeok 1972. Observe that it denotes semiosis in animals inclusive of the nonverbal semiosic component in man, in contrast to the anthroposemiosic component, which necessarily and additionally implicates language; for convenience, however, only the languageless creatures will be considered in this section. The literature on this subject—virtually nonexistent before the early 1960s—has since grown hugely: Sebeok's 1968 survey ran to almost 700 pages; his 1977b survey ran to more than 1,100; and it would now require a multivolume encyclopedia to encompass the accumulated scholarship. At the same time, no one has quite succeeded in producing a synthesis, in a biologically informed as well as semiotically interesting way, of the essential principles, taking fully into account what we know both of intraspecific, let alone the interspecific, aspects of how animals communicate. (Some useful texts on intraspecific communication are Smith 1977; Lewis and Gower 1980; and Bright 1984. Varieties of interspecific semiosis, with special emphasis on interactions between humans and animals, are discussed in Chapter 10 of this book, where further references can be found.) One overblown topic that received exaggerated media attention in the 1960s and 1970s, but which has proved a false trail and has since become essentially moribund, focuses on the search for verbal semiosis in four species of Great Apes, and perhaps in certain pelagic mammals as well. (For critical reviews of the mythology of language-endowed animals, see Sebeok and Umiker-Sebeok 1980; Umiker-Sebeok and Sebeok 1981; and Sebeok 1981a, Ch. 8.)

Recent instructive researches in animal communication tend to view groupings—in particular, in such social animals as some insects, dolphins, wolves and lions, and of course primates—in a holistic way, as global semiosic systems. For example, honeybee colonies are now perceived as possessing a "collective intelligence," but one that arises from fundamentally decentralized sign processing (cf. Seeley and Levien 1987). Complementing the traditional description of the operation of a honeybee colony as one wherein each bee processes information in serial fashion (say, in evaluating flower patches one at a time), the colony as a whole is seen as working in parallel (say, with many patches being rated at once). The analogy is to the massively parallel computers many artificial intelligence researchers are now using, on the assumption (which is in good conformity with neurophysiological facts) that the human brain is a fundamentally social structure, its semiosic capacity arising from the interaction of many relatively simple sign processors.

5. HOMINID FORMS

Cartmill, Pilbeam, and Isaac (1986) present a convenient, concise survey of developments in paleoanthropology during the last one hundred years. Hominid forms, which evolved out of the australopithecines, are commonly recognized in terms of three principal anatomical features: gradually increasing brain size; the modification of the limb and pelvic bones in adaptation to fully upright walking ("bipedal locomotion"); and a reduction in sexual dimorphism (that is, the difference in body size between males and females). Other important arguments derive, besides from fossils, from the archeological record. Forms which have thus far been identified include *Homo habilis* ("handy man," 2.4 to 2.0 million years ago), first described in 1964, which is now generally recognized as a transitional form ancestral to all later *Homo*. *H. habilis* is the first hominid with a distinctly enlarged brain (600–800 cm^3). It appears virtually certain that *habilis* had language, although not speech. (This corresponds, if roughly, to the distinction between *Kognition* and *Sprache* drawn in Müller 1987). Language at its inception was not used for exterior communication, but only as an interior modeling device. Members of early hominid species communicated with each other by nonverbal means, in the manner of all other primates (for details, see Sebeok 1986c and Sebeok 1989a). *Homo erectus* ("upright man," over 1.5 million years ago) had a brain volume of 800–1,200 cm³ and a far more elaborate tool kit, including fire, and there is no doubt that it had language (yet not speech). Hominids from the upper Middle Pleistocene, starting about 300,000 years ago, with brain volumes of about 1,200–1,400 cm³, were our own immediate archaic *sapiens* ("wise man") ancestors, with even more elaborate tools (for example, hafting), ritual burials, and central-place foraging. Evidence for rule-governed behaviors indicates that they not only had language but manifested it in the form of speech as well. Archaic *sapiens* divided into at least two subspecies, only one of which, modern *sapiens sapiens* (that is, ourselves), has continued to flourish, since about 40,000 years ago, with an average brain capacity of 1,500 cm³. (The latter, it is thought, also replaced *H. sapiens neanderthalensis* in Europe 35,000 years ago.) Thus verbal semiosis, or language-as-a-modeling-system—a modeling system being a tool wherewith an organism analyzes its surroundings—having emerged on the scene perhaps 2.5 or 3.0 million years ago, now survives solely in *H. sapiens sapiens* (a species that appeared only some 100,000 to 40,000 years ago), and seems always to have been an exclusive property of the genus *Homo* (Sebeok 1986a, 1986b); Jerison's observation (1986:155), and attendant discussion, of a "uniquely human experience" (meaning species-typical) which arose "from our use of a cognitive system as a communication system" is right on the mark. The exaptation of language into speech and, later still, into other linear manifestations, such as script—all topics that belong to anthroposemiotics—will not be discussed here, except to call attention to an important observation by Gould and Vrba (1982:13) that applies *a fortiori* to the relationship of language as a biological adaptation (its historical genesis) to its current added utility as a communicative tool: "Most of what the [human] brain now does to enhance our survival lies in the domain of exaptation." As to why this process of exaptation took several million years to accomplish, the answer seems to be that the adjustment of a species-specific mechanism for encoding language into speech, that is, producing signs vocally, with a matching mechanism for decoding it, that is, receiving and interpreting a stream of incoming verbal/vocal signs (sentences), must have taken that long to fine-tune, a process which is far from complete (since humans have great difficulties in understanding each other's spoken messages). Hence Geschwind's remark (1980:313) "that the forerunners of language were functions whose social advantages [that is, communicative function] were secondary but conferred an advantage for survival [the modeling function]" appears well taken.

6. BIOCOMMUNICATION, AND SOME IMPLICATIONS

The comprehensive (German) term *Biokommunikation* was employed by Tembrock (1971) to cover the flow of semiosis in the world of the living.

While the domain of semiosis is essentially the same, it can also encompass, in any communicative loop, a human artifact, such as a computer, a robot, or automata generally. Moreover, the bold futuristic vision of Margulis and Sagan (1986b:44), according to which it is inevitable that human life and nonliving, manufactured parts will commingle in new "life-forms" within the next few decades, with molecules that, instead of turning into cell material, "would turn [energy] into information," by a novel progression referred to as "cybersymbiosis," likewise opens doors for an extension of evolutionary semiosis thus far into an eventual "cybersemiosis."

6.1 The Gaia Hypothesis

"The Gaia hypothesis" refers to a unified planetary world view proposed by James Lovelock in 1979. According to this controversial hypothesis, the atmosphere, the hydrosphere, and the lithosphere interact with the biosphere of Earth, each being a compound component of a global unitary autopoietic, that is, a homeostatic self-regulating system. In this view, all living entities, from their smallest limits to their largest extent, including some ten million existing species, form parts of a single symbiotic ecological body dubbed Gaia. Greenstein (1988) is concerned with the more general proposition of the existence of a symbiosis between the universe on the one hand and life on the other. Should a view, along these lines, of a modulated biosphere prevail, it would in effect mean that all message generators/sources and destinations/interpreters could be regarded as participants in one gigantic semiosic web; and, if so, this would at the very least affect the style of future semiotic discourse.

NINE

Semiosis and Semiotics: What Lies in Their Future?

The distinction between "semiosis" and "semiotics" is easily drawn. Semiotics is an exclusively human style of inquiry, consisting of the contemplation—whether informally or in formalized fashion—of semiosis. This search will, it is safe to predict, continue at least as long as our genus survives, much as it has existed, for about three million years, in the successive expressions of *Homo*, variously labeled—reflecting, among other attributes, a growth in brain capacity with concomitant cognitive abilities—*habilis, erectus, sapiens, neanderthalensis,* and now *s. sapiens*. Semiotics, in other words, simply points to the universal propensity of the human mind for reverie focused specularly inward upon its own long-term cognitive strategy and daily maneuverings. Locke designated this quest as a search for "humane understanding"; Peirce, as "the play of musement."

Both the past and the future of semiotics, being co-terminous with human existence, are therefore inalienably linked to human biological fate. The several contemporary cultural manifestations of semiotics must, in this perspective, be regarded as but vanishingly short chapters of history. The future of semiosis, on the other hand, suggests both more speculative and withal intriguing questions. First, however, a glimpse at its past.

Just as semiotics is a heavily glosso-tinged activity that characterizes all normal hominid life, so semiosis, the ceaseless romp of any and all signs (with which the universe, as Peirce assured us, is perfused), hitherto defines any and all life (being, as far as anyone yet knows, tantamount to terrestrial life).

Life emerged on Earth more than four billion years ago. The beginnings of semiosis can be traced to the appearance of the first cell, composed, as it always appears to have been, of life's four or five elementary building blocks, the distinctive features chemists call amino acids. Cells, these littlest self-reproducing, membrane-bounded entities, are the minimal are-

This sketch was written at the invitation of Norma Backes Tasca, of the Associação Portuguesa de Semiótica, for the Portuguese magazine *Culture e Arte*, where it appeared (in that language) in no. 52 (April 23, 1989): 208. The original English version was later published in the *International Semiotic Spectrum*, no. 10 (October, 1989): 2. Then the piece was variously translated and published in German, Hungarian, Italian, and Norwegian.

nas for signs in action: they process inputs, interpret them, and then transform them into appropriate outputs of novel strings.

In their primitive but abundant surviving forms, all cells were and are prokaryotic. Their semiosis is breathtaking in its elegance and structural complexity. These qualities dramatically increased when—say, about 800 million years ago—some sets of prokaryotes, by dint of a process scientists call symbiosis (and which itself constitutes a special form of biosemiosis), became eukaryotes. Eventually, the latter split into four Superkingdoms, three of them multicelled. They now coexist and ceaselessly interact with the microcosmos as well as with one another. All make up together the biosphere, which, in a more parochial perspective, is the engulfing and sustaining matrix of everything that Jurij M. Lotman has lately been calling "semiosphere."

The three multicellular Superkingdoms are, in common parlance, plants, animals, and fungi. Plants are the producers: organisms which extract information out of our sun, converting, as provisionally delineated by Martin Krampen (1981), inorganic signals (photons) into phytosemiosic processes. Animals ingest plants proximally or indirectly, thereby transmuting the solar information pre-processed by chlorophyll into far subtler and more sophisticated zoosemiosic processes. Animals convert plant signs into a wide array of nonverbal outputs, which are studied by ethologists interested in aspects of such interpretative comportment. Fungi dissolve and absorb both of the former by mycosemiosic techniques, and dissipate the resultant strings into a temporary entropic state eventually reconstituted so as to fuel yet another cycle.

The (1a) concocting plants, (2a) transmogrifying animals, and (3a) putrefying fungi are homologous with the three widely postulated categories of Western semiotics: (1b) object-signs, (2b) signs which regressively refer (*renvoi*, in Roman Jakobson's usage) to such object-signs, and, progressively proliferating, (3b) usually novel but sometimes lethal interpretant-signs. In bold, this (here crudely sketched) state of affairs that has characterized terrestrial semiosis since life evolved from a single cell to its multiform present diversity already contains within it the seeds of already palpable further permutations.

At the nether end of time, semiosis began when life began, but it would be erroneous to assume that, as life, including human life, changes in the future and eventually terminates, semiosis will also come to a stop. Sign processes, fabricating unlimited interpretants, are likely to continue, independently of us, in machines. The following argument is in conformity with, as well as strongly reinforced by, an essay on how man-made objects may remake man, written by Lynn Margulis and Dorion Sagan, titled "Strange Fruit on the Tree of Life" (Margulis and Sagan 1986b). Their scenario anticipates that life and nonlife will blend and interbreed. Biotechnology and computer technology already provide humanity with an opportunity to redesign itself, but the new step will take place in the domain of robotics.

Cybersymbiosis, defined by Margulis and Sagan (ibid.:43) as "the commingling of human and manufactured parts in new life-forms," could also be dubbed cybersemiosis, to underline the exchange of signs between life forms, such as bacteria, for example, to activate biochips based not on silicon but on complex organic molecules. Indeed, *Homo sapiens sapiens,* these authors insinuate, "might survive only as a rudimentary organ, a delicately dissected nervous system attached to electronically driven plastic arms" (ibid.). The mechanisms of sign-transfer, by means of what is coming to be called "the brain code," or the set of fundamental rules concerning how signs are stored and transmitted from site to site within the brain—itself being a complex assemblage of interacting microscopic spirochetes—and which supplement the far better understood regulations of the "neuron code," have behavioral implications that extend beyond the whole organism, penetrating into its inorganic envelope.

Machines will thus become not merely the agents of evolutionary change—in some measure they already have—but also the loci for what Peirce has called "the essential nature and fundamental varieties of possible semiosis," which, as he also foresaw, "need not be of a mental mode of being."

TEN

"Animal" in Biological and Semiotic Perspective

Whatever else an animal may be, it is clear that each is a living system, or subsystem, a complex array of atoms organized and maintained according to certain principles, the most important among these being negative entropy. The classic statement emphasizing this fact is to be found in Schrödinger's famous book, *What Is Life?* (1946:77), where he addresses an "organism's astonishing gift of concentrating a 'stream of order' on itself and thus escaping the decay into atomic chaos—of 'drinking orderliness' from a suitable environment."

The importance of Schrödinger's formulation, with its stress on the generation of order, seems to me to derive from two crucial implications. First, in invoking the notion of entropy, which in statistical mechanics is fundamental to the Second Law of Thermodynamics, it authenticates that life conforms to the basic laws of physics (Ling 1984). Second, since negative entropy is closely coupled with the notion (or, more accurately, *a* notion) of information—that which "embodies, expresses, and often specifies order" (Medawar and Medawar 1983:205)—it demonstrates the salience of semiotics to an understanding of life. Schrödinger himself (1946:79) hints at the latter when he remarks on the power of a group of atoms—he calls them a "tiny central office"—to produce "orderly events" in the isolated cell, and then goes on to ask: "do they not resemble stations of a local government dispersed through the body, communicating with each other with great ease, thanks to the code that is common to all of them?"

If the subject matter of semiotics "is the exchange of any messages whatever and of the systems of signs which underlie them" (Sebeok 1985:1), the amount of information is "a measure of the degree of order which is peculiarly associated with those patterns which are distributed as messages in time" (Wiener 1950:21). In short, life couples two transmuta-

This chapter was written at the invitation of Tim Ingold for presentation at the World Archaelogical Congress, Southampton, England, September 1986. The theme of the session at which it was delivered was "Cultural Attitudes to Animals, including Birds, Fish and Invertebrates." It was published in *What Is an Animal?* ed. Tim Ingold (London: Unwin Hyman, 1988), 63–76. A version was published in my volume of Japanese essays on zoosemiotics, *Doubutsu Kigouron-shu* (Tokyo: Keiso Shobo, 1989).

tive processes, one energetic or physical, the other informational or semiosic. The former has to do with the conversion of low-entropy articles, integrating energy flowing from external sources, into high-entropy waste products disgorged into other open systems; the latter points to the transformation of signs into (as a rule) more developed signs (an identification of organisms with signs that goes back at least to Peirce 1868).

There are two striking properties of life. One of these is hierarchical organization (cf. Bonner 1969; and Salthe 1985). This is a universal characteristic which life shares with the rest of the cosmos and which defines, in the overall architecture of the universe, its position on a continuum of scale between the vanishingly small (leptons, photons, and quarks) and the indefinitely large (galactic superclusters).

The second conspicuous property lies in the contrast between, and fundamental invariance in, life's subjacent biochemistry (a virtually uniform pool of twenty amino acids) and the prodigal variety in the individual expressions thereof, the latter depending on shifts in the environmental context within the global biosphere.

Given that all animals are composed of matter in a "living state," it is equally clear that by no means all life forms are animals. Competing definitions of life abound (for example, Miller 1978), as well as miscellaneous paradigms to account for its origin (for example, Schopf 1983), but these need not be discussed here. Indeed, such an exercise may not even serve any useful purpose, as Pirie (1937) has argued, especially considering the existence of borderline phenomena, comparable with the transition from, say, green to yellow or acid to alkaline. The supposedly ironclad distinction between life and nonlife becomes fuzzy if you look not only back far enough in time, but also in the light of recent developments in commingling and breeding life forms (including humans) with manufactured objects, as is breathtakingly envisioned by Margulis and Sagan (1986b).

The place of animals among other living systems and their distinctive features do, however, require consideration. Macrotaxonomy, the craft of classifying, is a vast (if not always fashionable) field of endeavor, masterfully explored in the realm of biology by Mayr (1982). However, the sole biologically valid classification of animals, since Darwin, is of subordinate classes whose members are united by common heritage or descent at one level of ancestry into superordinate classes whose members are united at the next ascending level. In Darwin's own words, "all true classification is genealogical" (1859:420).

There are many competing representations of evolutionary relations on all levels, and all of these are doubtless provisional. For example, the Linnaean plant-versus-animal dichotomy has been argued on quite different grounds by naturalists since the eighteenth century. Mayr (1965:418–420) lists eleven clusters of distinctive features among the more important differences which have been variously adduced. This notwithstanding, he concludes by noting that "it is important to emphasize that the species of animals and plants are nevertheless essentially similar. Plants and animals are virtually identical in their genetic and cytological mechanisms." Thus, the choice of a classification scheme is ultimately (although, of course, within limits) a personal matter. I favor the one which seems to me to provide the maximum heuristic guidance. That is the codification proposed by Whittaker (1959) and refined by him a decade later (1969).

Whittaker reviews the broad, conventional two-way classification of all organisms—into plants and animals—and enumerates its drawbacks, as well as those of an alternative quadripartite scheme proposed by Copeland (for example, 1956). He then puts forward a pentad of his own, which, although having certain recognized deficiencies as well, seems to me the most comprehensive and cogent system worked out thus far. Whittaker's classification is based on a combination of two sets of distinctions, concerning respectively *levels* of organization and *types* of organization. The first is derived from the principle of hierarchy already mentioned. The second relates to three principal modes of nutrition, that is, to three different ways in which information (negentropy) is maintained by extracting order out of the environment. This second set of distinctions sorts macroscopic entities into three complementary categories, called Superkingdoms, within the pervasive latticed configuration of the terrestrial biosphere. These are—as discussed variously throughout this book—as follows:

1. *Plants*, or producers, which derive their food from inorganic sources, by photosynthesis.

2. *Animals*, or ingestors, which derive their food—preformed organic compounds—from other organisms. They may be subdivided into three classes:

(A) If they eat plants, we call them herbivores.
(B) If they eat animals that eat plants, we call them carnivores (or predators).
(C) If they eat both, we call them omnivores.

Animals are designated "ingestors" because they incorporate food into their bodies, where the intake is then digested.

3. *Fungi*, or decomposers in opposition to animals do not incorporate food into their bodies, but they "secrete digestive enzymes into the environment to break down their food externally and they absorb the resulting small molecules from solution" (Margulis 1981:32).

On this macroscopic scale animals can be catalogued as intermediate transforming agents midway between two polar opposite life forms: the composers, or organisms that "build up," and the decomposers, or organisms that "break down." Bernard (1878:1, 37) once coined a pair of slogans, paradoxically entailing both production, *La vie, c'est la création,* and decay, *La vie, c'est la mort.* Of animals, it may well be added, *La vie, c'est l'entremise!*[1]

Most remaining life forms can be negatively defined as nonplants, nonanimals, and nonfungi. By application of the first principle of hierarchy, these fall into one of two groups:

4. *Protoctists,* comprising the remaining eukaryotes, all of them being micro-organisms lacking embryogenesis but displaying alimentary heterogeneity, including the familiar triad of photosynthetic, ingesting as well as absorbing species (here belong algae, protozoa, slime molds and nets, and so forth).

5. *Prokaryotes,* the Monera, where bacteria belong, are generally single-celled creatures which, although nutritionally diverse, are incapable of ingestion (see also Margulis and Sagan 1986a).[2]

Let me now consider further the classification of animals. In addition to Whittaker's double characterization: first, by level of entitation—a term coined by the physiologist Gerard (1969:218–219) to mean "the identification of entity," and which he considered vastly more important than the concept of quantitation—and, second, by nutritional mode, two further principles may be introduced, one embryological, the other biosemiosic. The former is stated by Margulis (1981:32) thus: "in all animals, the zygote formed by the fertilization of the female by the male gamete develops into a ball of cells called a blastula," which unambiguously separates animals from all other forms by virtue of their development.

All animates are bombarded by signs emanating from their environment, which includes a *milieu intérieur,* as well as, of course, other animates sharing their environment, some conspecific, some not (for further pertinent particulars, see Sebeok 1986a, Ch. 3). Such inputs are eventually transmuted into outputs consisting of strings of further signs. This sign-process is called semiosis. The pioneer explorer of the decisive role of semiosis in the origin and operation of life processes was Jakob von Uexküll, also a preeminent founder of modern ethology. He advanced a highly original and integrated theory of semiosis in the framework of what came to be known as *Umwelt-Forschung,* the study of phenomenal worlds, self-worlds, or the subjective universe.[3]

Although *Umwelt* research has focused almost wholly on animals, including humans (for example, Sebeok 1979b), plants are also discussed, contrastively if briefly, and there have been allusions even to plasmodial slime molds—now in a phylum of the Protoctista, although classified by Uexküll and others among the fungi (Uexküll 1982:35f.). As Uexküll maintained (ibid.:33f.), and Krampen (1981) later greatly elaborated, plants differ from animals in that they lack a "functional cycle" (Thure von Uexküll 1980, Ch. 3) which would link receptor organs via a mesh of nerve fibers to effector organs. They are rather immersed directly in their habitat.

The relationships of a plant with its habitat, or casing, "are altogether different from those of the animals with their Umwelts." However, Krampen (1981:203) concludes that the "vegetative world is nevertheless structured according to a base semiotics which cuts across all living beings, plants, animals, and humans alike." He argues that while plants exhibit predominantly indexical signs, in animals both indexical and iconic signs appear, whereas human sign-processes encompass the entire gamut from indexicality via iconicity to symbolicity.[4] However this may be—and in my opinion the entire subject cries out for more empirical investigation—it is already obvious that one must suppose, at least as a working assumption, that there are bound to be substantive differences among the several branches of biosemiotics (or biocommunication, as in Tembrock 1971): endosemiotics (Thure von Uexküll 1980:291, 1986:204), zoosemiotics (Sebeok 1963), phytosemiotics (Krampen 1981), and, *in posse*, mycosemiotics.[5]

These and related subfields are very unevenly developed. The literature of zoosemiotics alone—even discounting human communication—is so prodigious that no summary can be attempted here, although one point pertinent to the topic of this chapter perhaps does need to be emphasized.

It seems to me beyond reasonable doubt that the symbiotic theory of the origin and evolution of cells is correct. This means that eukaryotic forms composed of nucleated cells—including such advanced forms as animals—evolved in consequence of certain symbioses between ancestral prokaryotes in the Proterozoic Aeon, by about 800 million years ago, and thereafter continued to diversify (see Margulis and Sagan 1986a, esp. Chs. 8, 9).

"Symbiosis," including commensalism, mutualism, and so forth, is plainly a form of semiosis: "mutual cooperation is often facilitated by simple forms of *communication* between the participants," as *The Oxford Companion* puts it, with undue caution (McFarland 1982:540). Biologists appear reluctant to describe it as such, yet the most obvious fact about symbionts is that they are types of communicants. They are organisms of different species living together, in ceaseless informative commerce, for most of the life cycles of each, and to their mutual benefit. "Semiochemical effects occur between organisms of all types" (Albone 1984:2; for the sharing of semiochemicals in human bonding-related behavior, see Nicholson 1984). Their exchanges are accomplished by chemical messengers of precision and subtlety; the topics of their "conversations" have to do largely with territory or reproduction. The exosemiotic chemical signals yoking micro-organisms together—hormonal and chemical neurotransmitters—evolved in life forms such as animals into specialized and localized endosemiotic cells within the body tissue (Krieger 1983:977). Such cells facilitate exceedingly complex mutual communicative interactions between the immune and nervous systems, known as "neuroimmunomodulation."

Research in this area has far-reaching clinical as well as philosophical implications, some of which I have reviewed elsewhere (Sebeok 1981b).

Mayr (1982:146) defines *taxonomy* as "the theory and practice of delimiting kinds of organisms and of classifying them." However, this kind of enterprise, fathered in its evolutionary perspective by Darwin, is but a segment of the far more venerable as well as unbounded science of *systematics* which, as Simpson (1961; cf. Mayr 1982:145) taught it, has diversity as its subject matter. Systems of classification may depend on a whole variety of alternative, presumably complementary, approaches. For example, given that multiple biochemical pathways emerged for the biosynthesis of chlorophyll, plants can be reclassified according to how they fabricate their photosynthetic pigments. As Lowenstein (1984:541), for one, has cogently claimed, comparisons based on DNA or on proteins can be vastly fecund, especially when it comes to "the inclusion of extinct species in phylogenies, the identification of species in fossil studies and museum collections, and broad systematic analysis of living animals and plants."

In short, all organisms—especially plants, animals, and fungi—pertain at once to a plurality of codes, each of which is capable of being transmuted into every other. To paraphrase a striking passage from one of Lévi-Strauss's latest books (1985:228), "like a text less intelligible in one language than in several, from many different versions, rendered simultaneously, there might flow a sense richer and more profound than each of the partial and distorted meanings that any single version, taken in isolation, might yield to us."[6] Although his observation was meant to apply to myths, viewed as formulaic networks, the same surely holds for groupings of animals into at once biologically relevant assemblages and anthropologically as well as semiotically relevant folk arrangements, such as were discussed, for instance, for English animal categories by Leach (1964) or, to adumbrate the "meaning of life" in assorted African societies, by Willis (1974). Lévi-Strauss (1962:57, 59 [1966:42–43]) has remarked on the "evidence of thought which is experienced in all the exercises of speculation and resembles that of the naturalists and alchemists of antiquity and the middle ages. . . . Native classifications are not only methodical and based on carefully built up theoretical knowledge. They are also at times comparable, from a formal point of view, to those still in use in zoology and botany." Thus, it is hardly surprising that Aristotle classified whales as fish and that, despite their replacement in 1693 by John Ray (refined by Linné in 1758) into that class of vertebrates biologists call the Mammalia, infraclass Eutheria, order Cetacea, most laymen still believe that whales are, indeed, fish. Whales are, of course, both, and other entities—such as Moby Dick—to boot.

The transience from code to code can become critical. In certain societies a plant can substitute for an animal, as a cucumber for an ox in the well-known case of the Nuer (Evans-Pritchard 1956) and, as elsewhere in

Africa, a token of a plentiful animal species can take the place of a religiously prescribed but rare one. *A fortiori* a beast can stand in, symbolically, for a human in a sacrificial rite. Nor should one overlook liminoid creatures belonging to overlapping codes—Turner (1974:253) singles out the centaur Cheiron as a classical prototype epitomizing such liminality—which render the would-be cataloguer's chore so wearisome. Just how much they do so is beautifully explored in Vercors's penetrating novel centering on an imaginary creature named *Paranthropus erectus* (Bruller 1953).

Brown (1984) is concerned with folk zoological life forms. Appendix B to his book contains a rich source of lexical data on zoological life-form coding from more than 220 globally scattered languages, postulating six stages of terminological growth, ranging, for example, from no zoological forms to a mammal-"wug" (that is worm + bug) dichotomy, on to a bird-fish-snake trichotomy, and so forth.

To appreciate what counts as an animal for humans, and in what ways, finally requires a concentrated semiotic enquiry, which can only be hinted at in the following paragraphs. An animal is upgraded to a cultural object, an object of value, as a by-product of structuring, ordering, and classifying: the animal, in short, becomes a *marker* in MacCannell's (1976:110) sense, a chunk of concentrated information, a signifier segregated from a signified by virtue of "the superimposition of a system of social values" (ibid.:119). From this point of view it seems promising to consider the many and varied circumstances under which humans may encounter animals. In what follows I shall identify and briefly comment on some of the most common situations. The following list is presented in no particular order, and is certainly not all-embracing. Moreover, the different situations are not necessarily exclusive, and may partially coincide.

1. The human *as predator*. Human beings prey upon or even annihilate animal species, for different reasons. Some, like antelopes, may be hunted down as game; certain carnivores, such as the East African crocodile, are condemned as "vermin" (a distancing label, discussed by Serpell [1986:159–162] under the heading of justificatory "misrepresentation"); primates are overused in medical research; marsupials are killed for their hides; and cetaceans are exploited for their oil. In effect, every time a population of animals is exterminated, the draining of the gene pool is concurrently and irreversibly accompanied by the elimination of a unique communicative code.

2. The human *as prey*. Human beings become the casualties of animals' depredations: for example, human malaria is caused by any of four sporozoites (parasitic protozoans). Each is transmitted from human to human by a female *Anopheles* mosquito, which injects saliva containing plasmodian sporozoites as it bites (even today, more people die every year of mosquito-borne disease than from any other single cause; cf. Stanier et al. 1985:646).

Another forceful illustration is provided by Geist's speculations on the prehistoric bears of native North America and their possible role in delaying human colonization of that continent (Geist 1986).

3. The human *as "partner."* Human beings coexist with animals in some sort of partnership (see Katcher and Beck 1983), as, for example, in a purely guest-host relationship (such as aquarium fish with their master) or in a nexus of mutual dependence (such as in beekeeping; a seeing-eye dog working in the service of a blind person; dogs used for hauling, such as Arctic sled dogs; dogs or cheetahs used for tracking; birds as fishing partners, such as a cormorant catching fish for a Japanese fisherman in exchange for a food reward matching the size of the catch; or as hunting partners, such as the raptors described by Frederick II [1194–1250] in his classic and innovative account. *De arte venandi cum avibus;* pets as therapists [Beck and Katcher 1983, Ch. 8; Serpell 1986, Ch. 6]; and the like).

A special set of subproblems in this category can be identified when animals are used as sexual partners by either men or women, a phenomenon known as "cross-species attachment" (Money 1986:75f.). Bestiality, or the carnal exploitation of animals, has been known at least since Apuleius (cf. an "ancient pre-Columbian custom among Indians of the Caribbean coast of Columbia," cited by Money [ibid.], "that associates the attainment of manhood with the exercise of copulating with donkeys"). Zoophilic acts, involving cattle, horses, or donkeys, dogs, monkeys, or barnyard fowl, are a common theme of pornographic literature; there is also a variant called "formicophilia," "in which arousal and orgasm are dependent on the sensations produced by small creatures like snails, frogs, ants or other insects creeping, crawling, or nibbling the genitalia and perianal area, and the nipples" (ibid.). In some urban environments, animals are used as social facilitators, or catalysts; thus, dogs are used by European female, as well as male, streetwalkers to assist in striking up conversations with potential clients. The curious Western phenomenon of pet cemeteries could further be mentioned here.

4. *Sport and entertainment.* Animals have been long and variously used for human amusement: in Roman circuses (gladiators wrestling with big cats), bullfighting rings, alligator wrestling, cockfights, and frog-jumping contests. Here, too, belong horse and dog races and, perhaps marginally, birdwatching, (urban) pigeon feeding, and, more generally, safaris with photographic intent.

5. *Parasitism.* This may work in either direction:

(A) The activities of humans in relation to the reindeer, for instance, can be described as those of a social parasite; interspecific associations, in relation to parasitism and other concepts, are discussed by Ingold (1980:30f.). He writes: "It is a matter of personal experience, since when I was first in the field in Lapland, an old reindeer named Enoch made a habit of coming round, at 11 o'clock every morning, to visit the place where I regularly urinated outside my cabin" (personal communication).

(B) Each of us has about as many organisms on the surface of our skin as there are people on earth. The mite *Demodex*, crab lice, fleas, and bedbugs are a few samples of the teeming miniature parasitic population sharing the ecological niche constituted by human bodies (Andrews 1976).[7]

6. *Conspecificity*. An animal may accept a human as a conspecific; this is also known as "zoomorphism." As early as 1910, Heinroth described the attachment of incubator-hatched greylag goslings to human beings. These goslings reject any goose or gander as parent objects, opting instead to look upon humans as their exclusive parents. Many other hand-reared birds were later found to have transferred their adult sexual behavior toward their human caretakers. Morris and Morris (1966:182f.) recount attempts by a "fully humanized" female panda, Chi-Chi, to mate with her keepers; and the sexual advances of a male dolphin, Peter, toward his female trainer, Margaret Howe, are recorded in her published protocol (Lilly 1967:282). The latter episode is represented as an accomplished, although fictional, aquatic congress in Ted Mooney's 1981 novel, *Easy Travel to Other Planets* (cf. also 3 above).

7. *Insentience*. An animal may define a human as a part of its inanimate *Umwelt*, as when young birds will perch on the keeper's head or even on his or her outstretched arm, as though it were a branch. Fascinating behaviors of this sort were extensively analyzed by Hediger (1969:81–83), who explains one of the tricks performed by snake charmers on the basis of this principle of misapprehending a human limb for an insensate substrate. According to Hediger, mammals such as the koala may also regard humans as a place for climbing, and make use of them accordingly. Especially intriguing is Hediger's discussion (ibid.:91–95) of the "centaur-like fusion" of man and motor vehicles, especially in the context of big-game reserves, and of how wild animals view such relatively novel combinations.

8. *Taming*, defined as the reduction or possibly total elimination of an animal's flight reaction from man, may be deliberately induced. This is an indispensable precondition for both training and domestication. In the latter, not only the care and feeding, but most particularly the breeding, of an animal—or the communication of genetic information from one generation to the next—have to some degree come under human control. When the biologically altered domesticated animal breeds out of control, it is referred to as "feral," as opposed to "wild."

9. *Training* of animals by humans may take one of two counterpolar forms:

(A) A rat forced to swim under water to escape drowning is taught to take the alley in a submerged Y-maze when the correct decision is indicated by the brighter of two alleys; a porpoise is brought under behavioral control to locate and retrieve underwater objects. Such efforts are called *apprentissage,* loosely rendered as "scientific" or "laboratory training" (cf. Silverman 1978) or, in German, *wissenschaftliche Dressur*.

(B) A horse is taught to perform a comedy act for the purposes of exhibition (cf. Bouissac 1985, Ch. 4); a porpoise is taught to play basketball. Such efforts are called *dressage,* or circus (namely, oceanarium) training, or *höhere Dressur* (as with the Lippizaners of the Spanish Riding School).

Note that *apprentissage* and *dressage* are fundamentally distinct ways of shaping behavior, although from a semiotic point of view they constitute complementary measures, in particular as regards their pragmatic import. This distinction was intuitively appreciated by Hediger as early as 1935, in his dissertation, and was later materially advanced in several of his published writings (for example, Hediger 1979:286). For instance, Hediger insightfully emphasized that *apprentissage* entails a reduction of the animal-man nexus to as close to zero as feasible. *Dressage,* conversely, requires a maximum intensification of the ligature, with the richest possible emotional involvement. This is one dimension of semiotic variation.

Apropos *dressage,* Breland and Breland (1966:108) relate an arresting informal observation concerning the emotional component of a parrot's vocalization. In the exhibition in question the bird picks up a toy telephone, holds it up to his ear, and says "Hello!" Afterward he receives a peanut. it was noted that every time the bird said "Hello!" "the pupils of his eyes contracted and dilated remarkably." The sign is emitted solely in an emotionally charged situation, for the pupil-size cue may not occur if the bird is "talking" merely for peanuts (kindred observations have been made of domestic cats).

A second dimension of semiotic variation lies, in Hediger's words, between "Dressur ohne Affektaufwand" (or without affective display) and "Dressur mit bedeutendem Affektaufwand" (or with significant affective display).

Many other juxtapositions of human and animal could fruitfully be examined; concerning some of these there of course already exist more- or less-substantial studies. These areas include the representation of animals in mythology, oral and written literature, cartoons, on the stage and in the performing arts generally (especially the cinema and television), and in the shape of dolls, puppets, toys, and robots. Animals are often featured, by design, in magazine and TV advertising.

Moreover, countless studies deal with interactions between humans and particular sets of demarcated animals, individual anthropomorphic animals, and classes of exploited captives, such as primates (Erwin et al. 1979), or species in the aggregate (Clutton-Brock 1981; Craig 1981; Houpt and Wolski 1982, Ch. 2), birds in general (Murton 1971), and horses in particular (Lawrence 1985). A synthesis of this vast literature, especially in its fascinating semiotic ramifications, is long overdue.

Saint Augustine was once asked: what is time? He answered: "If no one asks me, I know; if I wish to explain it to one that asks, I know not."

To recapitulate, the central purpose of this chapter is to inquire what, broadly speaking, an animal is. That question ought to be preceded by another: what is life? Although there may not be an absolutely rigorous distinction between inanimate matter and matter in a living state, it is clear enough that animates undergo semiosis, that is, they exchange, among other items, messages, which are strings of signs.

Paying heed, first, to biologically valid (meaning strictly genealogical) classificatory schemes, five major life forms were distinguished, among which, on the macro-level, the mediating position of animals between plants and fungi was accentuated. The critical relevance of *Umwelt-Forschung* to an understanding of animals was mentioned, but was not further developed. The recalcitrant term *Umwelt* had best be rendered in English by the word "model" (as recently expounded in Sebeok 1986c). The biologist's notion of symbiosis, it was also suggested, is equivalent to the philosopher's notion of semiosis.

Turning back to systematics, of which taxonomy is but one component, animals were reassessed from the standpoint of folk classification. In this perspective it was argued that an animal always belongs at once to a multiple array of codes, some natural, or "scientific," others disparately cultural. Far from being irreconcilable, such codes complement one another. Therefore, it is perfectly in order, as one illustration, to regard a whale as being simultaneously a mammal and a fish, as well as, moreover, an enigmatic creature of man's imagination.

The anthropological, or semiotic, definitions of "animal" acquire concreteness and saliency within different types of man-animal confrontation, but their enumeration cannot be carried out exhaustively in the compass of a brief essay such as this. Nevertheless, even the very incomplete and preliminary listing attempted here may serve to elicit further investigation.

Notes

1. In semiosis, signs tend to function in a trinity of mutually exclusive classes as the intermediate transforming agents between "objects" and "interpretants." This is highly pertinent to Peirce's man-sign (more broadly, animal-sign) analogy. (For a recent discussion by an anthropologist, see Singer 1984, esp. pp. 1–2, 55–56, 61.)

2. It is at present unclear whether the recently discovered thermophillic ("black smoker") bacteria of the East Pacific Rise, employing symbiotic chemosynthesis, thus surviving in utter independence of the sun (that is, of photosynthesis) and seemingly constituting the only closed geothermal (terrestrial) ecosystem not integrated with the rest of life, can or cannot be grouped with "ordinary" bacteria (see Baross and Deming 1983; and Jannasch and Mottl 1985). The giant worms subsisting, by absorption, upon these microbial symbionts thus also derive their energy from underwater volcanoes, not sunlight.

3. Among his many writings, Jakob von Uexküll (1982), creatively amplified by his elder son, Thure, is both one of the most important and one of the most readily accessible in English. (See also Thure von Uexküll 1980:291–388, "Die Umweltlehre als Theorie der Zeichenprozesse; Lorenz 1971:273–277; and Sebeok 1979b, Ch. 10.)

4. Peirce's trichotomous classification of signs into iconic, indexical, and symbolic is fundamental in semiotics. It has been discussed by many commentators, notably Burks (1949), Ayer (1968:149–158), Sebeok (1975), and, most recently, Hookway (1985, Ch. 4). (See also the entries under each of these three lemmata; and Joseph Ransdell's article on Peirce, in Sebeok 1986b.)

5. See Bonner 1963 for semiosis in the *Acrasieae*—however classified, they must be reckoned aggregation organisms *par excellence*. (See also Stanier et al. 1985:543f.)

6. "Comme un texte peu intelligible en une seule langue, s'il est rendu simultanément dans plusieurs, laissera peut-être émaner de ces versions differentes un sens plus riche et plus profond qu'aucun de ceux, partiels et mutilés, auqel chaque version prise à part eût permis d'accéder."

7. In the framework of Jakob von Uexküll, the ecological niche could best be described as "*Umwelt*-from-outside," from the standpoint of the observer of the subject concerned.

ELEVEN

Clever Hans Redivivus

Nobody knows the identity of Samuel Rid, or even whether this was his true name or is a literary pseudonym, conceivably of Reginald Scot (S. R. for R. S.?), the author of *Discoverie of Witchcraft* (1584). Some of that book was copied, word for word, into *The Art of Juggling or Legerdemain* (1612), Samuel Rid's only known work, which variously sets forth illusions with balls, coins, and cards—attributed by Scot to witchcraft—and tricks with dice, abridged from Gilbert Walker's *A Manifest Detection of Diceplay* (1580). Rid's guide, as was noted by Arthur F. Kinney (1973:263), belongs to the genre "of an instructional manual, forerunner of our how-to-do-it books." Its arrangement, being an exposé of a variety of discreditable rogues, while being also a handbook for magicians, reminds me of James Randi's *Flim-Flam: The Truth about Parapsychology and Other Delusions* (1980).

Rid unexpectedly turns, in his penultimate paragraphs (Kinney 1973:289f.), to "one pretty knack, which is held to be marvelous and wonderful," namely, "to make a horse tell you how much money you have in your purse." He leads into his concise account by way of a historical example, of a story of a performing ass of Memphis, in Egypt, followed by one meaty paragraph about a horse, unnamed, which is one "at this day to be seen in London." There is little doubt that the horse is none other than the celebrated "dancing horse" Morocco, exhibited by a confidence artist named John Banks, usually stated to be a Scot. "This horse," we are informed by J. O. Halliwell-Phillipps (1879:21; written in 1855), "was taught tricks and qualities of a nature then considered so wonderful, that the exhibitor was popularly invested with the powers of magic. . . ." Halliwell-Phillipps reviewed the contemporary literature pertaining to the exploits of Morocco and Banks because they were featured by such famous poets as John Donne and Ben Jonson, among others, and particularly because they are alluded to in William Shakespeare's *Love's Labour's Lost* (1598:I.ii.51).

Gervase Markham's curious *Cavelarice,* an early seventeenth-century work on horsemanship, explains in some detail how "strange Morocco's

This chapter is reprinted from *The Skeptical Inquirer* 10:4.314–318. It was written, by invitation of the editor, Kendrick Frazier, as a tenth-anniversary essay for the Committee for the Scientific Investigation of Claims of the Paranormal, of which the author is a Fellow.

dumbe arithmeticke" (as Bishop Hall spoke of its faculty in 1598:iv.2) was drummed into the horse:

> Now if you will teach your horse to reckon any number by lifting up and pawing with his feete, you shall first with your rodde, by rapping him upon the shin, make him take his foote from the ground, and by adding to your rod one certaine word, as *Up,* or such like, now when he will take up his foote once, you shall cherrish him, and give him bread, and when hee sets it uppon the ground, the first time you shall ever say *one,* then give him more bread, and after a little pause, labour him againe at every motion, giving him a bit of bread til he be so perfit that, as you lift up your rod, so he will lift up his foot, and as you move your rod downeward, so he will move his foot to the ground; and you shall carefully observe to make him in any wise to keep true time with your rod, and not to move his foot when you leave to move your rodde, which correcting him when he offends, both with stroakes and hunger, he will soone be carefull to observe. After you have brought him to this perfectnesse, then you shall make him encrease his numbers at your pleasure, as from one to two, from two to three, and so fourth, till in the end hee will not leave pawing with his foote, so long as ever you move your rod up and downe; and in this by long costume you shall make him so perfect that, if you make the motion of your rod never so little, or hard to bee perceived, yet he will take notice of it; and in this lesson as in the other, you must also dyrect him by your eie, fixing your eyes upon the rod and uppon the horsses feete all the while that you move it; for it is a rule in the nature of horsses, that they have an expeciall regard to the eye, face, and countenaunce of their keepers, so that once after you have brought him to know the helpe of your eye, you may presume he will hardly erre except your eye misguide him; and therefore ever before you make your horse doe any thing, you must first make him looke you in the face. Now after you have made him perfit in these observations, and that he knowes his severall rewardes, both for good and evill dooings, then you may adventure to bryng him into any company or assembly, and making any man think a number, and tell it you in your eare, you may byd the horse tell you what number the man did thinke, and at the end of your speech bee sure to saye last *Up:* for that is as it were a watch-worde to make him know what hee must doe, and whylest you are talking, you shall make him looke in your face, and so your eye dyrecting him unto your rodde, you may with the motions thereof make him with his foot declare the number before thought by the by-stander. From this you may create a world of other toyes, as how many maydes, howe many fooles, how many knaves, or how many rich men are amongst a mustitude of gazing persons, making the worlde wonder at that which is neyther wonderfull nor scarce artificiall [Halliwell-Phillipps 1879:39–42].

What is so remarkable about Samuel Rid's exposition five years afterward is its thoroughly modern aspect, couched in the terminology of current semiotic and nonverbal communication studies. Rid says that, for example, the horse's master

> will throw you three dice, and will bid his horse tell how many you or he have thrown. Then the horse paws with his foot whiles the master stands stone still.

> Then when his master sees he hath pawed so many as the first dice shews itself, then he lifts up his shoulders and stirs a little. Then he bids him tell what is on the second die, and then on the third die, which the horse will do accordingly, still pawing with his foot until his master sees he hath pawed enough, and then stirs. Which, the horse marking, will stay and leave pawing. And note, that the horse will paw an hundred times together, until he sees his master stir. And note also that nothing can be done but his master must first know, and then his master knowing, the horse is ruled by him by signs. This if you mark at any time you shall plainly perceive [Kinney 1973:290].

Every reader of this passage who is familiar with the Clever Hans phenomenon will instantly recognize Rid's description; some may wonder why Oskar Pfungst, so expert in the methodology of scientific research (Fernald 1984; Sebeok 1985d; and Sebeok 1985e), ignored Rid, so knowledgeable about elementary techniques of conjury.

Rid was not the only one the thorough Pfungst should have known about. The cunning Thomas Dekker, who knew this exhibition well, informs us (1606) that Banks's feats were accomplished "onely by the eye and the eare," that is, by nonverbal and verbal signs. Thomas Killigrew gave similar testimony in 1664, mentioning a woman who "governs them with signs and by the eye, as Banks breeds his horse." These are among many comparable accounts of wondrous horses and other learned domestic animals of all sorts preceding and following the authoritative studies of Pfungst (Christopher 1970:39–54, for instance, discusses some of these; see also Sebeok 1979a, and Sebeok 1981b).

In the 1950s, a distancing transformation took place: although domestic animals continued to be trained to perform seemingly miraculous acts, the emphasis decidedly shifted from the familiar to the exotic—to creatures that dwell in the depths of the oceans, especially dolphins, or in remote African and Indonesian jungles, including most of the great apes (two species of chimpanzees, the gorilla, and the orangutan). While John Banks and his fellows practiced outright deception, for the straightforward and honorable purpose to increase their income, the bully pulpit of today is the academic laboratory, supported with federal funding or by private corporate donations, connived at by irresponsible segments of the media. Lewis M. Branscomb (1985:421) has put the matter elegantly:

> I am afraid that a great many scientists deceive themselves from time to time in their treatment of data, gloss over problems involving systematic errors, or understate the contributions of others. These are the 'honest mistakes' of science, the scientific equivalent of the 'little white lies' of social discourse. But unlike polite society, which easily interprets those white lies, the scientific community has no way to protect itself from sloppy or deceptive literature except to learn whose work to suspect as unreliable. This is a tough sentence to pass on an otherwise talented scientist.

A host of problems stem from self-deception of this sort, as we have documented elsewhere (Sebeok and Umiker-Sebeok 1980; Sebeok 1981a; and Umiker-Sebeok and Sebeok 1981).

Perhaps of greatest interest to skeptical inquirers should be that both the logic and the cop-outs employed by those who seek to evoke a language propensity or arithmetic proclivity in wild Cetaceans, Pinnipeds, or Primates are, in many particulars, the same as those used by investigators of other paranormal tendencies. These parallels need to be spelled out in a further article.

TWELVE

Fetish

Wilcox: Why can't you people take things at their face value?
Robyn: Signs are never innocent. Semiotics teaches us that.
Wilcox: Semi-what?
Robyn: Semiotics. The study of signs.
Wilcox: It teaches us to have dirty minds, if you ask me.
—Lodge 1988:155

1. THE WORD "FETISH" AND ITS USES IN ANTHROPOLOGY

As everyone can ascertain from the *OED*, the English vocable *fetish* was directly adopted from the Portuguese substantive *feitiço*, "charm, sorcery." (Cf. Spanish *hechizo;* both from the Latin *facticius* "factitious," meaning "artificial, skillfully contrived.") Originally, the term was applied to any of the objects used by the Guinea Coast natives and in neighboring regions as talismans, amulets, or other means of enchantment, "or regarded by them with superstitious dread." Portuguese sailors allegedly minted the appellation in the fifteenth century when they observed the veneration that West Coast Africans had for such objects, which they wore on their person. The earliest English citation, as further reported in the *OED*, dates from a 1613 work by Samuel Purchas, *Pilgrimage* (VI.xv.651): "Hereon were set many strawen Rings called *Fatissos* or *Gods*."

Writers on anthropology, following Brosses (1760), began using fetish in the wider sense of an inanimate object being worshipped by "savages" on account of its supposed inherent magical powers, or as its animation by a spirit. More generally still, fetish referred to something irrationally reverenced.

In 1869, McLennan, who framed totemism as a theoretical topic, also invented the notorious formula: totemism is fetishism plus exogamy and matrilineal descent (but cf. Lévi-Strauss 1962:18). Van Wing then wrote (1938:131) an oft-cited amplification about the fetish, which is of particular interest here because of its relatively early employment, in this context, of the metaphor-metonym opposition:

This chapter was written at the invitation of Thaïs Morgan, of Arizona State University, for publication in a special issue on the semiotics of pornography which she edited for the *American Journal of Semiotics* (6:51–65). Versions have also been published in French, German, Italian, (Brazilian) Portuguese, and Spanish.

> Le "fétiche" *nkisi* est, chez les Kongo orientaux, un objet artificiel comportant des éléments métaphoriques empruntés aux trois règnes naturels: "herbes qui egratignent, blessent, guérissent; feuilles, écorces, racines qui guérissent ou tuent; becs et ongles, plumes, cornes, dents, queues et poils d'animaux divers, etc." L'élément vital (metonymique) d'un *nkisi* "est une argile prise au fond d'une rivière ou d'un étang, séjour des esprits des morts;" cette opération fixe l'un de ces esprits dans le charme, lui conférant son pouvoir effervescent.

The *nkisi,* Van Wing noted, assures the protection of its proprietor, the two being magically linked, "uni à lui par un lien de maître à sujet." He sums it all up in this couplet: "La gloire du nkisi, c'est d'avoir un maître en vie. / Le chef a son autorité, le féticheur a la sienne."

However, Herskovits, writing about a decade later (1950:368), objected:

> One word that has been applied to charms is *fetish,* and no term has proved more troublesome than this and its companion, *fetichism.* The derivation is from the Portuguese *feitiço* "something made," and was used by the early Portuguese to denote the charms and images of African peoples. These terms are mentioned here because they are encountered so often in the literature, as when it is said that "fetichism is the religion of Africa." When used at all, they should be employed in the sense of "charm" and "magic"; but they are far better omitted from any discussion of the means whereby man controls the supernatural.

That demurral notwithstanding, one fruitful way of classifying religions has been to ask in the case of each: where is the divine (the object of religious responses) primarily sought and located, and what sort of response is primarily made to it? According to this principle of division, religions may be partitioned into three major groups: sacramental, prophetic, and mystical. Details of this were spelled out by Alston (1967c), following a suggestion by William James; but Auguste Comte and Charles de Brosses specifically interpreted the fetish as a basis for their theories concerning the origin of religion.

The divine in the sacramental religion is said to be chiefly sought in things, which are thought of as capable of capturing natural forces—inanimate things, such as pieces of wood, relics of saints, statues, crosses; or food and drink, such as bread and wine or baptismal water; or living things, such as the totemic animal of the group, the sacred cow, the sacred tree; or processes, such as the movements of the sacred dance. In very primitive forms of sacramental religion, when the object itself, perhaps possessing animate existence in and of itself, is responded to as divine, that object has, in early anthropological practice, been designated a fetish. Such a fetish could be wrought to have positive effects—such as to heal or to cure sickness—and even used to induce erotic disposition, that is, to affect and alter "natural" social relations.

Clearly, it was the assignment of the latter capability that led to the eventual espousal of the term in clinical, thence in legal, discourse to describe the enhancement of sexual activity in the presence of a type of object which is, for others, not at all, or if so but weakly, endowed with a compulsively sexual (paraphiliac) connotation. Gebhard (1969:72) quite properly envisions "the whole matter of fetishism as a gradated phenomenon. At one end of the range is slight preference; next is strong preference; next is the point where the fethish item is a necessity to sexual activity; and at the terminal end of the range the fetish item substitutes for a living sexual partner." Indeed, as will become clear, sorting by degree is the only procedure that makes sense when the matter is viewed from the semiotic standpoint.

The notion of "fetishism of the commodities" (cf. Erckenbrecht 1976) has become one of the cardinal concepts and slogans of the Marxist heritage as applied to the analysis of the relationship between people and products, or between use-value and exchange-value. Geras (1971:71) sees the origins of this concept in the more fundamental distinction between "essence" (that is, "real" social relations) and its "appearance" (the outer manifestation of such relations). He writes:

> It is because there exists at the interior of capitalist society, a kind of internal rupture between the social relations which obtain and the manner in which they are experienced, that the scientist of the society is confronted with the necessity of constructing reality against appearances. Thus this necessity can no longer be regarded as an arbitrary importation into Marx's own theoretical equipment or something he merely extracted from other pre-existing sciences. . . . [It is] seen to lead, by a short route, to the heart of the notion of fetishism.

In short, to invest a commodity with powers which are not present or inherent is to elevate it to the status of a fetish; it is in this way that money, or capital in general, comes to be "fetishized." Jhally—whose concern is with fetishism in television and magazine advertising—(1987:29) reformulated this process in quasi-semiotic parlance when commenting that "fetishism consists of seeing the meaning of things as an inherent part of their physical existence when in fact that meaning is created by their integration into a *system* of meaning." Earlier, Baudrillard (1981:92) made a similar point when he noted that it is the sanctification of the system as such, "the commodity as system," that reinforces "the fetishist fascination."

2. THE FETISH IN PSYCHOLOGY AND IN SEXOLOGY

The forensic psychiatrist Richard von Krafft-Ebing's book, *Psychopathia sexualis* (1886), contained the first systematic collection of data relating to "pathological" fetishism. This text, with its view of sex as perverted and disgusting, came to exert a great, baleful, and seemingly perpetual, influence. He wrote extensively of sex crimes and sexual variations or deviations, which he considered based on genetic defects.

So far as I have been able to trace, it was Krafft-Ebing who first referred to the notion of the fetish as a "perversion," that is, something that requires shame and social sanctions to control it. According to his descriptions, a fetish is a nonhuman object—a part of the body or something contiguous to it, such as clothing—which serves as an impetus to sexual arousal and orgasm. The Teutonic doctor, in fact, considered all acts other than marital coitus for the purpose of procreation, and all surrogates for penile-vaginal intercourse—for example, voyeurism, exhibitionism, transvestitism, sadomasochism, and so forth—as "perversions" to be reprehended.

Krafft-Ebing's "method" is illustrated by his report of a case (no. 101) of hair fetishism, which I cite from Kunzle (1982:53n14), who, after the French police doctor Paul Garnier's monograph (1896:70), uses it to illustrate "the degree of moral vindictiveness" evinced by the authorities and approved of by Krafft-Ebing. According to this retold story, a seventeen-year-old boy was watching a show in the Tuileries gardens, while pressing up to a girl "whose hair he silently, amorously rolled between his fingers, so softly that she did not even notice. Suddenly two plainclothes policemen sprang upon him. One seized with his hand the boy's erect penis through his trousers, and cried, 'At last we got you . . . after all the time we've been watching you!' " The boy was then sentenced to three months in jail.

Freedman, Kaplan, and Sadock's standard comprehensive textbook *Psychiatry* (1972) likewise defines the use of fetishes (in an explicitly sexual context) in metonymic terms: "The process of achieving sexual excitement and gratification by substituting an inanimate object such as a shoe, piece of underwear, or other article of clothing for a human love object." This definition is substantially repeated under the rubric of *(sic)* "Other Sexual Deviations," where only "a foot or a lock of hair" is added to the enumeration of common sexual fetishes. (A recent conspicuous instance of foot fetishism is displayed in Martin Scorsese's short film *Life Lessons;* this is realized by his camera's—or the painter's—obsessive dwelling over Rosanna Arquette's feet.) In point of fact, it is very common in psychiatric literature to find references to the attraction a patient may have for an inanimate object as inordinate or pathological.

An exchange (March 6, 1987) from "The Kinsey Report," a syndicated newspaper column by my colleague June Reinisch, epitomizes the current scientific view of the subject:

> Q.—I am a male in my mid-20s. Since age 9, I have been strongly attracted to women's feet, shoes and stockings. I become sexually aroused thinking about foot odor and sometimes have erections in public places from fantasizing about this.
>
> I feel extremely guilty and think most people would think I'm perverted. Do you think I'm sick? Do I need professional help? Why am I this way?

A.—I think that you should consult a psychotherapist who is experienced in working with sexual problems. He or she can help you determine exactly what role these desires play in your life, and then the two of you can decide what type of therapy (if any) is necessary for you to form long-lasting, close relationships.

Fetishism is a behavior in which sexual arousal depends on an inanimate object, a certain body part or the like—in short, on something other than the whole person. This area has not been fully examined scientifically. Very little is known about the causes of fetishistic behavior, except that it is thought to originate early during psychosocial development.

Scientists also don't know how many people have sexual fetishes, but it is clear that this behavior is much more common in men than in women. A variety of body parts, items of clothing and odors have been mentioned in reports of individual fetishism.

Several points in this correspondence merit comment.

It is clear, first of all, that both parties in the exchange view the reported fetishistic comportment as constituting a sexual "problem," possibly even a "perverted" form of behavior, or one at least likely to require psychotherapeutic intervention. This is so despite Reinisch's concession that very little is known about the cause of the kind of behavior described or of its ontogeny.

Reinisch also echoes a common opinion among clinicians—that fetishism "is much more common in men than in women." This presumption was held by Freud (1927; cf. Vigener 1989), as well as by Alfred C. Kinsey and his collaborators, who considered fetishism to be an "almost exclusively male phenomenon" (1953:679). Freud and his epigones even held that fetishism is *the* male perversion *par excellence*. As Schor (1985:303) puts it, in a nutshell, "female fetishism is, in the rhetoric of psychoanalysis, an oxymoron."

For Schor's subject, George Sand, the female fetish happens to be a wound; but wounds, Schor asserts (p. 304), "are not generally fetishized by men"—a questionable claim. Fetishistic attraction to cripples or, more broadly, to "discredited" individuals who bear stigmata in Goffman's sense (1963), as also to one-legged females, and even crutch fetishism (cf. Schindler 1953), abound in the literature. For instance, Desmond Morris (1969:170) reports the following case: a young boy "was leaning out of a window when his first ejaculation occurred. As it happened, he saw a figure moving past in the road outside, walking on crutches. When he was married he could only make love to his wife if she wore crutches in bed."

Reinisch implicitly subscribes to the view of the fetish as an essentially indexical sign—especially a synecdochic sign ("something other than the whole person")—although, of course, her idiom is other than semiotic. Indeed, the fetish is, as here, commonly regarded as a fixation on the *pars pro toto*.

The most extensive recent study of the fetish in sexology is to be found in John Money's *Lovemaps* (1986). He once more offers the conventional definition, as "an object or charm endowed with magical or supernatural power; an object or part of the body charged, for a particular person, with special sexuoerotic power" (ibid.:261). In his lemma on "fetishism," however, there is a hint of a wider view (to which I shall return), when Money points out that there "is no technical term for the reciprocal paraphilic condition in which the fetish, for example, a uniform, must belong to the self" (ibid.:261).

Mainly, what we find in Money's book is a routine catalogue of some objects that have been pinpointed by numerous clinicians as typical fetishes. Pornographers fabricate and sell objects—including pictorial and written displays—arranged according to similar categories, designed to cater to every conceivable fetishistic taste.

Money classifies tangible objects, or, technically, imagery (ibid.:65f.), in addition to those appealing to the eye, as either haptic or olfactory, available in immediate perception or in fantasy. The former pertain to feelings of pressure, rubbing, or touch, which may be generated internally (as by an enema or other inserted artifact) or externally (by the application of fabrics, fur, hair, and so forth). A tactual token may also be a live creature, wriggling and/or furry; thus, in one reported case, a woman habitually placed a dog in her crotch, "as an adjunct to masturbation and orgasm," but she later substituted a small infant in the same position (ibid.:54).

Leather (for example, shoes, as in Figs. 12.1 and 12.2) and rubber or now plastic (for example, training pants) fetishes bridge the gap between touch and smell, as did James Joyce's fetish for soiled knickers. (For other paraphernalia employed by well-known writers, see Colin Wilson's book, *The Misfits: A Study of Sexual Outsiders*, 1988.) Olfactory fetishes characteristically carry the smell of some portion of the human body, especially of those garments that cover sexual parts (namely, fecal or urinary odor, odor of sweat, menstrual odor, smell of lactation). These garments are sometimes also sucked or chewed.

Although Money doesn't emphasize this, the use of fetishes by females seems considerably more prevalent than has been explicitly recognized in the literature thus far. Freud's judgment was obviously dictated by his theoretical preoccupation with the castration complex, according to which fixation or regression to prior psychosexual stages of development underlies deviations, so that castration anxiety is the central component of fetishism.

Kinsey's traditional supporting opinion may have been due to nothing more than a prejudicial sampling error. For instance, compulsive stealing of objects which are of no intrinsic value to the thief but which have obsessive semiotic significance—treated in sexology under the heading "kleptophilia"—seemingly does occur in women more often than in men,

Fig. 12.1. "Penaljo & Muscle." Color advertisement for Penaljo Shoe Corp. by Michael Meyers & Associates, Inc. *New York Times Magazine*, August 31, 1987. By permission.

Obsessive Footwear For The Female *Persuasion*
134 Chestnut Street Philadelphia (215)592-8004

Fig. 12.2. Merchant's logo and tag line on business card.

but the connection is not always explicitly recognized (cf., however, Zavitzianos 1971, relating female fetishism to exhibitionism and kleptomania).

Moreover, reports such as the following are not uncommon: "A young girl experienced her first orgasm when clutching a piece of black velvet as she masturbated. As an adult, velvet became essential to her sexually. Her whole house was decorated with it and she only married in order to obtain more money to buy more velvet" (Desmond Morris 1969:169–170). Similarly, the fixation of Imelda Marcos on her 500 bras and 3,000 pairs of shoes appears to be a well-publicized recent case of something more than run-of-the-mill female fetishism.

Children of both sexes frequently cling to an object—à la Linus and his celebrated blanket. Such an object may be related by contiguity to a parent or to the infant's early material surroundings. According to some psychiatrists (Freedman et al. 1972:637), this "is a security operation that should be distinguished from fetishism in which the normal sexual object is substituted by another." It is further asserted in this source that fetishism of this latter type "is not known to occur in childhood." However, this judgment may be due to psychiatrists' clinging to the prejudice that a fetish, in order to be defined as such, must produce genital sexual satisfaction (usually deemed "deviant" as well) and that the use of objects to produce a fetishistic effect necessarily occurs relatively late in adolescence. Nevertheless, earlier transitory objects present in the child's immediate environment may, eventually, be promoted to the status of a full fetish, so this again seems to be only a matter of degree (cf., for example, Sperling 1963; Roiphe 1973; and Bemporad et al. 1976).

In passing, a syndrome sometimes called "Pygmalionism," which refers to a fetish in the shape of a female statue or life-sized rubber doll, should be mentioned here. From a semiotic viewpoint, an object such as this would constitute an index that is strongly tinged with iconicity. (To a lesser degree, perhaps the rarer cases of tattoo fetishism, as reported by Weimann 1962, involve iconic indexes, too.)

Still other fetishes—as, for instance, diamond engagement rings, gold wedding bands, and class rings or pins exchanged as tokens of going steady in teen age (Money 1986:63)—can be taken as indexes overlaid, in an erotic frame of reference, with a pervasive, culturally widely understood symbolic significance. Money itself, or, more broadly, property, is commonly reported to turn into capitalistic fetish objects (cf. Becker and Schorsch 1975; and Stratton 1987, *passim*, for literary implications).

3. THE FETISH IN SEMIOTICS

I turn now to a fuller consideration of the fetish as a semiotic problem.

It is clearly the case that, as can be gleaned even from the discussion thus far, a fetish is (1) a sign; namely, that it is (2) a predominantly indexical sign; that, moreover, it is (3) an indexical sign of the metonymic species, usually a *pars pro toto* synecdoche; and that (4) this indexical sign is, as a rule, intermingled with both iconic and symbolic elements in various proportions, depending on the context of its use.

With respect to (4), an important consequence of the semiotic model of the fetish is that it is not necessary for the represented object to be fully present to the organism before information about it can influence internal semiosis ("thought") and induce what Peirce called (8.372) "gratific" action.

In another terminology, a fetish could be regarded as a model *(aliquid)*, but such that this simulacrum is often more potent than the object *(aliquo)* that it stands for *(stat pro)*. Its reference *(renvoi)* is, as it were, reminiscent in efficacy to that of a caricature to the subject that it represents. This accords with the view of Desmond Morris (1969:209f.) to the effect that the art of caricature is entirely concerned with the process of stimulus extremism. Features exaggerated in caricatures are, as a rule, supernormal equivalents of normal juvenile features, or of sexual parts, such as female breasts and buttocks.

As we have seen, the term "fetish" has hitherto been principally employed in the fields of anthropology and psychiatry (including especially psychoanalysis) and, in a narrower, more focused sense, yet quite extensively, in studies of erotic and sexual behavior in humans. The notion of "fetish" has to do, in all of these conceptions, with an obsessive maintenance of self-image.

To my knowledge, only Christian Metz has reflected thus far on the "fetish" in chiefly semiotic terms, but even he does so only in a strictly circumscribed technical environment, namely, in relation to photography. (His remarks hark back to Dubois 1983, which, in turn, is an elaboration and application of Peirce's notions about indexicality.) Metz (1985) feels that because of two features—relatively small size and the possibility of a look that may linger—a photograph (as opposed to the cinematic lexis) "is better fit, or more likely, to work as a fetish," that is to say, as something that signifies at once loss (Freudian "symbolic castration," which is metaphoric) and protection against loss (which is metonymic). However, let me set aside here the matter of the photograph-as-fetish, which Metz then ingeniously relates to death (or the fear of death) and conservation (embodied as looking, glancing, gazing). Instead, I would prefer to briefly review and ponder the implications of the more relevant ethological problem variously dealt with under such headings as the "supernormal signal/stimulus" or the "superoptimal sign." (On the relation of semiotics and ethology, see Sebeok 1979a, Ch. 2.)

The point I want to make about such signs is neatly captured by Oscar Wilde's celebrated aphorism (from *A Woman of No Importance,* III), "Nothing succeeds like excess," itself anticipated by Shakespeare's lines, "To gild refined gold, to paint the lily, / To throw perfume on the violet . . . / Is wasteful and ridiculous excess" (*King John,* IV.ii.11f.).

In short, a sign is deemed "supernormal" when it surpasses a "normal" sign in its effectiveness as a releaser (meaning, the discharge of appropriate behavior). According to Guthrie's excellent account of the anatomy of social organs and behavior (1976:19), so-called supernormal signs "occur in the form of extra-large social organs, i.e. increasing signal strength by increasing signal amplitude." Thus, in certain species of animals, antlers and horns are used as an estimation of rank, and therefore they either "grow to gigantic size among the older males, or develop specialized modifications, like filling in between the tines to form palms, thereby increasing the visual effect from a distance."

In particular, anal and genital organs—or just those about which humankind harbors so many taboos—tend to become modified into semiotic organs for several reasons: in part, because mammals, having, in general, a well-developed smelling apparatus, tend to use feces and urine as a part of their signing behavior ("Who was where and when?"); and, in part, because of the sexual overtones of different mammalian ways of urination. Genitalia have frequently acquired heavy semiotic import and have become ritualized into a set of signs conveying oppositions such as maleness-femaleness, aggression-submission, and so forth, while having been elaborated, as well, into specialized social ornamentation that is residually related to their ancestral copulatory role.

The phenomenon of the supernormal stimulus object has been demonstrated many times in animal-behavior studies, especially in one exemplary piece of work by Tinbergen and Perdeck (1950). In brief, these two investigators (among other interesting achievements) found that they could devise a supernormal stimulus object consisting of an artificial model in which some sign aspects are exaggerated relative to the natural object. Such a supernormal stimulus was provided by a long red knitting needle with three white rings near the tip. In the event, this was more effective than a naturalistic head and bill of an adult gull in evoking a pecking response from herring gull chicks.

It should also be noted that, in experiments such as this one, the strength of the response to the stimulus situation varies from context to context, including that of the internal state of the responding animals. In the famous experiment designed to identify the stimulus characters important for the male three-spined stickleback, the maximal effectiveness of the red belly display depends on the stage of the respondent's breeding cycle and whether or not he is in his territory.

Writing about domestic cats, the ethologist Leyhausen observed (1967) that "substitute objects" can become supernormal objects, as when a sated cat disports itself with a ball of paper in an intensive catching game, while perfectly "adequate" prey mice run around under its very nose. Indeed, fetishistic attachments are commonplace among vertebrates, in particular in mammals, as well as in many birds.

I would argue that a fetish is just such a supernormal sign, a "misplaced response" (Lorenz 1971:160), if you will, standing for, indeed amplifying by a process of ritualization, some natural object, upon which an individual has become preferentially imprinted in lieu of the object itself. (For a likely mechanism, see Leyhausen 1967.)

But this definition requires a considerable expansion of the concepts of fetish and of fetishism, encompassing erotic estheticism in general, as well as positive attachments which can only by interpretative extension, if at all, be considered to fall into the realm of the erotic (for example, saints' relics, a rabbit's-foot charm, and the like).

Such attachments normally occur between a child and its mother, and again when the child grows up and falls in love with another human being. Attachment to an exclusive love-object or sexual partner, eventuating in a relationship which animal behaviorists call pair-bonding, involves in fact a live fetish: the love-object is a *pars pro toto,* in the sense that, say, the female mate comes to stand for, say, all marriageable females. "The strongly sexual aesthetic responses to specific 'beautiful features' of the male and female body demand particular attention," for these are elicited by characters *"which are immediate indicators of hormonal sex functions"* (Lorenz 1971:159f.; italics in original). Lorenz goes on to give many examples from art and from fashion of the production of such "superoptimal dummies," pinpointing those characters which are exaggerated for this purpose; other instances are listed and discussed by Desmond Morris (1969).

In this perspective, what in the literature of the erotic and the sexological is called a fetishistic attachment may be viewed as a form of malimprinting. As Morris (1969:169) writes: "Most of us develop a primary pair-bond with a member of the opposite sex, rather than with fur gloves or leather boots . . . but the fetishist, firmly imprinted with his unusual sexual object, tends to remain silent on the subject of his strange attachment. . . . The fetishist . . . becomes isolated by his own, highly specialized form of sexual imprinting."

THIRTEEN

Indexicality

The poet Joseph Brodsky remarked that a study in genealogy "normally is owing to either pride in one's ancestry or uncertaintly about it" (1989:44). Indeed, most contemporary American workers in semiotics proudly trace their lineage, or try to, as do growing numbers abroad, to Peirce, whom Max Fisch once justly characterized as "the most original and versatile intellect that the Americas have so far produced" (1980:7). In this, he perhaps echoed Peirce's student and sometime collaborator in the early 1880s, Joseph Jastrow, who called his teacher "one of the most exceptional minds that America has produced" and "a mathematician of first rank" (1930:135).

Of course, intimations of Western semiotics—sometimes under the distinctly indexical *nom de guerre* "sem(e)iotic"—which, in a sense, culminated with Peirce, gradually sprouted out of the haze of millennia before him. And the doctrine of signs, to which Peirce imparted so critical a spin, today clearly continues to flourish almost everywhere. His reflection, that "human inquiries,—human reasoning and observation,—tend toward the settlement of disputes and ultimate agreement in definite conclusions which are independent of the particular stand-points from which the different inquirers may have set out" (8.41, 1885), holds surely no less for semiotics than it applies in other domains of study and research.

Fourteen years ago this month, The Johns Hopkins University hosted The Charles Peirce Symposium on Semiotics and the Arts. Featuring invited lectures by Eco, Jakobson, Geertz, and others, the papers were delivered in the presence of many distinguished discussants. My particular assignment had been to give the opening address, on a topic of my choice. Having had in mind at the time to prepare an interlinked trio of papers—one on iconicity, another on indexicality, a third on the symbol; in brief, to review the overall question: How do different categories of signs signify their objects?—I opted, because the time seemed ripe for this in Baltimore, to explore the mysteries of iconicity (Sebeok 1976; cf. Bouissac et al. 1986).

A condensed version of this invited address was read to the Charles Sanders Peirce Sesquicentennial International Congress, Harvard University, September 9, 1989, in the closing plenary session, "Peirce and Semeiotic." It is slated to appear in a collection of plenary papers, *Peirce and Contemporary Thought*, ed. Kenneth Laine Ketner (Lubbock: Texas Tech University Press). Versions are being translated for publication in German, Japanese, and Vietnamese.

Here, I should like to present some thoughts concerning the second category, indexicality. (The third subject has, at least for the nonce, been preempted by Eco's detailed analysis [1984, Ch. 4].)

It should go without saying that this Peircean category, like every other, cannot be well understood piecemeal, without taking into account, at much the same time, the veritable cascade of other irreducible triadic relational structures which make up the armature of Peirce's semiotic—indeed, without coming to terms with his philosophy in its entirety. But this ideal procedure would be mandatory only were I bent on exegesis rather than engaged—taking Peirce's ideas as a kind of beacon—in a quest of my own. I should nonetheless give at least one example of the dilemma of selectivity, and do so by noting how Peirce tied together his notions of deduction and indexicality:

> An Obsistent Argument, or *Deduction,* is an argument representing facts in the Premiss, such that when we come to represent them in a Diagram we find ourselves compelled to represent the fact stated in the Conclusion; so that the Conclusion is drawn to recognize that, quite independently of whether it be recognized or not, the facts stated in the premisses are such as could not be if the fact stated in the conclusion were not there; that is to say, the Conclusion is drawn in acknowledgment that the facts stated in the premisses constitute an Index of the fact which it is thus compelled to acknowledge . . . [2.96, c. 1902].

It was Rulon Wells who, in an article that even today amply rewards close study for its extraordinary fecundity, argued the following three interesting claims (1967:104): (1) that Peirce's notion of the icon is as old as Plato's (namely that the sign *imitates* the signified); (2) that Peirce's notion of the symbol is original but fruitless; and (3) that it is "with his notion of index that Peirce is at once novel and fruitful." I discussed some implications of the first of these statements in 1975; this is not the place to debate the second.

The third assertion is, I enthusiastically concur with Wells, doubtless true. Peirce's views on the index may in truth have been historically rooted in his interest in the realism of Scotus; "*hic and nunc,*" he once observed, "is the phrase perpetually in the mouth of Duns Scotus" (1.458, 1896). "The index," he later amplified, "has the being of present experience" (4.447, c. 1903). Whatever the attested sources of his ideas on this topic may have been, his innovativeness in respect to the index is, as Wells noted (ibid.), due to the fact that Peirce saw, as had no one before him, "that indication (pointing, ostension, deixis) is a mode of signification as indispensable as it is irreducible."

Peirce contended that *no* matter of fact can be stated without the use of some sign serving as an index, the reason for this being the inclusion of *designators* as one of the main classes of indexes. He regarded designations as "absolutely indispensable both to communication and to thought. No assertion has any meaning unless there is some designation to show whether the universe of reality or what universe of fiction is referred to" (8.368n23, from the undated "Notes on Topical Geometry"). Deictics of various sorts, including tenses, constitute perhaps the most clear-cut examples of designations. Peirce identified universal and existential quanitifiers with selective pronouns, which he classified with designations as well (2.289, c. 1893).

Peirce called his other main class of indexes *reagents.* Since reagents may be used to ascertain facts, little wonder they became the staple of detective fiction, as was dazzlingly demonstrated in the famous Sherlock and Mycroft Holmes duet in "The Greek Interpreter," and thereafter replayed by Conan Doyle's countless copycats.

Space permits but a single cited exemplification here of how this detectival method of abduction (alias "deduction") (cf. Eco and Sebeok 1983) works in some detail. The *rei signum* of my choice (Quintilian 8.6.22) involves (as it turns out) a bay mare, or yet another a horse, an animal which, for obscure reasons, has been favored in this context by dozens of novelists from the 1747 episode of the king's horse in Voltaire's *Zadig,* via the chronicle of Silver Blaze, John Straker's racehorse and the many ensuing racehorses of Dick Francis, to Baskerville's incident of the abbot's horse, by Eco (cf. Sebeok 1990a). My parodic pick comes from the Dorothy L. Sayers novel *Have His Carcase* (1932:209–210).

In Chapter 16, Harriet Vane hands over to Lord Peter Wimsey a shoe she has just found on the beach. He then proceeds to reconstruct—*ex alio aliud etiam intellegitur* (Quintilian 8.6.22)—a horse from this synecdoche:

> He ran his fingers gently round the hoop of metal, clearing the sand away.
>
> "It's a new shoe—and it hasn't been here very long. Perhaps a week, perhaps a little more. Belongs to a nice little cob, about fourteen hands. Pretty little animal, fairly well-bred, rather given to kicking her shoes off, pecks a little with the off-fore."
>
> "Holmes, this is wonderful! How do you do it?"
>
> "Perfectly simple, my dear Watson. The shoe hasn't been worn thin by the 'ammer, 'ammer, 'ammer on the 'ard 'igh road, therefore it's reasonably new. It's a little rusty from lying in the water, but hardly at all rubbed by sand and stones, and not at all corroded, which suggests that it hasn't been here long. The size of the shoe gives the size of the nag, and the shape suggests a nice little round, well-bred hoof. Though newish, the shoe isn't fire-new, and it is worn down a little on the inner front edge, which shows that the wearer was disposed to peck a little; while the way the nails are placed and clinched indicates that the smith wanted to make the shoe extra secure—which is why I said that a lost shoe was a fairly common accident with this particular gee. Still, we needn't blame him or her too much. With all these stones about, a slight trip or knock might easily wrench a shoe away."

"Him or her. Can't you go on and tell the sex and colour while you're about it?"

"I am afraid even I have my limitations, my dear Watson."

. . . .

"Well, that's quite a pretty piece of deduction. . . ."

Peirce pointed out that "A scream for help is not only intended to force upon the mind the knowledge that help is wanted, but also to force the will to accord it" (2.289, 1893). Perhaps Peirce's best known example of a reagent—although a disconcerting one, for it seems exempt from his general rule that an index would lose its character as a sign if it had no interpretant (Ayer 1968:153)—involved "a piece of mould with a bullet-hole in it as a sign of a shot; for without a shot there would have been no hole; but there is a hole there, whether anybody has the sense to attribute it to a shot or not" (2.304, c. 1901).

Here belong motor signs as well, when, as is commonly the case, they serve to indicate the state of mind of the utterer; however, if a gesture serves merely to call attention to its utterer, it is but a designation.

An index, as Peirce spelled this out further, "is a sign which refers to the Object that it denotes by virtue of being really affected by that Object" (2.248, c. 1903)—where the word "really" resonates to Scotus' doctrine of *realitas et realitas,* postulating a real world in which universals exist and general principles manifest themselves in the sort of cosmos that scientists try to decipher.

Peirce specified that, "insofar as the Index is affected by the Object, it necessarily has some Quality in common with the Object, and it is in respect to these that it refers to the Object" (2.305, c. 1901). He further noted that "a sign, or representation, which refers to its object not so much because of any similarity or analogy with it, nor because it is associated with general characters which that object happens to possess, as because it is in dynamical (including spatial) connection both with the individual object, on the one hand, and with the senses or memory of the person whom it serves as a sign, on the other hand." (Let it be recalled that all objects, on the one hand, and the memory, being a reservoir of interpretants, on the other, are also kinds of signs or systems of signs.)

Thus indexicality hinges on association by contiguity (a technical expression Peirce understandably disliked [3.419, 1892]), not, as iconicity does, by likeness; nor does it rest, in the manner of a symbol, on "intellectual operations." Indexes, "whose relation to their objects consists in a correspondence in fact, . . . direct the attention to their objects by blind compulsion" (1.558, 1867).

A grisly instance (only recently laid to rest) of association by contiguity was the right arm of the Mexican General Alvaro Obregón. Lost at the elbow during a battle in 1915, the limb had for fifty-four years, until the summer of 1989, been on display in a jar of formaldehyde at a large marble monument in Mexico City, where it acquired talismanic qualities referring to the ruthless former president. When the novelist Gabriel García Márquez suggested (Rohter 1989) that "they should just replace [the decaying appendage] with another arm," he was effectively advocating that the limb be transfigured from an index with a mystical aura into a symbol with historical significance.

Iconicity and indexicality were often, although never by Peirce, polarized with the same or comparable labels in the most various fields as if the two categories were antagonistic rather than complementary (Sebeok 1985a: 77, 132)—so that, for instance, James G. Frazer contrasted homeopathic with contagious magic, "the magical sympathy which is supposed to exist between a man and any severed portion of his person"; the Gestalt psychologist Max Wertheimer set apart a "factor of similarity" from a "factor of proximity"; the neuropsychologist Alexander Luria distinguished similarity disorders from contiguity disorders in aphasic patients; linguists in the Saussurean tradition differentiated the paradigmatic from the syntagmatic axis, opposition from contrast; and so forth.

Contiguity is actualized in rhetoric, among other devices, by the trope of metonymy: the replacement of an entity by one of its indexes. The possessive relation between an entity and its index is often realized in grammar by the genitive case (Thom 1973:95–98), as in these two Shakespearean couplets: "Eye of newt, and toe of frog / Wool of bat, and tongue of dog" *(Macbeth)*, with a preposition; and "O tiger's heart wrapp'd in a woman's hide" *(King Henry VI)*, without a preposition. The *pars pro toto* proportion is also at the core of the anthropological and, in particular, psychosexual semiotic category known as "fetish" (cf. Ch. 12, above). In poetics, entire genres have sometimes been professed, as lyric verse, to be imbued with iconicity, and, contrastively, epics with indexicality.

The closely related notion of ostension, launched by Russell in 1948, and later developed by Quine, in the sense of "ostensive definition," should be alluded to here, at least in passing. The Czech theater semiotician Ivo Osolsobě extensively analyzed this concept in the somewhat different context of "ostensive communication" (for example, in 1979). This is sometimes also called "presentation" or "showing." Osolsobe wants to distinguish sharply ostension from indexicality, deixis, natural signs, communication by objects, and the like. However, I find his paradoxical assertion that "ostension is the cognitive use of non-signs," and his elaboration of a theory of ostension as a theory of nonsigns, muddled and perplexing.

Temporal succession, relations of a cause to its effect, or vice versa, of an effect to its cause, or else some space-time vinculum between an index and its dynamic object, as Berkeley and Hume had already discovered but as Peirce went much further to elaborate, lurk at the heart of indexicality. Thus epidemiologists, responsible for investigating the outbreak of a disease (that is, an effect) impinging upon a large number of people in a given locality, seek a source carrier (that is, a causative agent), whom they call, in the root purport of their professional jargon, an "index case," who, and only who, had been exposed, say, to an unknown viral stockpile. It is in this sense that a Canadian airline steward, Gaetan Dugas, aka the infamous Patient Zero, was supposedly identified as *the* index case for AIDS infection in North America.

A given object can, depending on the circumstance in which it is displayed, momentarily function, to a degree, in the role of an icon, an index, or a symbol. Witness the Stars and Stripes: iconicity comes to the fore when the interpreter's attention fastens upon the seven red horizontal stripes of the flag alternating with six white ones (together identical with the number of founding colonies), or the number of white stars clustered in a single blue canton (in all, identical to the number of actual states in the Union); in a cavalry charge, say, the flag was commonly employed to point imperatively, in an indexical fashion, to a target; and the debates pursuant to the recent Supreme Court decision on the issue of flag burning behold our banner as an emotionally surcharged emblem, being a subspecies of symbol.

Peirce once stated uncommonly loosely that a sign "is either an *icon*, an *index*, or a *symbol*" (2.304, c. 1901). But this plainly cannot be so. Once Peirce realized that the utility of his trichotomy is greatly enhanced when, to allow for the recognition of differences in degree, not signs but rather *aspects* of signs are being classified, he emended his statement thus: "it would be difficult if not impossible, to instance an absolutely pure index, or to find any sign absolutely devoid of the indexical quality" (2.306, c. 1901) (although he did allow demonstrative and relative pronouns to be "nearly pure indices," on the ground that they denote things but do not describe them [3.361, 1885]). Ransdell rightly emphasized that one and the same sign can—and, I would insist, must—"function at once as an icon and symbol as well as an index" (1986:1.341); in other words, that all signs necessarily partake of Secondness, although this aspect is prominently upgraded only in certain contexts.

Peirce, who fully recognized that an utterer and an interpreter of a sign "need not be persons" at all (MS 318:205, c. 1907), would not in the least have been shocked to learn that semiosis, in the indexical relationship, or Secondness—along with its elder and younger siblings, Firstness and Thirdness—appeared in terrestrial evolution about 3.6×10^9 years ago. Too, in human ontogenesis, Secondness is a universal of infant prespeech communicative behavior (Trevarthen 1990). The reason for this is that the prime reciprocal implication between *ego*, a distinct sign maker, and *alter*, a distinguishable sign interpreter—neither of which, I repeat, need be an integrated organism—is innate in the very fabric of the emergent, intersubjective, dialogic mind (Braten 1988).

Signs, inclusive of indexes, occur at their most primitive, on the single-cell level, as a physical or chemical entity, external or internal with respect to the embedding organism as a reference frame, which they may "point" to, read, or microsemiosically parse—in brief, can issue functional instructions for, in the manner of an index. Such an index, which may be as simple as a change in magnitude, a mere shape, a geometric change in surface area, or some singularity, can be significant to a cell because it evokes memories, that is, exposes previously masked stored information.

The following striking example, from the life of the ubiquitous prokaryotic bacterium *E. coli*, was provided by Berg (1976), here paraphrased after an interpretation by Yates (in press). This single-celled creature has multiple flagellae that it can rotate either clockwise or counterclockwise. When its flagellae rotate clockwise, they fly apart, causing the organism to tumble. When they rotate counterclockwise, they are drawn together into a bundle which acts as a propeller to produce smooth, directed swimming. Roaming about in your gut, the bacterium explores a chemical field for nutrients by alternating—its context serving as operator—between tumbling and directed swimming until it finds an optimally appropriate concentration of chemical attractant, such as sugar or an amino acid, for its replication. In doing so, it relies on a memory lasting approximately 4 seconds, allowing it to compare deictically, over short times and distances, where it *was* with where it *is*. On that basis, it "decides," with seeming intentionality, whether to tumble (stay in place) or swim, searching for another indexical match somewhere else.

It may be pertinent to note that, with respect to their rhythmic movements, the *hic et nunc* that we humans perceive has a duration of 3 seconds. Poets and composers appear to have been intuitively aware of this fact (proved by Ernst Pöppel) in providing proper "pauses" in their texts. Recent ethological work in societies the world over on ostensive and other body posture movements of an indexical character revealed that there are no cultural differences in the duration of these kinds of behaviors, and that the time intervals last an average of 2 seconds for repeated gestures and 2.9 seconds for nonrepeated gestures. According to the researchers, the 3-second "time window" appears to be fully used up in these circumstances.

Jakob von Uexküll, laboring in Hamburg in a very different scientific tradition and employing a discrepant but readily reconcilable technical jargon, was laying down the foundations of biosemiotics and setting forth the principles of phytosemiosis and zoosemiosis at roughly the same time as Peirce was elaborating general semiotics in the solitude of Milford. Unfortunately, neither knew of the other.

It fell to a contemporary German semiotician, Martin Krampen, in collaboration with Uexküll's elder son, Thure, to show in detail why and precisely how the Peircean distinctions apply to plants. Krampen wrote in part:

> If one wants to extend this trichotomy to plants on the one hand, versus animals and humans on the other, the absence of the function cycle [which, in animals,

> connect receptor organs via a nervous system to effector organs] would suggest that, in plants, indexicality certainly predominates over iconicity. . . . Indexicality, on the vegetative level, corresponds to the sensing and regulating, in a feedback cycle, of meaningful stimulation directly contiguous to the form of the plant [1981:195–196].

After all, as Peirce once mused, "even plants make their living . . . by uttering signs" (MS 318:205, c. 1907).

Indexical behavior is found in abundance in animals, too. Here I must restrict myself to citing just a single avian example (one which I described in detail in Sebeok 1986a:136–139). The bird I speak of was presciently named *Indicator indicator* by its ornithologist taxonomer; its English name is "black-throated honeyguide." The honeyguide's singular habit of beckoning and pointing various large mammals, including men, toward nests of wild bees was first noted in Southeast Mozambique in 1569. When the bird discovers a hive, it may seek out a human partner, whom it then pilots to the hive by means of an elaborate audio-visual display.

The display proceeds in roughly the following manner. The normally inconspicuous honeyguide calls out, emitting a continuous sequence of churring notes. Then it flies, in stages, to the nearest tree, lingering motionless on an easily seen branch until the pursuit recommences. When embarking on a flight—which may last from two to twenty minutes, and extend from 20 to 750 meters—the bird soars with an initial downward dip, its white tail feathers saliently outspread. Its agitated ostensive comportment continues until the vicinity of the objective, a bees' nest, is reached. Avian escorts and their human followers are also capable of reversing their roles in this indexical *pas de deux:* people can summon a honeyguide by mimicking the sonancy of a tree being felled, thereby triggering the behavior sequence described.

Such words as "symptom," "cue," "clue," "track," "trail," and so forth, are among the high number of English quasi synonyms of "index." Peirce's telling example of Secondness—that the footprint Robinson Crusoe found in the sand, "and which has been stamped in the granite of fame, was an Index to him that some creature was on his island" (4.531, c. 1906)—implies, in such a typical case, a key attribute of indexicality, to wit: that the operation Jakobson dubbed *renvoi,* or referral, directs Robinson Crusoe back to some day, presumably prior to Friday, in the past. The index, as it were, inverts causality. In Friday's case, the vector of the index points to a bygone day in that a signans, the imprint of some foot in the sand, temporally rebounds to a signatum, the highly probable presence of some other creature on the island. Thom (1980) has analyzed some fascinating ramifications of parallels, or the lack of them, between semiotic transfers of this sort and physical causality, and the genesis of symbols—that footprint which, Peirce noted (ibid.), at the same time "as a Symbol, called up the idea of a man."

At least twice in his career, Peirce became entangled in true-life encounters with multitudes of indexical signs: once, in the company of his father, in 1867, in the Case of the Witch of Wall Street, for which the world is not yet prepared; and in 1879, in the singular adventure of the Tiffany lever watch. Alas, time does not now allow me to dwell on those fascinating experiences. But I intend to return elsewhere soon to the earlier episode; and we previously used the latter, a real detective story—a genre which, by the way, Caprettini (in Eco and Sebeok 1983:136) aptly defined as "a tale which consists of the *production of symptoms*"—as a springboard to provide a modest entry into Peirce's semiotic (Sebeok and Umiker-Sebeok, 1980).

The historian Carlo Ginzburg (1983) has exposed commonalities among art historians who study features of paintings by means of the so-called Morelli method, medical diagnosticians and psychoanalysts bent on eliciting symptoms, and detectives in pursuit of clues. Ginzburg invokes a canonical trio of physicians—Dr. Morelli, Dr. Freud, and Dr. Conan Doyle—to make out a very convincing case for their and their colleagues' parallel dependence on indexical signs. He shows that, as to their historical provenance, features, symptoms, clues, and the like, they are all based on the same ancient semiotic paradigm: the medical.

That model is, of course, implicit in the Hippocratic writings, as in the marvelous depiction of the *facies Hippocratica,* with its perhaps gruesome catalogue of indicial symptoms, in all sure signs of our mortality; and in this classic, everlasting, well-nigh exhaustive inventory of iatrical indexes, which I cannot refrain from quoting at length (from Epidemics I, after Heidel 1941:129):

> The following were the circumstances attending the diseases, from which I formed my judgments, learning from the common nature of all and the particular nature of the individual, from the disease, the patient, the regimen prescribed and the prescriber—for these make a diagnosis more favorable or less; from the constitution, both as a whole and with respect to the parts, of the weather and of each region; from the customs, mode of life, practices and age of each patient; from talk, manner, silence, thoughts, sleep or absence of sleep, the nature and time of dreams, pluckings, scratchings, tears; from the exacerbations, stools, urine, sputa, vomit, the antecedents of consequents of each member in the succession of diseases, and the absessions to a fatal issue or a crisis, sweat, rigor, chill, cough, sneezes, hiccoughs, breathing, belchings, flatulence, silent or noisy, hemorrhages, and hemorrhoids. From these things we must consider what their consequents also will be.

The same model was later made amply explicit by Galen (c. A.D. 130–201), who not only systematized semiotics in one of his treatises as one of the six principal branches of medicine, but who also showed in the same chapter how the formulation of a clinical diagnosis, with an eventual prognostic extrapolation therefrom, based on subjective symptoms and objective "signs" yoked together into coherent syndromes, mandate strict causal thinking by means of indexical signs.

Indexes included for Peirce "all natural signs and physical symptoms. . . . a pointing finger being the type of the class" (3.361, 1885). The "signs which become such by virtue of being really connected with their objects" comprehended for him "the letters attached to parts of a diagram" as much as "a symptom of disease" (8.119, c. 1902). Writing to Lady Welby, he contrasted "the occurrence of a symptom of a disease, . . . a legisign, a general type of a definite character," with its "occurrence in a particular case [which is] a sinsign" (8.335, 1904). This surely means that a symptom is a type, or an indexical legisign, apart from its individual expression, but that it becomes a token, or indexical sinsign, when displayed in an actual, particular patient. (See also Short 1982.)

Ginzburg adroitly traces the origins of this medical model based on the decipherment and interpretation of clues, clinical and otherwise, to two coupled sources: early man's hunting practices, as he retrogressed from the effects, an animal's tracks and other leavings—"prints in soft ground, snapped twigs, droppings, snagged hairs or feathers, smells, puddles, threads of saliva"—to their actual cause, a yet unseen quarry; and Mesopotamian divinatory techniques, progressing magically from an actual present cause to a prognosticated future effect—"animals' innards, drops of oil in water, stars, involuntary movements" (1983:88–89).

Ginzburg's subtle arguments, which make learned use of the overarching medieval and modern comparison between the world—metaphorically, the Book of Nature—and the book, both assumed to lie open ready to be read once one knows how to interpret indexical signs, draws comprehensively upon Old World sources. But he could as easily have cited nineteenth-century American fiction, such as James Fenimore Cooper's Leatherstocking saga or other mythic accounts of Noble Savages, to illustrate their dependence on sequences on indexical cues, available to immediate perception, which enabled the art of pathfinding through the wilderness landscape. Thus alone Uncas, the last of the Mohicans, is able to read a language, namely, the Book of Nature, "that would prove too much for the wisest" of the white men, Hawkeye; so also Uncas's crucial discovery of a footprint, in one of Cooper's novels, makes it possible for Hawkeye confidently to assert, "I can now read the whole of it." (Cf. Sebeok 1990.)

So also Robert Baden-Powell, who, in his military manual *Reconnaissance and Scouting* (1884), adapted Sherlock Holmes's technique of "deduction," that is, inferring important conclusions from seemingly insignificant clues, when teaching his young troopers how to interpret enemy locations and intentions by studying indexic topographical signs, including footprints.

For the farmer, forester, and professional gardner, it is essential, if only for reasons of economy, to be able to sort out animal tracks (for details, see Bang and Dahlstrom 1972). We know from contemporary field naturalists' accounts that Nature continually provides, printed in the ground for anyone who cares to follow it, a record of the previous night's activities. Thus Tinbergen used to spend many an hour "in 'countryside detection', reading these stories written in footprint code, revelling in the patterns of light and shade in the stillness of early morning" (Ennion and Tinbergen 1967).

The body of any vertebrate, including human, is composed of a veritable armamentarium of more or less palpable indexical markers of unique selfhood. Certain mantic practices, such as haruspication from patterns of liver flukes, and palmistry, but also some highly consequential pseudosciences—graphology today (Furnham 1988), phrenology in the past—hinge pivotally on Secondness, as when, according to Kevles's awesome account (1985:6), the chief of the London Phrenological Institution told Francis Galton, himself to become no mean biometrician, that men of his head type—his skull measured twenty-two inches around—"possessed a sanguine temperament, with considerable 'self-will, self-regard, and no small share of obstinacy,' " and that "there is much enduring power in such a mind as this—much that qualifies a man for 'roughing it' in colonising."

Some forms of entertainment, such as stage conjury and circus animal acts, rely crucially on the manipulation of indexical signs. So do certain crafts, such as handwriting authentication (à la Benjamin and Charles Peirce); and of course identification, criminal or otherwise, by fingerprinting (Moenssens 1971), mentioned no less than seven times by Sherlock Holmes, according to a phenotypic system devised by Galton in the 1890s. In 1894, Mark Twain's fictional character Pudd'nhead Wilson became the first lawyer in the world to use fingerprints in a criminal case, antedating Scotland Yard by eight years. Such indexes are called in the business "professional signs"; the distinguished sociologist Erving Goffman called them "positive marks" or "identity pegs" (1963:56). Preziosi (1989:94–95) further connects the methods of Morelli, Voltaire's Zadig, Sherlock Holmes, and Freud with Hyppolyte Taine's *petits faits*, or his system of cultural and artistic indexes, and with Peirce.

All such devices likewise richly hinge on Secondness, as was already evident in such protosemiotic works as Alphonse Bertillon's *Service de signalements* (1888) and *Instructions signalétiques* (1893). He dubbed his system of measurements of parts of the body "anthropometry." On the genotypic plane, so-called DNA fingerprinting can (arguably so) now in fact identify with a discrimination far beyond anything available in forensics heretofore, in fact with absolute certainty (if properly used), every individual (excepting an identical twin), even by a single hair root on a small piece of film displaying his or her unique sequence of indexical DNA molecules.

Natural sciences in general work empirically by decoding indexes, then interpreting them. The crystallographer Alan Mackay (1984) in particular has shown how his field shares with divination "a belief that nature can be made to speak to us in some metalanguage about itself, a feeling that nature is written in a kind of code," and how augurers decode nature's indexical messages by magic, scientists by logic. Crystallographers are strongly and consciously influenced by techniques of decryption and they have heavily borrowed from the semiotic vocabulary of the cryptographers; for example, they speak of X-ray diffraction photographs as message texts.

The study of the distinctive pheromonal function (cf. Toller and Dodd 1989), nowadays subsumed under a newly designated scientific rubric, "semiochemistry," of human chemical signatures, has in fact been compared with individual fingerprints. Patrick Süskind based his novel *Das Parfum* entirely on the indexical facets of human semiochemistry with its devastating repercussions. This field encompasses the study of odors,[1] of which Peirce wrote in an amazingly lyrical yet seldom remembered passage that these "are signs in more than one way," which "have a remarkable tendency to *presentmentate* themselves . . . namely, by contiguous association, in which odors are particularly apt to act as signs." He continued in this personal vein:

> A lady's favorite perfume seems to me somehow to agree with that of her spiritual being. If she uses none at all her nature will lack perfume. If she wears violet she herself will have the very same delicate finesse. Of the only two I have known to use rose, one was an artistic old virgin, a *grande dame;* the other a noisy young matron and very ignorant; but they were strangely alike. As for those who use heliotrope, frangipanni, etc., I know them as well as I desire to know them. Surely there must be some subtle resemblance between the odor and the impression I get of this or that woman's nature [1.313, c. 1905].

Our immune system utilizes approximately as large a number of cells dispersed throughout our body as the number of cells that composes a human brain. These endosymbiotic—or, as I would prefer, endo*semiotic*—aggregations of spirochetal remnants, functioning (as Jerne has shown [1985]) in the open-ended manner of a finely tuned generative grammar, constitute an extremely sensitive, sophisticated repertory of indexical signs, circumscribing, under normal conditions, our unique biological selfhood. Sadly, Secondness can go awry under pathological conditions, when for instance, one is afflicted, with certain types of carcinoma, an autoimmune disease, or ultimately even when administered immunosuppressors after an organ transplant.

Most of the huge literature on indexicality has been played out either in the verbal arena or else in the visual (for one discussion of the latter, see Sonesson 1989:38–65). Peirce was right as usual in arguing for the predominance of indexicality over iconicity, in respect to the mode of production, in photographs: "they belong to the second class of signs, those by physical connection" (2.281, c. 1895). This has now been documented in Philippe Dubois's outstanding study, *L'acte photographique* (1988). And it has long been obvious that metonymy—especially the indexical method of *pars pro toto*—far outweighs the uses of metaphor in films.

In the verbal domain, indexicality has chiefly preoccupied, although with rather differing emphases, philosophers of language and professional linguists. Surveying, by one who is not, the contributions of the philosophers—say, Hilary Putnam's insight that lexemes (beyond such obvious deictics as personal or demonstrative pronouns) tend to have an "unnoticed" indexical component, especially as this led to Putnam's startling convergence with Saul Kripke's doctrine concerning natural-kind words; let alone attempting to assess the writings of classic figures of the stature of Russell, Wittgenstein, Reichenbach, Bar-Hillel, or Strawson—would be an act of supererogation, as well as carrying water, or suchlike rigid designators (alias indexical legisigns), from Twin Earth up to Cambridge.

Suffice it to say that I generally found Bar-Hillel's conspectus (orginally published in 1954, later variously developed; see 1970, *passim*) personally useful. He of course knew that it was Peirce who had launched the terms "indexical sign" and "index." He went on to remind his readers that Russell used instead "ego-centric particulars" (earlier: "emphatic particulars"), though without resolving whether Russell rediscovered indexicality independently of Peirce or simply relabeled it. He further recalled that "Nelson Goodman coined 'indicator', and Hans Reichenbach 'token-reflexive word'." Gale later (1967) compared and contrasted Peirce's, Russell's, and Reichenbach's approaches. Bar-Hillel himself, in his elegant critical investigation (mainly on the sentence level) stuck—if not to all of his claims—with Peirce's terminology, "since it provides an adjective easily combined with 'sign', 'word', 'expression', 'sentence', 'language', 'communication' alike" (ibid.:79).

The overall interest of philosophers in indexical expressions is bound up, as I understand it, with their search for an ideal language, consisting of a set of context-free sentences as an instrument to employ for probing the universe *sub specie aeternitatis*.

In Ayer's phrasing (1968:167), the argument has been about "whether language can be totally freed from dependence upon context." Ayer was unable to decide this for himself, and I believe that the matter is still wide open. However, whether or not this indecision has any serious consequences for indexicality in general or for Peirce's view of this matter in particular seems to me quite doubtful. For, as Ayer thought as well (ibid.), "although a reference to context within the language may not be necessary for the purposes of communication, there will still be occasions, in practice, when we shall need to rely upon the clues which are provided by the actual circumstances in which the communications are produced."

Peirce once insisted that an index is quite essential to speech (4.58, 1893). So what do linguists mean by an index? For many of us, this term simply and broadly refers to membership-identifying characteristics of a group, such as regional, social, or occupational markers; for others, more narrowly, to such physiological, psychological, or social features of speech or writing that reveal personal characteristics as the voice quality or handwriting in a producing source. Indexicals of these sorts, sometimes also called expressive features, have been analyzed for many languages and in a wide range of theoretical contributions.

In addition, there is a vast, separate literature, not as a rule subsumed by linguists under indexicality, devoted to different types of deixis. By this, linguists refer to a whole range of commonly grammaticalized roles in everyday language behavior, that is, to the way in which interlocutors anchor what they talk about to the spatiotemporal context of their utterance. Person deixis, social deixis, place deixis, time deixis, discourse deixis are the major types distinguished in the literature (Levelt 1989:44–58). Karl Bühler (1934:149) called the relevant context of the utterance *Zeigfeld*, or indexical field, and the anchoring point of this *hic and nunc* field its *Origo*, or origin (ibid.:107; on Bühler's role in the study of deictics, cf. Jarvella and Klein 1982).

Deictics can vary considerably from language to language, and can often be—as, for example, in Wolof (Wills 1990)—very knotty in structure. One examination of the typological and universal characteristics of personal pronouns in general, over a sample of 71 natural languages, claimed the existence of systems ranging from 4 to 15 persons (Ingram 1978). In this array, the English 5-person system is highly atypical, which, if true, would lead to fundamental questions about Peirce's and other philosophers' seemingly natural "I-It-Thou" tripartition.

Only a native speaker of Hungarian can appreciate, if not always articulate, the richly differentiated set of terms of address which speakers must control to produce utterances appropriate to various roles and other contextual variables. For instance, to simplify, but not much, two academics of the same sex and approximate rank and age are unable to converse at ease in Hungarian without knowing each other's exact date of birth, because seniority, even if by one day, strictly determines the terms of address to be used in that dialogue. (John Lyons reviewed matters of this sort in his useful 1977 compendium on semantics.)

Otto Jespersen casually coined the term "shifter" in 1922 to refer to grammatical units which cannot be defined without a reference to the message. In 1957, Jakobson reassigned shifters to the Peircean syncretic category of indexical symbols, which are, in fact, complex syncategorematic terms, where code and message intersect (1971:132).

In a remarkable study of a single four-word sentence consisting of a modal auxiliary, a person-deictic pronoun, and a verb and its complement, Fillmore (1973) hints at the incredible intricacy demanded of a linguistic theory if it is adequately to capture the conceptual richness of even the simplest sentences. Such a theory must incorporate principles for deriving at least the complete syntactic, semantic, and pragmatic description of a sentence, a theory of speech acts, a theory of discourse, and a theory of natural logic. Although all of these are foci of a considerable amount of research today, I know of no overarching theory which meets all of those demanding conditions.

Barwise and Perry (1983:32–39) coined the expression "efficiency of language" for locutions—even though these retain the same linguistic meaning—which different speakers use in different space-time locations, with different anchoring in their surroundings, capable of different interpretations. To put it another way, the productivity of language depends decisively on indexicality, which is therefore "extremely important to the information-carrying capacity of language" (ibid.:34). These authors convincingly argued that philosophical engrossment with context freedom, that is, with mathematics and the eternal nature of its sentences, "was a critical blunder, for efficiency lies at the very heart of meaning" (ibid.:32). However this may be, linguists at present have no inkling of, let alone a comprehensive theory to account in general for, how this commonplace, global human enterprise is carried out.

In my pessimistic conclusion, I return briefly to Jakob von Uexküll's *Umweltlehre* (Thure von Uexküll 1989). Reality, according to Uexküll, reveals itself in *Umwelten,* those parts of the environment—*die Natur*—that each organism selects with its species-specific sense organs, each according to its biological needs. Everything in this phenomenal world, or self-world, is labeled with the subject's perceptual cues and effector cues, which operate via feedback loop that Uexküll called the functional cycle. Nature (the world, the universe, the cosmos, true reality, and so forth) discloses itself through sign processes, or semioses. These, according to him, are of three distinct types: (1) semioses of information, emanating from the inanimate environment; (2) semioses of symptomatization, where the source is alive (this is equivalent to George Herbert Mead's "unintelligent gestures"); and (3) semioses of communication (Mead's "intelligent gestures").

The first and second form indispensable, complementary steps in each biosemiosis. The observer reconstructs the exterior sign processes of the observed from the perceived stream of indexes, but never their interior structures, which necessarily remain private. The transmutation of such sign processes into verbal signs are meta-interpretations which constitute objective connecting structures that remain outside the subjective self-world of the observed living entity; these are "involved in its sign processes only as an inducing agency for its perceptual sign and as a connecting link to its operational sign" (ibid.:151).

How reference—the index-driven circuit between the semiosphere (Lotman 1984) and the biosphere (Vernadsky 1926)—is managed by sign users and sign interpreters remains, despite the best efforts of Peirce and his many followers, a profound enigma. What then of anchoring? "The forms of things unknown, the poet's pen / Turns them to shapes, and gives to airy nothing / A local habitation and a name" *(A Midsummer Night's Dream).*

Theories of mapping and modeling have not progressed beyond disciplined speculation. Notwithstanding that I remain intuitively attracted to John Archibald Wheeler's closed loop of the world viewed as a self-synthesizing system of existences (for example, 1988), his teacher, Niels Bohr, considered, rightly in my opinion, such questions as how concepts are related to reality as ultimately sterile. Bohr once replied to this very question: "We are suspended in language in such a way that we cannot say what is up and what is down. The word 'reality' is also a word, a word which we must learn to use correctly" (French and Kennedy 1985:302).

Note

1. Cf. this surprising passage in a letter by Mallarmé (1989) to his friend Henri Cazalis: " 'Gracious me! Madame Ramaniet ate asparagus yesterday.' "How can you tell?' 'From the pot she's put outside her window.' . . . that ability to see clues in the most meaningless things—and such things, great gods!"

FOURTEEN

Messages in the Marketplace

1. PREAMBLE

One week prior to this meeting, I had firmly in mind the points I wanted to convey to this unprecedented assembly: I would speak, of course, from that side of the porous fence labeled "semiotics," the perennial focus of which is the casual or guided circulation of messages—that is, of signs or strings of signs—among participants in any marketplace.

What I had intended to say was, however, to a degree sidetracked by dint of an accident that I suffered two days prior to coming to address this meeting. The particulars are personal and thus irrelevant. What is pertinent is that I showed up here walking with a cane, and that this gave me an opportunity to open with a reminder of a yarn—no doubt apocryphal but eminently plausible in the context—about a habit of Sigmund Freud's, obsessive and ultimately fatal, of continual cigar smoking. When he entered the classroom one day to deliver one of his introductory lectures on psychoanalysis, flourishing a big cigar, the assembled medical students burst out laughing. Freud, not in the least perturbed, is reported to have said, "sometimes a cigar is nothing but a cigar." If Freud had really said that, he was thoroughly mistaken, for a cigar, as any other object in the universe, is, for the interpreter, always and unavoidably a semiotic entity. My walking "stick" is, for you, first and foremost, a walking *shtick,* which is a show business expression for a particular method of doing something, as is, for instance, Henry Youngman's fiddle or Michael Jackson's glove.

The distinction is between what semioticians call an *object* (the cigar or the stick) and a *sign* (the phallic symbol or the "shtick"), although, on deeper analysis, the former turns out, as well, to be a kind of sign, in a universe which, in one of Peirce's most memorable expressions, "is perfused with signs." (I recently discussed this fundamental identity in Sebeok 1986a; see also Sebeok 1977.)

This chapter was written for delivery at the First International Conference on Marketing and Semiotics, J. L. Kellogg Graduate School of Management, Northwestern University, July 10–12, 1986. It was first published in a book based on that meeting, *Marketing and Semiotics: New Directions in the Study of Signs for Sale* (Berlin: Mouton de Gruyter, 1987), 21–30, edited by Jean Umiker-Sebeok, who was also the principal organizer of the meeting. An Italian version was dedicated to the memory of Ferruccio Rossi-Landi and published in 1988.

The walking stick moreover serves, in this frame of reference, a specific semiotic function, called by such rhetoricians as Cicero *captatio benevolentiae*—the man in the Hathaway shirt, Baron Wrangel, used his spurious eyepatch in this way, to enlist sympathetic attention. The great early rhetorical treatises, such as Quintilian's elaborate *Institutes of Oratory*, can be profitably reread as "how to" manuals for such ancient but no less valid marketing techniques.

Such manuals embodied, as well, old-fashioned, indeed classical, political theory, armed with semiotic tactics. According to this theory, a marketplace was a forum where anyone who had anything on his mind could express and perhaps dispose of it. The objective was to give free play to ideas as marketable commodities and to disseminate them as effectively as the tutored application of adroit semiotic craftsmanship would allow.

2. IDOLS OF THE MARKETPLACE

The notion of a "marketplace" as that arena of a society in which signs are bought and sold, in a word, bartered, was already explicit in Francis Bacon's theory of the Great Instauration. Bacon, early in the seventeenth century, discerned several profound kinds of fallacies in the mind of man that he thought needed to be rectified for the advancement of learning. He named these Idols (for example, 1973:XIV, §§9–11).

His third category of such bad habits of mind he called "Idols of the market-place" (or of the forum). Here he was alluding to errors that arise during the process of interaction among human beings, that is, in the course of their undergoing what Peirce was later to broaden and more exactly identify as "semiosis" (himself elaborating on Greek usage, of at least as early as Cicero's time; cf. Peirce 1933–1966:5.484). Friedrich Nietzsche's nice phrase, the "prison-house of language," needs, however, to be generalized, in the light of Bacon's critique, to some such expression as "the tyranny of *semeiosy*" (after Peirce 1935–66:5.473), a term by which the American philosopher meant any action of any sign, whether verbal or nonverbal. Bacon was alluding to the inherent ambiguity of signs: unwittingly, humans use the same signs differently yet do not realize what they are doing. When they are in seeming agreement, they are not agreed; and, contrariwise, they seemingly disagree when they really do not. Worst of all, signs that refer to fictions they tend to treat as if these stood for "real" entities. For Bacon, then, the improvement, or the freeing, of the human mind hinged upon a revision of the human attitude to the world. It is therefore a vital part of the reform of knowledge, particularly insofar as this bears on ethics, and that, especially, in its relation with rhetoric.

Bacon's comments about the Idols of the marketplace are worth careful attention in the context of this international gathering. For Bacon did not commit the vulgar error of identifying language with communication; on the contrary, he viewed "language" (namely, semiosis) as rendered effable either by verbal or by nonverbal means—Bacon named signs of the latter variety "notes"—and as an instrument for *transmission:* "We are handling here the currency (so to speak) of things intellectual," he insisted, "and it is not amiss to know that as moneys may be made of other material besides gold and silver, so other Notes of Things may be coined besides words and letters." (Cf. Rossi 1968:167.)

Language is clearly a semiotic system, but only one, which is composed of signs in the generic sense: "This then may be laid down as a rule; that whatever can be divided into differences sufficiently numerous to explain the variety of notions (provided those differences be perceptible to the sense) may be made a vehicle to convey the thought of one man to another" (after ibid.:167).

Bacon was thus perhaps the first to recognize explicitly that, as Philip Kotler came to write in his perceptive foreword to Fine's 1981 now classic *The Marketing of Ideas and Social Issues,* "there is a marketplace of ideas just as there is a marketplace of goods," and that the purveyors of ideas "use modern channels of communication and distribution to reach their audiences" (in Fine 1981:v). Ideas, in brief, are marketable as is any other commodity. All commodities are fascicles of marketable messages, which are composed of strings of signs. (It is no accident that Fine concludes his book [ibid.:193–194] with a two-page excerpt from John Dewey, the pragmatist philosopher who most heavily elaborated Peirce's maxim and applied it to the language of value!)

3. GAMES OF COMMUNICATION

The Idols of the marketplace, which are imposed by signs, are not, as Bacon had reminded us, to be trusted, for either they are "names of things which exist but yet confused and ill-defined, and hastily and irregularly derived from realities," or—more injurious because more intricate and deeply rooted—they are "names of things which do not exist" (after Rossi 1968:171).

It was actually Claude Lévi-Strauss (for example, 1963:296) who clearly and persuasively pointed to the reciprocal give-and-take between the communication of goods and services (economics, broadly speaking), on the one hand, and that of "pure" semiotic entities (the usual subject of general semiotics, including linguistics), on the other, both firmly situated within an integrated science of communication. He pictured culture as consisting of "*rules* stating how the 'games of communication' should be played both on the natural and on the cultural levels." He added that the juxtaposition of these two modalities of exchange, namely, of economics and semiotics, "cannot hide the fact that they refer to forms of communication which are on a different scale." Marketing and semiotics (conjointly with some other disciplines) are therefore revealed as approaches to the same kinds of problems according to different strategic operations. Subtly hierarchical and other proportional relationships, which are yet to be fully explored, prevail among them. Thus, in the marketing of goods, services, and ideas, auxiliary verbal and nonverbal messages are normally implied—in marketing, semiotics plays necessarily a relevant, if only auxiliary, role. Such, however, is not the case vice versa. The domain of semiotics is, accordingly, more general than the province of marketing, the symbolic aspects of which can fruitfully be thought through as *applied* semiotics; the groundwork for any such analyses has already been laid in the excellent but insufficiently known publications of Rossi-Landi (for example, 1974), which must serve as the starting point for continued collaboration between the two fields of endeavor.

While, in Bacon's view, signs correspond to notions (that is, "objects"), and, thus, where a notion is impaired, so, necessarily, is the sign derived from that notion, such signs, whether faulty or not, do influence the mind and are at the root of self-deception: they "cast their rays or stamp their impressions on the mind itself, and they do not only make discourse tedious, but they impair judgment and understanding"; and, further, "that which is the remedy for this evil (namely definitions) is in most cases unable to cure it," for definitions themselves consist of strings of signs, and signs beget signs (after Rossi 1968:171; cf. Peirce 1935–1966:2.302, *Omne symbolum de symbolo*).

4. THE CONCEPT INDUSTRY

In this early, or "cottage," manifestation of what Fine calls the "concept industry" (1981:188), semiosis began at the source, which was, in the event, an individual person. The pluriform destination, the public in the forum, could find out about the "state of affairs" from this solitary source, looking out upon and then inwardly contemplating the world, reflecting on what he or she perceived to be the case.

Mulling over the "state of affairs," one could, if one so chose, bring the fruits of one's cogitations to the marketplace, there to display the end product in competition with the harvest of others' labors. The public could thus pick and choose, with little constraint, what it liked, and reject what it did not.

This underlying dialectic principle of marketing is shifting from a quintessentially cottage industry to a high-tech, refluent concept industry. A crucial change now permeates it, infecting activities that go under headings "such as education, gossip, rumor, public relations, public opinion, propaganda, lobbying, [and] advocacy" (Fine 1981:188), in brief, the entire gamut of social and political marketing.

A good example of impending change centers on the troubles that beset the *CBS Evening News Program,* and the reverberations of its ratings successes or failures. As set forth by Boyer (1986), when a recent crisis arose as the program's popularity began to drift and fall behind NBC's, a high-level staff meeting was called, which included the vice president of advertising for CBS News and TV stations, a man with whom the evening news group had refused ever to meet before.

This man's expertise, according to Boyer's report, is similar to that of "news consultants," whom Boyer portrays as "program doctors so prevalent in local television news who, to understate the case, have always been anathema to network journalists." What such program doctors do, apparently, is to study the composition and profile of the actual target audience, and then make recommendations to the news anchor and his or her staff how to modify, or "reform," in the light of such information, the presentation of the news in such a way as to increase their ratings. Still viscerally sticking by the old-fashioned principle, anchorman Dan Rather is quoted as having recalled telling himself on the flight home from this meeting, "Dan, you'd better do what you feel good about doing. If we go another millimeter down the road of trying to figure out what it is the audience wants and then try to deliver it to them, we're lost souls on the ghost ship forever. At my age and stage, I ain't gonna do it." Indeed, this is an exceptional counterexample: for staff changes were then made, "leading the way," in Boyer's words, "to old values." (Not by accident, the people at CBS who "turned backward" have been named the "Red Guard"!)

5. POLITICAL APPLICATIONS

According to the modern principle which clearly pervades the American political process today, if not yet all corporate management, the individual looks outward to the intended destination—to public opinion—rather than, specularly and speculatively, inward. What would the public like to hear? Whatever it wants to hear is what the observer then attempts to replicate. Then, having replicated what his measurements indicated that the public wants to hear, he or she wraps up that product to be peddled in the marketplace, which, however, is already teeming with competitors eager to do the same.

But how does the public decide what *it* wants to buy? In this cultural forum, there is no product available other than its own specular image, albeit perhaps in several, more or less distorted, versions. Public opinion polls investigate—what else?—public opinion. The news media then inform us what the polls have revealed. And what did they reveal? What the public already thinks, of course. And it is a further fact of political life that, once such a candidate gets elected in the light of this new verity, he or she has to continue to function in conformity with his or her own set of messages. There is, in other words, little or no room left for invigorating novelty.

6. MESSAGE SOURCE OR DESTINATION?

All this is a story not only familiar to us all, but, as I have described and illustrated nearly a decade ago (Sebeok 1978), it strikes at the roots of a particular kind of destructive self-deception, well known to semioticians who deal with commonplace, everyday aspects of nature and culture. It is becoming an omnipresent and, I think, dangerous Idol of the marketplace. Thus the assignment of predominance, in dyadic encounters, to the destination over the source is, as I have tried to show in that earlier essay, a baleful begetter of errors.

Let me conclude with just one example, which, however, can be taken as paradigmatic. It is especially interesting in this context because, although it is based on time-honored observations (and is, moreover, deeply anchored in mammalian physiology), its earliest formulations chance to have come, not from science, but from the marketplace. The formal domain of this case in point is derived from what is known as Pupillometry, or "the psychology of the pupillary response" (cf., for example, Janisse 1977). The most fascinating early "pupillometric report," testifying that the pupils often unwittingly convey critical information to the "interactant," is by Richard Gump (1962), a scion of, and jade buyer in, pre-Revolutionary China in this century for, Gump's of San Francisco.

Mr. Gump tells how he learned, from an experienced fellow businessman named Allen Newell, the subtler aspects of the pursuit of jade objects when dealing with Oriental merchants: "It was harder," he noted (Gump 1962:229), "to learn to disguise his natural joy upon examining a beautiful object. The Chinese were aware that the pupils of the eyes dilated when one's interest was aroused and acted accordingly. Newell had earlier solved this problem by wearing dark glasses." Middle Eastern rug merchants were likewise aware of the pupil responses of their would-be customers. So-called psychic readers routinely derive critical information from their clients' nonverbal behavior, specifically including such alterations as "pupillary enlargement" (Hyman 1981:178). So do also professional card players (concealing, however, their own pupil responses, and preserving their "poker face," by wearing eyeshades). Many close-up magicians are also privy to such stock techniques. Scientific research has amply borne out that pupil-size changes—dilations and constrictions—are short-range mood signals, affected by emotional fluctuations in the sender, and that they are, in general, emitted out of control of the source, as well as received unbeknown to the destination.

There is a host of revealing laboratory experiments with the pupil response, involving, for instance, sexual or racial attitudes, or in the area of food preferences, which have been shown to tell quite a different story from what the subjects verbally asseverated.

Middle-class Hungarian ladies of my mother's generation—as also did Spanish women of the Middle Ages, for example—injected an atropine drug, aptly named *belladonna* ("fair lady," actually a tincture derived from the "deadly nightshade"), into their eyes, solely for the cosmetic purpose of dilating their eyes, wanting thereby to seem more attractive. They knew very well that one of the reasons lovers spend so much time gazing closely into each other's eyes is to monitor unwittingly one another's pupil dilations: "The more her pupils expand with emotional excitement, the more it makes his expand, and vice versa" (Desmond Morris 1977:172). This was, of course, conscious steering on the part of the message source, though presumably beyond the cognizance of the destination.

One of Thomas Mann's more memorable fictional characters went even further, calculatingly training himself as a youth for his hoped-for career in adult life as a confidence man:

> I would stand in front of my mirror, concentrating all my powers in a command to my pupils to contract or expand, banishing every other thought from my mind. My persistent efforts . . . were, in fact, crowned with success. At first as I stood bathed in sweat, my colour coming and going, my pupils would flicker erratically; but later I succeeded in contracting them to the nearest points and then expanding them to great, round, mirror-like pools. [*Confessions of Felix Krull Confidence Man*].

Inverse cases, where the message source is innocent but the destination is obliged to keep careful track of the sources' pupil responses, come from zoosemiotics. They are repeatedly confirmed by articulate circus trainers who work with large felines—whence the expression "cool cat," in reference to a hip dude wearing shades—in the ring.

Again I join with Fine (1981:39) in his critique of marketers of ideas, new style, for being in violation of the pristine marketing concept by distributing views which are "not necessarily those most beneficial to society," in other words, reselling public opinion ascertained by their ever more powerful instruments of measurement. Leo Tolstoy, in a famous passage in *Anna Karenina*, pictured vividly the degenerate "state of unthinking conformism" Fine (ibid.:38) writes of:

> Stepan Arkadyevitch took in and read a liberal paper, not an extreme one, but one advocating the views held by the majority. And in spite of the fact that science, art, and politics had no special interest for him, he firmly held those views on all these subjects which were held by the majority and by his paper, and he only changed them when the majority changed them—or, more strictly speaking, he did not change them, but they imperceptibly changed of themselves within him. Stepan Arkadyevitch had not chosen his political opinions or his views, these political opinions and views had come to him of themselves. . . . he liked his newspaper, as he did his cigar after dinner, for the slight fog it diffused in his brain.

FIFTEEN

The Sign Science and the Life Science

In the celebrated passage in which Saussure referred to *une science qui étudie la vie des signes au sein de la vie sociale,* the term *science* is, as a rule, loosely, arguably, and, in my view, misleadingly rendered by the English quasi-cognate "science" (for example, by Harris, in Saussure 1983:15). Saussure went on to say that this *science*—that is, semiotics (alias semiology)—"does not yet exist," nor can one "say for certain that it will exist." If so, the status of semiotics as a science (in the strict sense, rather than meaning simply *savoir*) would be comparable with that of, say, exobiology, a sanguine term coined by Joshua Ledeberg at a meeting in Nice in 1957 for the study of extraterrestrial life (Ponnamperuma 1972:viii); but this "science" of exobiology remains, to this day, void of a palpable subject matter.

Such is not, however, the case if semiotics is defined—as all of us echo here, after the variegated usage of the Schoolmen, the Latin expression *doctrina signorum*—according to Locke in 1690, Berkeley in 1732, Peirce in c. 1897, and others, as a "doctrine" (cf., generally, "On the Notion 'Doctrine of Signs,' " Deely 1982:127–130). When viewed as a "teaching maneuver combined with a learning stratagem" (Sebeok 1986d), semiotics is found to be at least as richly infused with content as what is today practiced under the label "cognitive sciences," the domain of which is in fact essentially conterminous in gist and problematic, if not necessarily in methodology, with that of semiotics.

In this essay, I juxtapose, as a framing and heuristic device, "sign science" with "life science." The latter is a general phrase "comprehending all the Sciences . . . that have to do with the structures, performances and interactions of living things." These are enumerable as the conventional biological sciences but additionally subsume several "interfacial" sciences, such as biochemistry, biophysics, and bioengineering, the last of which, Medawar and Medawar (1977:7), claim, "also establishes a common frontier between biology and communications theory."

Ten years ago, I noted a libration in the annals of semiotic inquiry

This piece was written for *Modern Semiotics/Nyere semiotik,* ed. Jørgen Dines Johansen and Svend Erik Larsen, where it is scheduled to appear in 1991 under the Danish title "Videnskaben om tegn og videnskaben om liv."

between two seemingly antithetical tendencies: a major tradition, in which semiosis is taken to be a steadfast, indeed bedrock, hallmark of life; and a minor, predominantly glottocentric trend, in which semiosis is tied to human existence alone. As a matter of personal conviction, I then declared myself in the former camp, stating that "the scope of semiotics encompasses the whole of the *oikoumene*, the entirety of our planetary biosphere," adding that semiosis "must be recognized as a pervasive fact of nature as well as of culture" (Sebeok 1977:180–183). In what follows, I propose to explore this claim further.

I begin with two interlinked queries: what is semiosis (or, as Peirce sometimes put it [5.473], *semeiosy*); and what is life?

Peirce adapted the designation "semiosis" (in a variant transcription) from Philodemus's fragmentary Herculanean papyrus *On Signs*, where the Greek equivalent occurs at least thirty times (1978:141), to represent a type of reasoning or inference from signs. He endowed the term with a definition of his own as an action, or influence, "which is, or involves, a cooperation of *three* subjects, such as sign, its object, and its interpretant, this tri-relative influence not being in any way resolvable into actions between pairs" (1935–1966:5.484). The "action of a sign" is the semiosic function that sets an inferential process in motion.

Morris gave a somewhat different definition of semiosis, as a sign process, "that is, a process in which something is a sign to some organism (1971:366). His precept gives ample scope for pinpointing the locus where the process takes place, to wit, in anything alive. It follows that the notion of semiosis is yoked to the notion of animate existence and, as a corollary, that there could have been no semiosis before the appearance of life in the universe (or, for all practical purposes, the emergence of terrestrial life).

This leads to the second query, cogently formulated and addressed in Schrödinger's pathbreaking book (1946), *What Is Life?* Elsewhere (see above, Ch. 10) I had occasion to raise this same question, taking Schrödinger's discussion as my lodestar, but also taking duly into account Pirie's strictures (1937), according to which—especially considering borderline phenomena between the inanimate and the animate—such an inquiry may not even serve a useful purpose. The crux of Schrödinger's classic formulation has to do with the Second Law of Thermodynamics, particularly with the principle of negative entropy, which is often, if hitherto far from satisfactorily, coupled with a notion of information (more accurately, the lack of it) about the statistical structure of a semiotic system (cf., for example, Brillouin 1950). In any event, Schrödinger's discussion points to the salience of semiotics in the understanding of life processes; or, as Wiener put it (1950:21)—keeping the common opinion in mind that the subject matter of semiotics is the exchange of messages (that is, time series)—the amount of information is a measure "of the degree of order which is peculiarly associated with those patterns which are distributed as messages in time."

There are several additional noteworthy properties of life. One of these is its hierarchical organization, "a universal characteristic which life shares with the rest of the cosmos and which defines, in the overall architecture of the universe, its position on the genealogical tree." The hierarchy of nature appears as an ontological interpretation of data from the "real world," a pattern of relations which obviously extends up through semiotic systems, including particularly the verbal (cf. Jakobson 1963). This problem usually appears in the guise of messages-in-the-superimposed context, where the terminal noun is to be read as the equivalent of Leibniz's metaphysical concept of a monad, involving an indefinite series of perceptive acts coordinated by a unique point of view; or of Jakob von Uexküll's (1982:3) semiotically more patently pertinent biological concept of *Umwelt.*

Another conspicuous property emerges from the interplay between the fundamental invariance in life's subjacent biochemistry and the prodigal variability of singular realizations thereof, paralleling the conjugate ideas of global semiotic universals and local, or so-called cultural, variables.

"Meaning," the cosmologist Wheeler argues (1986a:vii)—or, better, "significance" (Saussure's *significativité,* or *pouvoir de signifier,* as in Godel 1957:276; cf. Peirce 1935–1966:8.314)—"is important, is even central"; and "meaning itself powers creation" (Wheeler 1986b:372; Wheeler 1984 develops this productive idea further). In semiotics, then, *a fortiori,* significance is at once the cardinal and the most haunting of concepts, yet the significance circuit must, in turn, be based on construction by the observer-participancy of some carbon-based life.

The first traces of life detected so far date from the so-called Archaean Aeon, which began 3,900 million years ago; the progress of the animation of inert matter is expertly portrayed by Margulis and Sagan (1986:47–57). In the course of evolution, according to the convincing, if speculative, metaphor of Dawkins (1976, Ch. 2), DNA replicators—a replicator being anything in the universe of which copies are made, thus any portion of chromosome, as well as a sign-and-its-interpretant, or, for that matter, a printed page and a facsimile thereof—cocoon themselves in "survival machines." These comprehend all prokaryotes, that is, cells, such as bacteria, in which the genes are not packaged into a membrane-bound nucleus; and all four eukaryotic superkingdoms, unicellular and multicellular organisms, such as plants, animals and fungi, in which they are. Such molecular replicators behave as nonverbal signs, which constrain and command the behavior of all living organisms, including ourselves (Sebeok 1979b:xiii), who are members of one genus, *Homo,* only a sole species of which, *sapiens sapiens* survives, endowed with the unique propensity to call additionally into action, when needed, an interwoven repertoire of verbal signs.

Bodies, Dawkins's survival machines, were in due course equipped by evolution with on-board computers called brains, the function of which is to facilitate message exchanges with comparable equipment in other bodies. (Dawkins also coined the word "meme" [1976:296] to designate nongenetic replicators, capable of flourishing only in environments provided by communicating brains.) Although this hypothesis is not yet proven, the brain does appear to be a highly complex amalgam of microscopic spirochetes, densely packed together in a symbiotic existence, a colony which itself feeds and thrives on a ceaseless traffic of sign input and sign output.

The universal RNA/DNA-based genetic code is commonly referred to as a "language," as, for instance, by Beadle and Beadle (1967:216): "the deciphering of the DNA code has revealed our possession of a language much older than hieroglyphics, a language as old as life itself, a language that is the most living language of all—even if its letters are invisible and its words are buried deep in the cells of our bodies." But this figurative equation is unfortunate, for it would be more accurate to call both the molecular code and the verbal code *semiotic systems* or, in Jakobson's parlance [1974:50], "two informational systems"), explicitly recognizing that they radically differ from one another on, to use Hjelmslev's terminology, the expression plane: the former is an object of study in chemistry, the latter in phonology.

The genetic code is but one of several endosemiotic systems. Bodies are made up of semiotically intertwined subsystems, such as cellular organelles, cells, tissue, organs, organ assemblages. Endosemiotic sign processes, Thure von Uexküll (1986:204) amplifies,

> use chemical, thermal, mechanical and electrical processes as sign carriers. They make up an incredible number. If one reflects upon the fact that the human body consists of 25 trillion cells, which is more than 2000 times the number of people living on earth, and that these cells have direct or indirect contact with each other through sign processes, one gets an impression of the amount. Only a fraction are known to us. Yet this fraction is hardly comprehensible. . . . The *messages* that are transmitted include information about the meaning of processes in one system of the body . . . for other systems as well as for the integrative regulation systems (especially the brain) and the control systems (such as the immune system).

Semiosis is the fulcrum around which another emerging interfacial discipline—recently dubbed "semioimmunology" or "immunosemiotics"—turns. The central problem immunologists keep struggling with is how the healthy immune system manages to recognize and respond to an almost infinite number of alien organisms and yet fails to assail components of self. What has become reasonably clear is that a single line of defense against potential pathogens is not enough and that there are dissimilitudes between antigen recognition by T cells and that by B cells. Jerne has proposed (1985:1058) a model of particular interest to semioticians, including especially linguists, with his claim that the immense repertoire of the vertebrate immune system functions as an open-ended generative grammar, "a vocabulary comprised not of words but of sentences that is capable of responding to any sentence expressed by the multitude of antigens which the immune system may encounter." The human immune system consists of about 10^{12} cells, dissipated over the entire body, excepting only the brain, but the former and the nervous system are known to exercise pervasive mutual sway one over the other by means of two-way electrochemical messages.

The metabolic code constitutes still another fascinating set of endosemiotic properties, because, as Tomkins (1975) showed in his brilliant article completed just prior to his death, complex regulation is characterized by two entities not operating in simple mechanisms: these are metabolic symbols and their domains, where the former "refers to a specific intracellular effector molecule which accumulates when a cell is exposed to a particular environment" (ibid.:761). For example, cyclic adenosine monophosphate (cAMP) acts, in most micro-organisms, as a symbol for carbon-source starvation, or ppGpp acts as a symbol for nitrogen or amino acid deficiency. Without going into details, the conspicuous point to note here is that, while a simple regulatory mode, that is, a direct chemical relationship between regulatory molecules and their effects, is a clear instance of Peirce's "secondness, or dependence," the complex mode is an instance of "thirdness, or mediation" (3.422). This insight was foreshadowed by Peirce himself in his observation that a "rhema is somewhat closely analogous to a chemical atom" (3.421). Tomkins's reasoning (1975:761) is highly semioticized: "Metabolic symbols need bear no structural relationship to the molecules which promote their accumulation," and, since a particular environmental (or contextual) condition is correlated with a corresponding intracellular symbol, the imputed "relationship between the extra- and intracellular events may be considered as a 'metabolic code' in which a specific symbol represents a unique state of environment."

The endocrine and the nervous systems, as noted above, are intimately fastened together via signs. As for the neural code itself, semiosis is what neurobiology is all about. "The modes of communication include membrane conductances, patterns of neural spikes and graded potentials, electric coupling between cells, electrical and chemical transmission at synapses, secretion, and modification of neural function" (Prosser 1985:118). The basic principle for understanding most sign use by neurons comes down to the selective permeability of their plasma membrane to ions (charged atoms), which seem to penetrate through specific pores, or channels, in the membrane. Another newly labeled interfacial field of research is "neurocommunications," which aims to portray in a current jargon the (human) mind, or "software level," and brain, or "hardware level," as a pair of semiotic coupled engines, namely, computational devices for verbal-nonverbal sign processing.

Beyond endosemiotics, the literature of biosemiotics distinguishes among phyto-, cyto-, and zoosemiotics, the latter comprising a specially marked branch, anthroposemiotics, to reflect its predominantly glottocentric emphasis, amounting at times to an obsession. These distinctions correspond exactly to the standard classification of eukaryotic multicellular organisms into the plant, fungus, and animal superkingdoms, the last including the *animal loquens*. The minor tradition I cited above concentrates on anthroposemiotics to the exclusion of all the other divisions; it excludes, that is, almost all of the rest of nature.

The plant-animal-fungus trichotomy (see also other chapters this book) is based on the manifold but complementary nutritional pattern of each group, which is to say on the manner in which information, or negentropy, is maintained by extracting order from the environment. It is therefore at bottom a semiosic taxonomy. Plants, deriving their food from inorganic sources by means of photosynthesis, are *producers*. Animals, ingesting their food—performed organic compounds—from other organisms, are *transformers*. Fungi, breaking their food down externally and then absorbing the resulting small molecules from solution, are *decomposers*. On this macroscopic scale, plants and fungi are two polar-opposite life forms: the composers, or organisms that build up, and the decomposers, or the organisms that break down. Animals are the mediators between the other two. By reason of their go-between status, animals have become incomparable virtuosi at semiosis, and that on several levels: in the interactions among their multitudinous cells; among members of their own species; and with members of all other life forms extant within their *Umwelten*. It is even possible to postulate provisionally a fruitful analogy between the systematists' P-A-F model and the classic semioticians' O-S-I model: according to this, in general, a fungus/interpretant is mediately determined by an animal/sign, which is determined by a plant/object (but plant/fungus are likewise variant life forms, of course, just as object/interpretant are both sign variants; cf. Peirce to Welby, in Hardwick 1977:31, 81).

As one would expect, the literature of zoosemiotics (a surprisingly productive term coined in 1963), dealing with both semiosis in the speechless animals and nonverbal semiosis in *Homo*, is immense. (Two encyclopedic overviews are to be found in Sebeok 1968 and Sebeok 1979b.) Many investigators consider separately aspects of intraspecific animal communication (see, for example, Lewis and Gower 1980; and Bright 1984) and aspects of interspecific communication, which are further partitioned into communication with members of other animal species and, as a specially elaborate case thereof, two-way communication between animals and men; the latter further impinges on a host of problems of animal taming, training, and domestication. One particular subtopic which, abetted by much media brouhaha, continues to excite the public, but also on which work has now reached a perhaps unsurmountable impasse, has focused on a search for language propensity in three African and one Asian species of apes, and/or also in certain pelagic mammals (for critical reviews, see Sebeok and Umiker-Sebeok 1980; Umiker-Sebeok and Sebeok 1981a; and Sebeok 1986b.)

Semiosis in the vegetative world has been accorded much less discussion, but the principles underlying phytosemiotics are thoughtfully assessed by Krampen (1981; cf. also the remarks of Thure von Uexküll 1986:211–212). Krampen (ibid.:203) argues that their code differs from those of zoosemiotics "in that the absence of effectors and receptors does not allow for the constitution of [Jakob von Uexküll's] functional cycles, of object signs and sign objects, or of an Umwelt," yet that the world of plants "is nevertheless structured according to a base semiotics which cuts across all living beings, plants, animals, and humans alike." For instance, plants, though brainless and solipsistic systems they may be, are capable of distinguishing self/nonself. Plant semiosis incorporates the ancient microcosmos, a circumstance that accounts for botanical success, and they do have significant interactions with both animals and fungi.

Semiosis in fungi, or cytosemiosis, is not yet well understood, although their modes of interaction with other life forms—especially algae, green plants, insects, and warm-blooded animals (to which they are pathogenic)—by such means as secretion, leakage, and other methods are basically known. One of the most fascinating forms of semiosis has been described in the cellular slime mold, where the sign carrier turns out to be the ubiquitous molecule cAMP, mentioned above.

There exists a massive and very ramified literature, though shockingly uneven in quality, on the biological bases of human nonverbal semiosis; for two excellent general accounts, see Guthrie (1976) and Morris (1977). By contrast, since Lenneberg's masterful (though sadly neglected) 1967 synthesis, there has been no similarly comprehensive discussion of the biological foundations of language. For a recent discussion of the main issues relating to the origin of language, see Sebeok (1986c). That article argues that language emerged as an evolutionary adaptation over two million years ago, in the guise of a mute semiotic modeling system—briefly, a tool wherewith hominids analyze their surroundings—and was thus present in *Homo habillis* and all successor species. Speech, the paramount linear display of language in the vocal-auditory mode, appeared as a secondary exaptation probably less than 100,000 years ago, the minimum time required to adjust a species-specific mechanism for encoding sentences with a matching mechanism for decoding and interpreting them in another brain. The fine-tuning process continues.

The overall scenario sketched out in that article is in good conformity with Thom's (1975:309–311) judgment about the double origin of language, in response to two needs, one personal—"aiming to realize the permanence of the ego"—and the other social—"expressing the main regulating mechanisms of the social group." And it is likewise so with Geschwind's equivalent view (1980:313) "that the forerunners of language were functions whose *social* advantages [that is, communicative function] were secondary but conferred an advantage for survival [that is, the modeling function]."

The Stoics were well aware that "animals . . . communicate with each other by means of signs" (Sebeok 1977:182). By the thirteenth century, Thomas Aquinas had concluded that animals make use of signs, both natural and those founded on second nature, or custom. Virtually every major thinker about semiotic issues since, from Peirce to Morris to Thom, and, above all, Jakob von Uexküll, have reaffirmed and generalized this fact to encompass the totality of life. Only a stubborn but declining minority still believes that the province of semiotics is coextensive with the semantic universe known as human culture; but this is not, of course, to deny Eco's dictum (1976:22) that "the whole of culture *should* be studied as a communicative phenomenon based on signification systems."

REFERENCES

Albone, Eric S. 1984. *Mammalian Semiochemistry: The Investigation of Chemical Signals between Mammals.* Chichester: Wiley.

Alston, William P. 1967a. Language. *The Encyclopedia of Philosophy* 4:384–386. New York: Macmillan and Free Press.

———. 1967b. Sign and Symbol. *The Encyclopedia of Philosophy* 7:437–441. New York: Macmillan and Free Press.

———. 1967c. Religion. *The Encyclopedia of Philosophy* 7:140–145. New York: Macmillan and Free Press.

Andrews, M. 1976. *The Life that Lives on Man.* New York: Taplinger.

Anobile, Richard J., ed. 1974. *Casablanca.* New York: Avon Books.

Armstrong, Robert L. 1965. John Locke's "Doctrine of Signs": A New Metaphysics. *Journal of the History of Ideas* 26:369–382.

Ayer, A. J. 1968. *The Origins of Pragmatism: Studies in the Philosophy of Charles Sanders Peirce and William James.* London: Macmillan.

Bacon, Francis. 1973. *The Advancement of Learning.* London: J. M. Dent.

Bailes, Kendall E. 1990. *Science and Russian Culture in an Age of Revolutions: V. I. Vernadsky and His Scientific School, 1863–1945.* Bloomington: Indiana University Press.

Bailey, Hilary. 1988. *As Time Goes By.* London: Constable.

Bang, Preben, and Preben Dahlstrom. 1972. *Collins Guide to Animal Track and Signs.* London: Collins.

Bar-Hillel, Yehoshua. 1970. *Aspects of Language: Essays and Lectures on Philosophy of Language, Linguistic Philosophy and Methodology of Linguistics,* 69–88. Jerusalem: Magnes Press.

Baross, J. A., and J. W. Demming. 1983. Growth of "Black Smoker" Bacteria at Temperatures of At Least 250°C. *Nature* 303:423–426.

Barrow, John D., and Joseph Silk. 1983. *The Left Hand of Creation: The Origin and Evolution of the Expanding Universe.* New York: Basic Books.

Barthes, Roland. 1967. *Elements of Semiology.* New York: Hill & Wang.

Barwise, Jon, and John Perry. 1983. *Situations and Attitudes.* Cambridge: MIT Press.

Bateson, Gregory. 1968. Redundancy and Coding. In *Animal Communication: Techniques of Study and Results of Research,* ed. Thomas A. Sebeok, 614–626. Bloomington: Indiana University Press.

Baudrillard, Jean. 1981. *For a Critique of the Political Economy of the Sign.* St. Louis: Telos Press.

Beadle, George W., and Muriel Beadle. 1966. *The Language of Life: An Introduction to the Science of Genetics.* Garden City: Doubleday.

Beck, Alan, and Aaron Katcher. 1983. *Between Pets and People: The Importance of Animal Companionship.* New York: G. P. Putnam's Sons.

Becker, Nikolaus, and Eberhard Schorsch. 1975. Geldfetischismus. In *Ergebnisse zur Sexualforschung,* ed. E. Schorsch and G. Schmidt, 238–256. Cologne: Wissenschafts Verlag.

Bemporad, Jules, Donald Dunton, and Frieda H. Spady. 1976. Treatment of a Child Foot Fetishist. *American Journal of Psychotherapy* 30:303–316.

Beniger, James R. 1986. *The Control Revolution: Technological and Economic Origins of the Information Society.* Cambridge: Harvard University Press.

Bentley, Arthur F. 1941. The Human Skin: Philosophy's Last Line of Defense. *Philosophy of Science* 8:1–19.

Benveniste, Emile. 1971. *Problems in General Linguistics.* Coral Gables: University of Miami Press.

Berg, H. C. 1975. Does the Flagellar Rotory Motor Stop? *Cell Motility, Cold Spring Harbor Conf.* 3:47–56.

Berlinski, David. The Language of Life. In *Complexity, Language, and Life: Mathematical Approaches,* ed. John L. Casi and Anders Karlqvist, 231–267. Berlin: Springer Verlag.

Bernard, Claude, 1878. *Leçons sur les phénomènes de la vie communs aux animaux et les végéaux.* Paris: Baillière.

Bloomfield, Leonard. 1939. Linguistic Aspects of Science. *International Encyclopedia of Unified Science.* 1:215–278. Chicago: University of Chicago Press.

Blumenberg, Hans. 1981. *Die Lesbarkeit der Welt.* Frankfurt am Main: Suhrkamp Verlag.

Bonner, John Tyler. 1963. How Slime Molds Communicate. *Scientific American* 209:2.84–93.

———. 1969. *The Scale of Nature.* New York: Harper & Row.

———. 1980. *The Evolution of Culture in Animals.* Princeton: Princeton University Press.

Bouissac, Paul. 1985. *Circus and Cultures: A Semiotic Approach.* Lanham: University Press of America.

——— et al., eds. 1986. *Iconicity: Essays on the Nature of Culture.* Tübingen: Stauffenburg Verlag.

Boyer, Peter J. 1986. CBS News in Search of Itself. *New York Times Magazine,* December 28, pp. 14–34.

Branscombe, Lewis M. 1985. Integrity in Science. *American Scientist* 73:5.421–423.

Braten, Stein. 1988. Dialogic Mind: The Infant and the Adult in Protoconversation. In *Nature, Cognition, and System I: Current Systems-Scientific Research on Natural and Cognitive Systems,* ed. Marc E. Carvallo, 187–205. Dordrecht: Kluwer Academic.

Breland, Keller, and Marian Breland. 1966. *Animal Behaviour.* London: Collier-Macmillan.

Bright, Michael. 1984. *Animal Language.* London: British Broadcasting Corporation.

Brillouin, Leon N. 1950. Thermodynamics and Information Theory. *American Scientist* 38:4.594–599.

Brodsky, Joseph. 1989. Isaiah Berlin at Eighty. *New York Review of Books* 36:13.44–45 (August 17).

Brooks, Daniel R., and E. O. Wiley. 1986. *Evolution as Entropy: Toward a Unified Theory of Biology.* Chicago: University of Chicago Press.

Brosses, Charles de. 1760. *La culte des dieux fétiches.* Paris.

Brown, C. H. 1984. *Language and Living Things: Uniformities in Folk Classification and Naming.* New Brunswick: Rutgers University Press.

Bruller, Jean [Vercors]. 1953. *You Shall Know Them.* Boston: Little, Brown.

Bruner, Jerome. 1983. *Child's Talk: Learning to Use Language.* New York: W. W. Norton.

Bühler, Karl. 1934. *Sprachtheorie: Die Darstellung-funktion der Sprache.* Stuttgart: Gustav Fischer.

Bullowa, Margaret, 1979. Prelinguistic Communication: A Field for Scientific Research. In *Before Speech: The Beginning of Interpersonal Communication,* ed. Margaret Bullowa. Cambridge: Cambridge University Press.

Burks, A. W. 1949. Icon, Index, Symbol. *Philosophy and Phenomenological Research* 9:673–689.

Burnett, J. H. 1968. *Fundamentals of Mycology.* London: Edward Arnold.

Buyssens, Eric. 1943. *Les langages et le discours.* Brussels: Office de Publicité.

Cairns-Smith, A. G. 1985. *Seven Clues to the Origin of Life: A Scientific Detective Story.* Cambridge: Cambridge University Press.

Carnap, Rudolf. 1942. *Introduction to Semantics.* Cambridge: Harvard University Press.

Cartmill, Matt, David Pilbeam, and Glynn Isaac. 1986. One Hundred Years of Paleoanthropology. *American Scientist* 74:410–420.

Cassirer, Ernst. 1944. *An Essay on Man: An Introduction to a Philosophy of Human Culture.* New Haven: Yale University Press.

Chance, Michael R. A., and Ray R. Larsen, eds. 1976. *The Social Structure of Attention.* London: Wiley.

Chao, Yuen Ren. 1962. Models in Linguistics and Models in General. In *Logic, Methodology and Philosophy of Science: Proceedings of the 1960 International Congress,* ed. Ernest Nagel, Patrick Suppes, and Alfred Tarski, 558–566. Stanford: Stanford University Press.

Chomsky, Noam. 1980. *Rules and Representations.* New York: Columbia University Press.

Christopher, Milbourne. 1970. *ESP, Seers & Psychics.* New York: Thomas Y. Crowell.

Clutton-Brock, Juliet. 1981. *Domesticated Animals from Early Times.* London: British Museum (Natural History).

Cook, Norman D. 1986. *The Brain Code.* London: Methuen.

Coover, Robert. 1987. *A Night at the Movies: Or, You Must Remember This.* London: Heinemann.

Copeland, H. F. 1956. *The Classification of Lower Organisms.* Palo Alto: Pacific Books.

Copeland, James E., ed. 1984. *New Directions in Linguistics and Semiotics.* Houston: Rice University Studies.

Craig, J. V. 1981. *Domestic Animal Behavior: Causes and Implications for Animal Care and Management.* Englewood Cliffs: Prentice Hall.

Culler, Jonathan. 1983. *Roland Barthes.* New York: Oxford University Press.

Darwin, Charles. 1859. *On the Origin of Species by Means of Natural Selection or the Preservation of Favoured Races in the Struggle for Life.* London: John Murray.

Dawkins, Richard. 1976. *The Selfish Gene.* Oxford: Oxford University Press.

Deely, John N. 1980. The Nonverbal Inlay in Linguistic Communication. In *The Signifying Animal: The Grammar of Language and Experience,* ed. Irmengard Rauch and Gerald F. Carr, 201–217. Bloomington: Indiana University Press.

———. 1982. *Introducing Semiotic: Its History and Doctrine.* Bloomington: Indiana University Press.

———. 1985. Semiotic and the Liberal Arts. *The New Scholasticism* 59:296–322.

Devreotes, Peter N. 1982. Chemotaxis. In *The Development of Dictyostelium discoideum,* 117–168. San Diego: Academic Press.

Dorit, Robert L., Lloyd Schoenbach, and Walter Gilbert. 1990. How Big Is the Universe of Exons? *Science* 250:1377–1382.

Dubois, Philippe. 1988. *L'acte photographique.* Brussels: Labor.

Ebert, Roger. 1984. *A Kiss Is Still a Kiss.* Kansas City: Andrews, McMeel & Parker.

Eccles, John C. 1979. *The Human Mystery.* New York: Springer International.

Eco, Umberto. 1976. *A Theory of Semiotics.* Bloomington: Indiana University Press.

———. 1977. The Influence of Roman Jakobson on the Development of Semiotics. In *Roman Jakobson: Echoes of His Scholarship,* ed. Daniel Armstrong and C. H. van Schoonefeld, 39–58. Lisse: Peter de Ridder Press.

———. 1984. *Semiotics and the Philosophy of Language.* Bloomington: Indiana University Press.

———. 1986. *Travels in Hyperreality: Essays.* New York: Harcourt Brace Jovanovich.

———, and Thomas A. Sebeok, eds. 1983. *The Sign of Three: Dupin, Holmes, Peirce.* Bloomington: Indiana University Press.

Edelman, G. M. 1987. *Neural Darwinism: The Theory of Neuronal Group Selection.* New York: Basic Books.

Ennion, E. A. R., and N. Tinbergen. 1967. *Tracks.* Oxford: Clarendon Press.

Erckenbrecht, Ulrich. 1976. *Das Geheimnis des Fetischismus: Grundmotive der Marxschen Erkenntiskritik.* Frankfurt am Main: Europäische Verlaganstalt.

Erwin, J., T. L. Maple, and G. Mitchell. 1979. *Captivity and Behavior: Primates in Breeding Colonies, Laboratories, and Zoos.* New York: Van Nostrand Reinhold.

Evan-Pritchard, E. E. 1956. *Nuer Religion.* Oxford: Oxford University Press.

Ewen, David. 1966. *American Popular Songs.* New York: Random House.

Fernald, Dodge. 1984. *The Hans Legacy: A Story of Science.* Hillsdale: Lawrence Erlbaum.

Fillmore, Charles. 1973. May We Come In? *Semiotica* 9:97–116.

Fine, Seymour H. 1981. *The Marketing of Social Issues.* New York: Praeger.

Fisch, Max. 1980. Foreword to Thomas A. Sebeok and Jean Umiker-Sebeok, *"You Know My Method,"* 7–13. Bloomington: Gaslight Publications.

Fiske, John. 1982. *Introduction to Communication Studies.* London: Methuen.

Fox, Sidney. 1988. *The Emergence of Life: Darwinian Evolution from the Inside.* New York: Basic Books.

Francisco, Charles. 1980. *You Must Remember This . . .: The Filming of Casablanca.* Englewood Cliffs: Prentice Hall.

.130Freedman, Alfred M., Harold I. Kaplan, and Benjamin Sadock. 1972. *Modern Synopsis of Comprehensive Textbook of Psychiatry.* Baltimore: Williams & Wilkins.

French, A. P., and P. J. Kennedy, eds. 1985. *Niels Bohr: A Centenary Volume.* Cambridge: Harvard University Press.

Freud, Sigmund. 1927. Fetishism. In *The Standard Edition of the Complete Psychological Works,* ed. James Strachey 21:149–157. London: Hogarth Press.

———. 1933. *New Introductory Lectures in Psychoanalysis.* New York: Norton.

Füller, H. 1958. *Symbiose im Tierreich.* Wittenberg-Lutherstadt: Ziemsen.

Furnham, Adrian. 1988. Write and Wrong: The Validity of Graphological Analysis. *The Skeptical Inquirer* 13:1.64–69.

Gale, Richard M. 1967. Indexical Signs, Egocentric Particulars, and Token-Reflexive Words. *The Encyclopedia of Philosophy* 4:151–155. New York: Macmillan and The Free Press.

Galilei, Galileo. 1957. "The Assayer." Trans. Stillman Drake. In *Discoveries and Opinions of Galileo.* Garden City: Doubleday Anchor Books.

Gardiner, Alan H. 1932. *The Theory of Speech and Language.* Oxford: Clarendon Press.

Gardner, Howard. 1983. *Frames of Mind: The Theory of Multiple Intelligences.* New York: Basic Books.

Garnier, Paul. 1896. *Fétichistes: Pervertis et invertis sexuel.* Paris: J. B. Baillière.

Garver, Newton. 1986. Review of Shapiro 1983. *Transactions of the Charles S. Peirce Society* 22:68–74.

Gatlin, Lila L. 1972. *Information Theory and Living Systems.* New York: Columbia University Press.

Gebhard, Paul H. 1969. Fetishism and Sadomasochism. *Science and Psychoanalysis* 15:71–80.

Geist, V. 1986. Did Large Predators Keep Humans Out of North America? Precirculated Paper. In *Cultural Attitudes to Animals Including Birds, Fish and Invertebrates.* World Archaelogical Congress 1 (mimeo.).

Gerard, W. Ralph. 1969. Hierarchy, Entitation, and Levels. In *Hierarchical Structures,* ed. L. L. Whyte, A. G. Wilson, and D. Wilson, 215–228. New York: American Elsevier.

Geras, Norman. 1971. Essence and Appearance: Aspects of Fetishism in Marx's *Capital. New Left Review* 65:69–85.

Geschwind, Norman. 1980. Some Comments on the Neurology of Language. In *Biological Studies of Mental Processes,* ed. David Caplan, 301–319. Cambridge: MIT Press.

Ginzburg, Carlo. 1983. Morelli, Freud, and Sherlock Holmes. In Eco and Sebeok 1983:81–118.

Gipper, Helmut. 1963. *Bausteine zur Sprachinhaltfoschung: Neuere Sprachbetrachtung im Austausch mit Geistes- und Naturwissenschaft.* Düsseldorf: Pädagogischer Verlag Schwann.

Godel, Robert. 1957. *Les sources manuscrites de Cours de Linguistique Générale.* Geneva: Librairie E. Droz.

Goffman, Erving. 1963. *Stigma: Notes on the Management of Spoiled Identity.* Englewood Cliffs: Prentice Hall.

———. 1971. *Relations in Public: Microstudies of the Public Order.* New York: Basic Books.

Gorbman, Claudia. 1987. *Unheard Melodies: Narrative Film Music.* Bloomington: Indiana University Press.

Gould, Stephen J., and Elizabeth S. Vrba. 1982. Exaptation—A Missing Term in the Science of Form. *Paleobiology* 8:1.4–15.

Greenstein, George. 1988. *The Symbiotic Universe: Life and Mind in the Cosmos.* New York: Morrow.

Greimas, A. J., and J. Courtés. 1982. *Semiotics and Language: An Analytical Dictionary.* Bloomington: Indiana University Press.

Grinker, Roy R. 1966. The Psychosomatic Aspects of Anxiety. In *Anxiety and Behavior,* ed. Charles D. Spielberger, Ch. 5. New York: Academic Press.

Gump, Richard. 1962. *Jade: Stone of Heaven.* Garden City: Doubleday.

Guthrie, R. Dale. 1976. *Body Hot Spots: The Anatomy of Human Social Organs and Behavior.* Englewood Cliffs: Prentice Hall.

Hadamard, Jacques. 1945. *An Essay on the Psychology of Invention in the Mathematical Field.* Princeton: Princeton University Press.

Hailman, Jack P. 1977. *Optical Signals: Animal Communication and Light.* Bloomington: Indiana University Press.

Halliwell-Phillips, James O. 1879. *Memoranda on Love's Labour's Lost, King John, Othello, and on Romeo and Juliet.* London: James Allard.

Hardwick, Charles S., ed. 1977. *Semiotic and Significs: The Correspondence between Charles S. Peirce and Victoria Lady Welby.* Bloomington: Indiana University Press.

———. In press. *Ein Leben mit Tieren im Zoo und in aller Welt.* Zurich: Werd Verlag.

Harrison, Phyllis A. 1983. *Behaving Brazilian: A Comparison of Brazilian and North American Social Behavior.* Rowley: Newbury House.

Hediger, Heini. 1959. Die Angst des tieres. *Studien aus dem C. G. Jung-Institut* 10:7–34.

———. 1969. *Man and Animal in the Zoo: Zoo Biology.* New York: Delacorte Press.

———. 1979. *Beobachtungen zur Tierpsychologie in Zoo und im Zirkus.* Berlin: Henschelverlag.

———. 1980. *Tiere verstehen: Erkenntnisse eines Tierpsychologen.* Munich: Kinder Verlag.

Heidel, William A. 1941. *Hippocratic Medicine: Its Spirit and Method.* New York: Columbia University Press.

Heinroth, O. 1910. Beiträge zur Biologie, namentlich Ethologie und Psychologie der Anatiden. *Verhandlungen des V. Internationalen Ornithologen-Kongress,* 589–702. Berlin.

Herskovits, Melville. 1950. *Man and His Works.* New York: Knopf.

Hesse, Mary. 1967. Models and Analogy in Science. In *The Encyclopedia of Philosophy* 5:354–359. Macmillan and Free Press.

Hjelmslev, Louis. 1963. *Prolegomena to a Theory of Language.* Madison: University of Wisconsin Press.

Hoage, R. J., ed. 1989. *Perceptions of Animals in American Culture.* Washington: Smithsonian Institution Press.

Holm, Serge-Christophe. 1982. *Le Bonheur-liberté.* Paris: Presses Universitaires de France.

Hookway, Christopher. 1985. *Peirce.* London: Routledge & Kegan Paul.

Houpt, K. A., and T. R. Wolski. 1982. *Domestic Animal Behavior for Veterinarians and Animal Scientists.* Ames: Iowa State University Press.

Hyman, Ray. 1981. In Sebeok and Rosenthal 1981, 169–181.

Ingold, Tim. 1980. *Hunters, Pastoralists and Ranchers: Reindeer Economies and Their Transformations.* Cambridge: Cambridge University Press.

Ingram, David. 1978. Typology and Universals of Personal Pronouns. In *Universals of Human Language,* ed. Joseph H. Greenberg, 3:213–247. Stanford: Stanford University Press.

Jacob, François. 1974. *The Logic of Living Systems: A History of Heredity.* London: Allen Lane.

———. 1982. *The Possible and the Actual.* Seattle: University of Washington Press.

———. 1988. *The Statue Within.* New York: Basic Books.

Jakobson, Roman. 1960. Linguistics and Poetics. In *Style in Language,* ed. Thomas A. Sebeok, 350–377. New York: Wiley.

———. 1963. Parts and Wholes in Language. In *Parts and Wholes,* ed. Daniel Lerner, 157–162. New York: Free Press.

———. 1971. *Selected Writings: Word and Language* 2:130–147. The Hague: Mouton.

———. 1974. *Main Trends in the Science of Language.* New York: Harper & Row.

———. 1980. *The Framework of Language.* Ann Arbor: Michigan Studies in the Humanities.

Janisse, Michel Pierre. 1977. *Pupillometry: The Psychology of the Pupillary Response.* New York: Wiley.

Janković, Branislav D., Branislav M. Marković, and Novera Herbert Spector. 1987. *Neuroimmune Reactions: Proceedings of the Second International Workshop on Neuroimmunomodulation.* Annals of the New York Academy of Sciences 496. New York: New York Academy of Sciences.

Jannasch, H. W., and M. J. Mottl. 1985. Geomicrobiology of Deep-Sea Hydrothermal Vents. *Science* 229:717–725.

Jarvella, Robert H., and Wolfgang Klein, eds. 1982. *Speech, Place, and Action: Studies in Deixis and Related Topics.* New York: Wiley.

Jastrow, Joseph. 1930. Joseph Jastrow [Autobiography]. In *A History of Psychology in Autobiography,* ed. Carl Murchison, 1:135–162.

Jerison, Harry J. 1986. The Perceptual World of Dolphins. In *Dolphin Cognition and Behavior: A Comparative Approach,* ed. Ronald J. Schusterman, Jeanette A. Thomas, and Forrest G. Wood, 141–166. Hillsdale: Lawrence Erlbaum.

Jerne, Niels K. 1985. The Generative Grammar of the Immune System. *Science* 229:1057–1059.

Jespersen, Otto. 1922. *Language: Its Nature, Development, and Origin.* London: Allen & Unwin.

Jhally, Sut. 1987. *The Codes of Advertising: Fetishism and the Political Economy of Meaning in the Consumer Society.* New York: St. Martin's.

Johnson, Sahnny. 1979. *Nonverbal Communication in the Teaching of Foreign Languages.* Ph.D. diss., Indiana University.

Jones, Edwin. 1989. *Reading the Book of Nature: A Phenomenological Study of Creative Expression in Science and Painting.* Athens: Ohio University Press.

Katcher, A. H., and A. M. Beck, eds. 1983. *New Perspectives on Our Lives with Companion Animals.* Philadelphia: University of Pennsylvania Press.

Kergosien, Y. L. 1985. Sémiotique de la nature. *Actes du IVe Séminaire de l'école de*

biologie théorique, ed. G. Benchetrit and J. Demongeot, 11–26. Paris: Editions du Centre National de la Recherche Scientifique.
Kevles, Daniel J. 1985. *In the Name of Eugenics: Genetics and the Uses of Human Heredity*. New York: Knopf.
Kinney, Arthur E., ed. *Rogues, Vagabonds, & Sturdy Beggars*. Barre, MA: Imprint Society.
Kinsey, Alfred C., Wardell B. Pomeroy, Clyde E. Marshall, and Paul H. Gebhard. 1953. *Sexual Behavior in the Human Female*. Philadelphia: Saunders.
Klein, Peter S., et al. 1988. A Chemoattractant Receptor Controls Development in Dictyostelium discoideum. *Science* 241:1467–1472.
Koch, Walter. 1986. *Philosophie der Philologie und Semiotik*. Bochum: Studienverlag Dr. Norbert Brockmeyer.
Krafft-Ebing, Richard von. 1886. *Psychopathia sexualis*. Stuttgart: Ferdinand Enke.
Krampen, Martin. 1981. Phytosemiotics. *Semiotica* 36:187–209.
Krieger, D. T. 1983. Brain Peptides: What, Where, and Why? *Science* 222:975–985.
Kunzle, David. 1982. *Fashion and Fetishism: A Social History of the Corset, Tight-Lacing and Other Forms of Body-Sculpture in the West*. Totowa: Rowman and Littlefield.
Lambert, Johann Heinrich. 1764. *Semiotik oder Lehre von der Bezeichnung der Gedanken und Dinge*. Leipzig: Johann Wendler.
Lawrence, E. A. 1985. *Hoofbeats and Society: Studies in Human-Horse Interactions*. Bloomington: Indiana University Press.
Leach, Edmund. 1964. Anthropological Aspects of Language: Animal Categories and Verbal Abuse. In *New Directions in the Study of Language*, ed. E. H. Lenneberg, 23–63. Cambridge: MIT Press.
Lecky, Prescott. 1945. *Self-Consistency: A Theory of Personality*. New York: Island Press.
Lee, Benjamin, and Greg Urban, eds. 1989. *Semiotics, Self, and Society*. Berlin: Mouton de Gruyter.
Lees, Robert B. 1980. Language and the Genetic Code. In *The Signifying Animal: the Grammar of Language and Experience*, ed. Irmengard Rauch and Gerald F. Carr. Bloomington: Indiana University Press.
Lekomcev, Ju. K. 1977. Foundations of General Semiotics. In *Soviet Semiotics*, ed. Daniel P. Lucid, 39–44. Baltimore: Johns Hopkins University Press.
Lenneberg, Eric H. 1967. *Biological Foundations of Language*. New York: Wiley.
Levelt, Willem J. M. 1989. *Speaking: From Intention to Articulation*. Cambridge: MIT Press.
Lévi-Strauss, Claude. 1958. *Anthropologie structurale*. Paris: Librairie Plon.
———. 1962a. *Le Totémisme aujourd'hui*. Paris: Presses Universitaires de France.
———. 1962b. *La Pensée sauvage*. Paris: Plon.
———. 1963. *Structural Anthropology*. New York: Basic Books.
———. 1966. *The Savage Mind*. Chicago: University of Chicago Press.
———. 1985. *La potière jalouse*. Paris: Plon.
Lewis, D. Bryan, and D. Michael Gower. 1980. *Biology of Communication*. New York: Wiley.
Leyhausen, Paul. 1967. Biologie von Ausdruck und Eindruck. *Psychologische Forschung* 31:177–227.
Lilly, John. 1967. *The Mind of the Dolphin: A Nonhuman Intelligence*. Garden City: Doubleday.
Linden, Eugene. 1986. *Silent Partners*. New York: Basic Books.
Ling, G. N. 1984. *In Search of the Physical Basis of Life*. New York: Plenum Press.
Locke, John. 1975 [1690]. *An Essay concerning Human Understanding*, ed. P. H. Nidditch. Oxford: Clarendon Press.

Lorenz, Konrad. 1971. *Studies in Animal and Human Behaviour* 2. Cambridge: Harvard University Press.
Lotman, Ju. M. 1977. Primary and Secondary Communication-Modeling Systems. In Lucid 1977, 95–98. Baltimore: Johns Hopkins University Press.
———. 1984. O Semiosfere. In *Trudy po znakovym sistemam* 17:5–23. Tartu: Tartu Riikliku Uikooli Toimetised 641.
———. 1991. *Universe of the Mind: A Semiotic Theory of Culture,* trans. Ann Shukman. Bloomington: Indiana University Press.
———, and B. A. Uspensky. 1978 [1971]. On the Semiotic Mechanism of Culture, *New Literary History* 9:211–232.
Lovelock, James E. 1979. *Gaia: A New Look at Life on Earth.* Oxford: Oxford University Press.
Lowenstein, J. M. 1984. Molecular Approaches to the Identification of Species. *American Scientist* 73:541–547.
Lucid, Daniel P., ed. 1977, 1988. *Soviet Semiotics: An Anthology.* Baltimore: Johns Hopkins University Press.
Lyons, John. 1977. *Semantics.* Cambridge: Cambridge University Press.
MacCannell, Dean. 1976. *The Tourist: A New Theory of the Leisure Class.* New York: Schocken Books.
McFarland, David, ed. 1982. *The Oxford Companion to Animal Behaviour.* Oxford: Oxford University Press.
Mackay, Alan L. 1984. The Code Breakers. *The Sciences* 24:3.13–14.
McLennan, J. F. 1869. The Worship of Animals and Plants. *Fortnightly* Review 12 (NS6): Pt. I, 407–427; Pt. II, 562–582.
Mallarmé, Stéphane. 1989. *Selected Letters of . . .,* ed. and trans. Rosemary Lloyd. Chicago: University of Chicago Press.
Margulis, Lynn. 1981. *Symbiosis in Cell Evolution: Life and Its Environment on the Early Earth.* San Francisco: Freeman.
———, and Dorion Sagan. 1986a. *Microcosmos: Four Billion Years of Microbial Evolution.* New York: Summit Books.
———, and Dorion Sagan. 1986b. Strange Fruit on the Tree of Life: How Man-Made Objects May Remake Man. *The Sciences* 4:2.38–45.
———, and Karlene V. Schwartz. 1988. *Five Kingdoms: An Illustrated Guide to the Phyla of Life on Earth.* New York: Freeman.
Maritain, Jacques. 1943. Sign and Symbol. *Redeeming the Time,* 191–224, 268–276. London: Geoffrey Bles.
———. 1957. Language and the Theory of Sign. In *Language: An Enquiry into Its Meaning and Function,* ed. Ruth Nanda Anshen, 86–101. New York: Harper.
Marrone, Gianfranco, ed. 1986. Dove va la semiotica? *Quaderni del Circolo Semiologico Italiana* 24:149–151.
Maturana, Humberto R., and Francisco G. Varela. 1980. *Autopoiesis and Cognition: The Realization of the Living.* Boston: D. Reidel.
Mayr, Ernst. 1965. *Animal Species and Evolution.* Cambridge: Harvard University Press.
———. 1982. *The Growth of Biological Thought: Diversity, Evolution, and Inheritance.* Cambridge: Harvard University Press.
Mead, George Herbert. 1934. *Mind, Self, and Society from the Standpoint of a Social Behaviorist,* ed. Charles Morris. Chicago: University of Chicago Press.
Medawar, P. B., and J. S. Medawar. 1977. *The Life Science: Current Ideas of Biology.* New York: Harper & Row.
———, and J. S. Medawar. 1983. *Aristotle to Zoos: A Philosophical Dictionary of Biology.* Cambridge: Harvard University Press.

Metz, Christian. 1974. *Film Language: A Semiotics of the Cinema*. New York: Oxford University Press.
———. 1985. Photography and Fetish. *October* 34:81–90.
Miller, J. G. 1978. *Living Systems*. New York: McGraw-Hill.
Moenssens, Andre A. 1971. *Fingerprint Techniques*. Philadelphia: Chilton Books.
Money, John. 1986. *Lovemaps: Clinical Concepts of Sexual/Erotic Health and Pathology, Paraphilia, and Gender Transposition in Childhood, Adolescence, and Maturity*. New York: Irvington.
Montalverne, Gol. 1984. A vida secreta das plantas. *Atlantas* 4:4.8–13.
Mooney, Ted. 1981. *Easy Travel to Other Planets*. New York: Farrar, Straus, Giroux.
Morris, Charles. 1946. *Signs, Language and Behavior*. New York: Prentice Hall.
———. 1964. *Signification and Significances: A Study of the Relations of Signs and Values*. Cambridge: MIT Press.
———. 1970. *The Pragmatic Movement in American Philosophy*. New York: Braziller.
———. 1971. *Writings on the General Theory of Signs*, ed. Thomas A. Sebeok. The Hague: Mouton.
Morris, Desmond. 1969. *The Human Zoo*. New York: McGraw-Hill.
———. 1977. *Manwatching: A Field Guide to Human Behaviour*. London: Jonathan Cape.
Morris, Ramona, and Desmond Morris. 1966. *Men and Pandas*. New York: New American Library.
Mounin, Georges. 1970. *Introduction à la sémiologie*. Paris: Les Editions de Minuit.
Müller, Horst M. 1987. *Evolution, Kognition, und Sprache*. Berlin: Paul Parey.
Murton, R. K. 1971. *Man and Birds*. London: Collins.
Nicholson, B. 1984. Does Kissing Aid Human Bonding by Semiochemical Addiction? *British Journal of Dermatology* 111:623–627.
Nöth, Winfried. 1985. *Handbuch der Semiotik*. Stuttgart: J. B. Metzlersche Verlagsbuchhandlung.
———. 1990. *Handbook of Semiotics*. Bloomington: Indiana University Press.
Oates, Joyce Carol. 1987. *You Must Remember This*. New York: Harper & Row.
Ogden, C. K., and I. A. Richards. 1938. *The Meaning of Meaning: A Study of the Influence of Language upon Thought and of the Science of Symbolism*. New York: Harcourt, Brace.
Osolsobě, Ivo. 1979. On Ostensive Communication. *Studia Semiotyczne* 9:63–75.
Peirce, Charles S. 1868. Some Consequences of Four Incapabilities. *Journal of Speculative Philosophy* 2:140–151.
———. 1935–1966. *Collected Papers of Charles Sanders Peirce*, ed. Charles Hartshorne, Paul Weiss, and Arthur W. Burks. Cambridge: Harvard University Press. [References are to volumes and paragraphs, not to pages.]
Philodemus. 1978 [c. 54 B.C.]. *On Methods of Inference*, ed. with trans. and comm. Phillip Howard De Lacy and Estelle De Lacy. Naples: Bibliopolis.
Pirie, N. W. 1937. The Meaninglessness of the Terms Life and Living. In *Perspectives in Biochemistry*, ed. J. Needham and D. E. Green, 11–22. Cambridge: Cambridge University Press.
Ponnamperuma, Cyril, ed. 1972. *Exobiology*. Amsterdam: North-Holland.
Popper, Karl R., and John R. Eccles. 1977. *The Self and Its Brain: An Argument for Interactionism*. Berlin: Springer International.
Premack, David. 1986. *Gavagai! Or the Future History of the Animal Language Controversy*. Cambridge: MIT Press.
Preziosi, Donald. 1989. *Rethinking Art History: Meditations on a Coy Science*. New Haven: Yale University Press.
Prieto, Luis J. 1975. *Etudes de linguistique et de sémiologie générales*. Geneva: Librairie Droz.

Prodi, Giorgio. 1977. *Le basi materiali della significazione*. Milan: Bompiani.
Prosser, C. Ladd. 1985. Modes of Communication. In *Comparative Neurobiology*, ed. Melvin J. Cohen and Felix Sturmwasser, 117–118. New York: Wiley.
Putnam, Hilary. 1973. Meaning and Reference. *Journal of Philosophy* 70:19.699–711.
Ransdell, Joseph. 1986. Index. *Encyclopedic Dictionary of Semiotics* 1:340–341. Berlin: Mouton de Gruyter.
Rector, Mônica, and Aluizio R. Trinta. 1985. *Comunicacão não-verbal: A gestualidade Brazileira*. Petrópolis: Editor Vozes.
Rhodes, Henry T. F. 1956. *Alphonse Bertillon: Father of Scientific Detection*. New York: Abelard Schuman.
Rohter, Larry. 1989. Macabre Relic Is Laid to Rest by Mexicans. *New York Times*, December 10, p. 9.
Roiphe, Herman. 1973. The Infantile Fetish. *Psychoanalytic Study of the Child* 28:147–166.
Rosenfeld, Israel. 1988. *The Invention of Memory: A New View of the Brain*. New York: Basic Books.
Rossi, Paolo. 1968. *Francis Bacon: From Magic to Science*. London: Routledge & Kegan Paul.
Rossi-Landi, Ferruccio. 1974. Linguistics and Economics. In *Current Trends in Linguistics* 12, ed. Thomas A. Sebeok, 1787–2017. The Hague: Mouton.
Roth, Jesse, and Derek LeRoith. 1987. Chemical Crosstalk. *The Sciences* 27:3.51–54.
Rudy, Stephen. 1986. Semiotics in the U.S.S.R. In *The Semitoic Sphere*, ed. Thomas A. Sebeok and Jean Umiker-Sebeok, Ch. 25. New York: Plenum Press.
Salthe, S. N. 1985. *Evolving Hierarchical Systems: Their Structure and Representation*. New York: Columbia University Press.
Sapir, Edward. 1929. The Status of Linguistics as a Science. *Language* 5:207–214.
———. 1931. Communication. *Encyclopedia of the Social Sciences* 4:78–81. New York: Macmillan.
Saussure, Ferdinand de. 1983. *Course in General Linguistics*, trans. and annot. Roy Harris. London: Duckworth.
Savage-Rumbaugh. 1986. *Ape Language: From Conditioned Response to Symbol*. New York: Columbia University Press.
Savan, David. 1983. Toward a Refutation of Semiotic Idealism, *Recherches Sémiotiques/Semiotic Inquiry* 3:1–8.
Sayers, Dorothy L. 1932. *Have His Carcase*. New York: Harcourt, Brace.
Schindler, Walter. 1953. A Case of Crutch Fetishism as the Result of a Literal Oedipus Complex. *International Journal of Sexology* 6:3.131–135.
Schmeck, Harold M., Jr. 1974. *Immunology: The Many-Edged Sword*. New York: Braziller.
Schneirla, T. C. 1965. Aspects of Stimulation and Organization in Approach/Withdrawal Processes Underlying Vertebrate Behavioral Development. In *Advances in the Study of Behavior*, ed. Daniel S. Lehrman, Robert A. Hinde, and Evelyn Shaw, 1:1–74. New York: Academic Press.
Schopf, J. William, ed. 1983. *Earth's Earliest Biosphere: Its Origin and Evolution*. Princeton: Princeton University Press.
Schor, Naomi. 1985. Female Fetishism: The Case of George Sand. *Poetics Today* 6:301–310.
Schrödinger, E. 1946. *What Is Life?* Cambridge: Cambridge University Press.
Schutz, Alfred. 1955. Symbol, Reality and Society. In *Symbols and Society*, ed. Lyman Bryson, Louis Finkelstein, Hudson Hoagland, and R. M. MacIver, 135–203. New York: Harper.
Sebeok, Thomas A. 1963. Communication among Social Bees; Porpoises and Sonar; Man and Dolphin. *Language* 39:448–466.

———, ed. 1968. *Animal Communication: Techniques of Study and Results of Research.* Bloomington: Indiana University Press.
———. 1972. *Perspectives in Zoosemiotics.* The Hague: Mouton.
———. 1975. Six Species of Signs: Some Propositions and Strictures. *Semiotica* 13:233–260.
———. 1976. Iconicity. *Modern Language Notes* 91:1427–1456.
———. 1977. Ecumenicalism in Semiotics. In *A Perfusion of Signs,* ed. Thomas A. Sebeok, 180–206. Bloomington: Indiana University Press.
———. 1978. Looking in the Destination for What Should Have Been Sought in the Source. *Diogenes* 104:112–137.
———. 1979a. *The Sign & Its Masters.* Austin: University of Texas Press.
———, ed. 1979b. *How Animals Communicate.* Bloomington: Indiana University Press.
———. 1981a. *The Play of Musement.* Bloomington: Indiana University Press.
———. 1981b. The Ultimate Enigma of "Clever Hans": The Union of Nature and Culture. In *The Clever Hans Phenomenon: Communication with Horses, Whales, Apes, and People,* ed. Thomas A. Sebeok and Robert Rosenthal, 199–205. Annals of the New York Academy of Sciences 364. New York: New York Academy of Sciences.
———. 1984a. Symptom. In Copeland 1984:211–230.
———. 1984b. *Communication Measures to Bridge Ten Millennia.* Technical Report BMI/ONWI-532. Columbus, OH: Office of Nuclear Waste Isolation, Battelle Memorial Institute.
———. 1985a [1976]. *Contributions to the Doctrine of Signs.* Lanham: University Press of America.
———. 1985b. Vital Signs. *American Journal of Semiotics* 3:1–27.
———. 1985c. Modern Man, Communication and Language. In *The Phylogeny and Ontogeny of Communication Systems,* ed. Clive Thomson, 163–169. Kingston: Queen's University.
———. 1985d. A Scientific Quibble. *Semiotica* 57:117–124.
———. 1985e. Amazements Explained. *Times Literary Supplement,* no. 4,275 (March 8), p. 268.
———. 1986a. *I Think I Am a Verb: More Contributions to the Doctrine of Signs.* New York: Plenum Press.
———, ed. 1986b. *Encyclopedic Dictionary of Semiotics* 1–3. Berlin: Mouton de Gruyter.
———. 1986c. The Problem of the Origin of Language in an Evolutionary Frame. *Language Sciences* 8:169–176.
———. 1986d. A Signifying Man. *New York Times Book Review* 91:13.14–15.
———. 1988. [2d corr. and exp. ed.] *The Sign & Its Masters.* Lanham: University Press of America.
———. 1989a. Darwinian and Lamarckian Evolution of Semiosis. Lecture prepared for delivery at the International Colloquium on the Evolution of Culture, September 22, 1988, Villa Vigoni. Bochum: Norbert Brockmeyer.
———. 1989b. Fetish. *American Journal of Semiotics* 6:51–65.
———. 1989–1990. *Essays in Zoosemiotics,* ed. Marcel Danesi. Toronto: Toronto Semiotic Circle Monographs Series 5.
———. 1990. *American Signatures.* Norman: University of Oklahoma Press.
———. 1990a. Why a Horse? In *Ajukawa and the 13 Mysteries of 1990.* Tokyo: Tokyo Sogen Sha. (In Japanese.)
———. 1991. *Semiotics in the United States: The View from the Center.* Bloomington: Indiana University Press.

———. 1991a. *American Signatures: Semiotic Inquiry and Method,* ed. Iris Smith. Norman: University of Oklahoma Press.

———, and Jean Umiker-Sebeok, eds. 1980. *Speaking of Apes: A Critical Anthology of Two-Way Communication with Man.* New York: Plenum Press.

Seely, Thomas D., and Roger A. Levien. 1987. A Colony of Mind. *The Sciences* 27:4.39–42.

Serpell, James. 1986. *In The Company of Animals: A Study of Human-Animal Relationships.* Oxford: Blackwell.

Shands, Harley C. 1976. Malinowski's Mirror: Emily Dickinson as Narcissus. *Contemporary Psychoanalysis* 12:300–334.

Shannon, Claude E. 1948. A Mathematical Theory of Information. *Bell System Technical Journal* 27:379–423, 623–656.

———, and Warren Weaver. 1949. *The Mathematical Theory of Communication.* Urbana: University of Illinois Press.

Shapiro, Michael. 1983. *The Sense of Grammar: Language as Semeiotic.* Bloomington: Indiana University Press.

Short, Thomas L. 1982, Life among the Legisigns. *Transactions of the Charles S. Peirce Society* 18:4.285–310.

Silk, Joseph. 1980. *The Big Bang: The Creation and Evolution of the Universe.* San Francisco: Freeman.

Silverman, P. 1978. *Animal Behaviour in the Laboratory.* New York: Pica Press.

Simpson, George Gaylord. 1961. *Principles of Animal Taxonomy.* New York: Columbia University Press.

Singer, Milton. 1984. *Man's Glassy Essence: Explorations in Semiotic Anthropology.* Bloomington: Indiana University Press.

Skupien, Janet. 1980. Interview. *The Kinesis Report: News and Views of Nonverbal Communication* 3(1):1–4.

Smith, W. John. 1977. *The Behavior of Communicating: An Ethological Approach.* Cambridge: Harvard University Press.

Sommer, Robert. 1969. *Personal Space.* Englewood Cliffs: Prentice Hall.

Sonea, Sorin. 1988. The Global Organism. *The Sciences* 28:4.38–45.

———. 1990. Bacterial (Prokaryotic) Communication. In *The Semiotic Web 1989,* ed. Thomas A. Sebeok and Jean Umiker-Sebeok, 639–662. Berlin: Mouton de Gruyter.

———, and Maurice Panisset. 1983. *A New Bacteriology.* Boston: Jones and Bartlett.

Sonesson, Göran. 1989. *Pictorial Concepts: Inquiries into the Semiotic Heritage and Its Relevance for the Analysis of the Visual World.* Lund: University Press.

Sperling, Melitta. 1963. Fetishism in Children. *Psychoanalytic Quarterly* 32:374–392.

Stanier, R. Y., J. L. Ingraham, M. L. Wheelis, and P. R. Painter. 1985. *The Microbial World.* Englewood-Cliffs: Prentice Hall.

Stepanov, Ju. S. 1971. *Semiotika.* Moscow: Nauka.

Stewart, Ann Harleman. 1976. *Graphic Representation of Models in Linguistic Theory.* Bloomington: Indiana University Press.

Stratton, Jon. 1987. *The Virgin Text: Fiction, Sexuality, and Ideology.* Norman: University of Oklahoma Press.

Suskind, Patrick. 1986. *Perfume: The Story of a Murderer,* trans. John E. Woods. New York: Knopf.

Telegdi, Zsigmond. 1976. Zur Herausbildung des Begriffs "sprachliches Zeichen" und zur stoischen Sprachlehre. *Acta Linguistica Scientiarum Hungaricae* 26:267–305.

Tembrock, Gunter. 1971. *Biokommunication: Informationsübertragung im biologischen Bereich.* Berlin: Akademie-Verlag.

Terrace, Herbert S. 1986 [1979]. *Nim.* New York: Columbia University Press.

Thom, René. 1973. De l'icône au symbole: Esquisse d'une théorie du symbolisme. *Cahiers Internationaux de Symbolisme* 22–23:85–106.

———. 1974. *Modèles mathémathiques de la morphogenèse: Recueil de textes sur la théorie des catastrophes et ses applications.* Paris: Union Générale d'Editions.

———. 1975. *Structural Stability and Morphogenesis: An Outline of a General Theory of Models.* Reading: W. A. Benjamin.

———. 1980. L'espace et les signes. *Semiotica* 29:193–208.

Tinbergen, N., and A. C. Perdeck. 1950. On the Stimulus Situation Releasing the Begging Response in the Newly Hatched Herring Gull Chick (*Larus argentatus argentatus* Pont). *Behaviour* 3:1–39.

Todorov, Tzvetan. 1982. *La Conquête de l'Amérique* Paris: Seuil.

Toller, Steve Van, and George H. Dodd, eds. 1989. *Perfumery: The Psychology and Biology of Fragrance.* New York: Routledge Chapman & Hall.

Tomkins, Gordon M. 1975. The Metabolic Code. *Science* 189:760–763.

Trabant, Jürgen. 1981. *Die Welt als Zeichen: Klassiker der modernen Semiotik,* ed. Martin Krampen, Klaus Oehler, Roland Posner, and Thure von Uexküll, 145–171. Berlin: Severin & Siedler.

Trevarthen, Colwyn. 1990. Signs before Speech. In *The Semiotic Web 1989,* ed. Thomas A. Sebeok and Jean Umiker-Sebeok, 689–755. Berlin: Mouton de Gruyter.

Tsuda, Aoi. 1984. *Sales Talk in Japan and the United States: An Ethnographic Analysis of Contrastive Speech Events.* Washington: Georgetown University Press.

Turner, Victor. 1974. *Dramas, Fields, and Metaphors: Symbolic Action in Human Society.* Ithaca: Cornell University Press.

Uexküll, Jakob von. 1909. *Umwelt und Innenwelt der Tierre.* Berlin: Springer Verlag.

———. 1973 [1928]. *Theoretische Biologie.* Frankfurt: Suhrkamp.

———. 1982. *The Theory of Meaning,* ed. Thure von Uexküll. *Semiotica* 42:1–87.

Uexküll, Thure von. 1978. Terminological Problems of Medical Semiotics. Ms.

———, ed. 1980. *Kompositionslehre der Natur: Biologie als undogmatische Naturwissenschaft,* by Jakob von Uexküll. Frankfurt am Main: Verlag Ullstein (Propyläen).

———. 1986. Medicine and Semiotics. *Semiotica* 61:201–217.

———. 1989. Jakob von Uexküll's Umwelt-Theory. In *The Semiotic Web 1988,* ed. Thomas A. Sebeok and Jean Umiker-Sebeok, 129–158.

———. In press. Biosemiotics. *Semiotica.*

———, and Wolfgang Wesiack. 1988. *Theorie der Humanmedizin: Grundlagen ärtzlichen Denkens und Handelns.* Berlin: Urban & Schwarzenberg.

Umiker-Sebeok, Jean, and Thomas A. Sebeok. 1981. Clever Hans and Smart Simians: The Self-Fulfilling Prophecy and Kindred Methodological Pitfalls. *Anthropos* 76:89–165.

Van Wing, R. P. J. 1938. *Etudes bakongo II, Religion et magie.* Brussels: G. van Campenhout.

Vernadsky, V. I. 1926. *Biosfera.* Leningrad.

Vigener, Gerhard. 1989. Dieser Schuh ist kein Schuh—zur Semiotik des Fetischs. In *Semiotik der Geschlechter. Akten des 6. Symposiums der österreichischen Gesellschaft für Semiotik, Salzburg* 1987, ed. Jeff Bernard, Theresia Klugsberger, and Gloria Withalm, 341–352. Stuttgart: Heinz.

Waddington, C. H. 1961. *The Nature of Life.* London: Allen & Unwin.

Walther, Elizabeth. 1984. Die Beziehung zwischen Semiotik und Linguistik. *Semiotica* 52:111–117.

Ward, Leo, and Walburga von Raffler-Engel. 1980. The Impact of Nonverbal Behavior on Foreign Language Teaching. In *Aspects of Nonverbal Communication,* ed. Walburga von Raffler-Engel, 287–304. Lisse: Swets and Zeitlinger.

Weimann, W. 1962. Über Tatowierungsfetischismus. *Archiv für Kriminologie* 130:106–109.

Weinreich, Uriel. 1968. Semantics and Semiotics. *International Encyclopedia of the Social Sciences* 14:164–169. New York: Macmillan and Free Press.

Wells, Rulon. 1967. Distinctively Human Semiotic. *Social Science Information* 6:6.103–124.

Welte, Werner. 1974. *Moderne Linguistik: Terminologie/Bibliographie: Ein Handbuch und Nachschlagewerk auf der Basis der generativ-transformationellen Sprachtheorie.* Munich: Max Huber Verlag.

Wheeler, John Archibald. 1984. Bits, Quanta, Meaning. In *Problems in Theoretical Physics,* ed. A. Giovanni, F. Mancini, and M. Marinaro, 121–141. Salerno: University of Salerno Press.

———. 1986a. How Come the Quantum? New York Academy of Sciences Conference on New Techniques and Ideas In Quantum Measurement Theory. Ms.

———. 1986b. Foreword to John D. Barrow and Frank J. Tipler, *The Anthropic Principle,* vii–ix. Oxford: Clarendon Press.

———. 1986c. Herman Weyl and the Unity of Knowledge. *American Scientist* 74:366–375.

———. 1988. World as System Self-Synthesized by Quantum Networking. *IBM Journal of Research and Development* 32:1.1–15.

Whitfield, I. C. 1984. *Neurocommunications: An Introduction. Chichester: Wiley.*

Whittaker, R. H. 1959. On the Broad Classification of Organisms. *Quarterly Review of Biology* 34:210–266.

———. 1969. New Concepts of Kingdoms of Organisms. *Science* 163:150–160.

Wicken, Jeffrey S. 1987. *Evolution, Thermodynamics, and Information: Extending the Darwinian Program.* New York: Oxford University Press.

Wiener, Norbert. 1950. *The Human Use of Human Beings.* Boston: Houghton Mifflin.

Willis, R. G. *Man and Beast.* London: Hart-Davis, MacGibbon.

Wills, Dorothy Davis. 1990. Indexifiers in Wolof. *Semiotica* 78:193–218.

Wilson, Colin. 1988. *The Misfits: A Study of Sexual Outsiders.* London: Grafton.

Wintsch, Susan. 1979. The Vocabulary of Gestures: Nonverbal Communication in Foreign Languages. *Research & Creative Activity* 3:6–11.

Wright, Robert. 1988. *Three Scientists and Their Gods: Looking for Meaning in an Age of Information.* New York: Times Books.

Yates, F. Eugene. In press. Microsemiosis. In *Semiotik: Ein Handbuch zu den zeichentheoretischen Grundlagen von natur und Kultur,* ed. Roland Posner, Klaus Robering, and Thomas A. Sebeok. Berlin: Walter de Gruyter.

———, and Peter N. Kugler. 1984. Signs, Singularities and Significance: A Physical Model for Semiotics. *Semiotica* 52:49–77.

Young, John Z. 1977. *What Squids and Octopuses Tell Us about Brains and Memories.* Forty-sixth James Arthur Lecture on the Evolution of the Human Brain. New York: American Museum of Natural History.

Zavitzianos, George. 1971. Fetishism and Exhibitionism in the Female and Their Relationship to Psychopathy and Kleptomania. *International Journal of Psycho-Analysis* 52:297–305.

INDEX OF NAMES

THOMAS A. SEBEOK is a Distinguished Professor of Linguistics and Semiotics and Chairman of the Research Center for Language and Semiotic Studies, Indiana University. His many publications include *The Play of Musement, How Animals Communicate* (two different editions), and *Sight, Sound, and Sense.* He is also editor of the important Indiana series Advances in Semiotics.